Ernest Hemingway's
A Farewell to Arms

Ernest Hemingway's
A Farewell to Arms

A Reference Guide

LINDA WAGNER-MARTIN

Greenwood Guides to Literature

GREENWOOD PRESS
Westport, Connecticut • London

1-2015

Library of Congress Cataloging-in-Publication Data

Wagner-Martin, Linda.
    Ernest Hemingway's A farewell to arms : a reference guide / Linda Wagner-Martin.
        p. cm.—(Greenwood guides to literature, ISSN 1543–2262)
    Includes bibliographical references and index.
    ISBN 0–313–31702–X (alk. paper)
    1. Hemingway, Ernest, 1899–1961. Farewell to arms. 2. World War,
1914–1918—United States—Literature and the war. 3. War stories, American—
History and criticism. I. Title. II. Series.
    PS3515.E37F366 2003
    813'.52—dc21   2002028442

British Library Cataloguing in Publication Data is available.

Library of Congress Catalog Card Number: 2002028442
ISBN: 0–313–31702–X
ISSN: 1543–2262

First published in 2003

Greenwood Press, 88 Post Road West, Westport, CT 06881
An imprint of Greenwood Publishing Group, Inc.
www.greenwood.com

Printed in the United States of America

The paper used in this book complies with the
Permanent Paper Standard issued by the National
Information Standards Organization (Z39.48–1984).

10 9 8 7 6 5 4 3 2 1

Copyright Acknowledgments

The author and the publisher gratefully acknowledge permission for use of the
following material:

Scattered excerpts reprinted with permission of Simon & Schuster from *A Farewell to Arms*
by Ernest Hemingway. Copyright © 1929 Charles Scribner's Sons. Copyright renewed 1957
by Ernest Hemingway.

Scattered excerpts from *A Farewell to Arms* by Ernest Hemingway © Hemingway Foreign
Rights Trust.

Every reasonable effort has been made to trace the owners of copyright material in this
book, but in some instances this has proven impossible. The author and publisher will be
glad to receive information leading to more complete acknowledgments in subsequent printings of the book and in the meantime extend their apologies for any omissions.

Contents

Preface

All readers of novels like to believe that their opinions matter. They do, whether the reader is a literary critic—paid by a publisher or a newspaper for written opinions—or someone who borrows a book from a public library and reads it entirely for pleasure. The latter reader may be the more important, in fact, for it is that borrowing—that keeping the book's title and the author's name alive—that creates the most lasting opinion.

It can truly be said that it has been readers of every nationality and persuasion who have kept Ernest Hemingway's A Farewell to Arms at the top of the list of serious American novels of the twentieth century. Even without the several film treatments of the evocative study of war and people's escape from it, this novel makes a significant statement about the way civilized human beings try to find their "separate peace" in the midst of chaos and despair.[1] One does not have to live in a war-torn country to understand the pathos of displacement, the fear of death, or the attractions of a steady—if fragile—romantic love.

When Ernest Hemingway published A Farewell to Arms in 1929, he was barely thirty years old, but he had been planning to write about World War I for more than a decade. The Great War had ended with the November 11 Armistice in 1918; Hemingway's own war service had ended with his multiple leg and groin injuries in the summer of that year. The fruition of his emotional devastation, coupled with the hundreds of stories he had heard from veterans similarly disillusioned and/or wounded, provided the young writer with a deep well of material from which to draw. By 1929, Hemingway was comparatively well known. He had published *Three Stories and Ten Poems* and three other collections of short fiction as well as two novels: the satiric comedy, *The Torrents of Spring*, which he had written to break his three-book commitment to Liveright publishing house, and the much-acclaimed 1926 *The Sun Also Rises*. Through his artfully built narratives and his astute political ties with such influential writers as Ezra Pound, F. Scott Fitzgerald, Sherwood Anderson, Gertrude Stein, Ford Madox Ford, and others, Hemingway was gaining a reputation as a writer to watch. And read.

Reviewers had already been kind to his slim collection of prose poems, *in our time*, which appeared in 1924, and, in 1925, to its more complete version, *In Our Time*, in which the prose poems about bravery, fear, and death in World War I and the Spanish bullfights as religious rites appeared as one-page interchapters between the fourteen stories he had written. His fictions about the young Nick Adams, doctor's son and a surrogate Ernest Hemingway, who grows up in the Middle West and spends his summers on Michigan lakes; and about a young married couple traveling through Europe were brilliantly realized. "Indian Camp," "The End of Something," "The Battler," "Soldier's Home," and "Big Two-Hearted River" were some of those early stories. And with his first serious novel, *The Sun Also Rises*, Hemingway became known as the quintessential modernist—a writer who went for highly crafted polish and yet captured honest emotion as well. In the shocking and very contemporary exposé of postwar expatriate life, *The Sun Also Rises* described the way the British and American characters lived on holiday in Paris and Pamplona, replete with heavy drinking, sex, and an almost existential search for meaning as its primary themes. His second major story collection, the 1928 *Men Without Women*, carried those themes through into studies of the modern angst that seemed valid to survivors of the debacle of World War I.

Yet just as he was becoming known as the novelist of keen despair, Hemingway reversed readers' expectations by writing a book that had as one of its primary ingredients the somewhat unfashionable attitude of hope. In his alternation of the narrative of war and its destruction with the luminous story of Frederic Henry's great love for Catherine Barkley, a love reciprocated without question, Hemingway created a book that drew much of its momentum from the reader's involvement. It is the reader who finds the hope in the rhythmic juxtaposition of war and love, fear and disappointment set against the lyric moments of genuine, selfless love.

For a writer who had been something of a "writer's writer," with his earlier work praised—for the most part—by other writers and critics who appreciated cryptic modern expression, Hemingway found himself in 1929 close to best-sellerdom. A *Farewell to Arms*, in fact, was leading the best-seller lists a few weeks after its autumn publication. Sales after seven weeks had reached 45,000 copies, and interest was so high that Scribner's renegotiated Hemingway's original contract.[2] Max Perkins, his editor at the house, offered him a supplemental advance of $25,000 (sales figures continued at this rate even after the market crash in late October of 1929). It seemed clear that A *Farewell to Arms* had captured the imaginations of many more readers than the young author—or his publishing house—had anticipated.

This reference guide is aimed at describing the way the novel has achieved its audience, as well as helping readers understand Hemingway's important book from a variety of perspectives. *Ernest Hemingway's* A Farewell to Arms: *A Reference Guide* exists for a number of reasons, all of them implicitly tied to the reader who is interested in good narratives that tell important stories—for more than just readers contemporary with the first publication. To that end, the book is divided into a number of relatively short chapters, each with a focus that is announced at the start. Readers looking for one kind of information can look under appropriate headings; the book also provides a careful index.

In the "Introduction," for example, I provide enough Hemingway biography to make readers question the critical argument that the author was writing simply from his own life experiences during the war. Like most of Hemingway's creative process, his employment of characters, events, and details from his personal autobiography into his fiction or memoir was complex and intricate—and mysterious. Just as the author was not a part of the retreat from Caporetto, neither did he and a lover row across the impossibly wide lake to the safety of Switzerland. Severely wounded during the first weeks of his duty as a Red Cross aide and ambulance driver, Hemingway did not—obviously—desert from the Italian army; he had never been in service to that army at all. Knowing the biography of the writer during the years from the beginning of the twentieth century through the publication date of the novel, 1929, enables the reader to clarify some of the discrepancies between the stories that are told about Hemingway, the purported veteran of World War I, and the factual events of his life.

In the "Introduction" as well are placed discussions about what kind of fiction A *Farewell to Arms* is. Among literary typology, the book is, most apparently, a war novel. Because the reason for Frederic Henry's being away from home is his military standing, the reader remains conscious of his involvement in the worldwide conflict throughout the book. Even after he deserts, an act which Hemingway makes justifiable in the execution scene during the Caporetto retreat, he and Catherine are still under military rule. Whereas previously Catherine Barkley was also in service, contributing her life to the care of the wounded after the death of her own fiancé, in order to accompany Henry, she also must leave her post. In effect, she deserts as well. No matter how involved the reader becomes in the story of the Henry-Barkley love, the shadow of the war (and Henry's possible court-martial, or worse) is omnipresent.

As part of that war novel structure, Hemingway includes scenes from battle, scenes from behind the lines, scenes in the officers' quarters. Although not many enlisted or drafted men are prominent in the action, the Italian ambulance drivers are treated as well-defined characters, and the officers, particularly the young priest and the Italian doctor, Rinaldi, are significant figures. Hemingway convinces the reader that this is a genuine war; it does not exist merely in the minds of Frederic and Catherine. It is much more than an abstract worry for them. It is the continuing threat of death.

A Farewell to Arms, as its ambiguous title hints, is also the story of Frederic Henry's great love—and loss. The arms that he loses are Catherine's, and the arms he never had can be said to be those of his son, the child who never lived even though he was, in fact, born. One of Hemingway's strikingly apt choices for narrative method in writing the novel is that the story is told by the bereaved, by Frederic Henry himself, and its entire meditative and mournful tone underscores the sense of impending disaster. The voice of the man who has been so damaged by both the war and the unexpected loss of his contrived separate peace remains a constant in the telling of the story. Unlike a Shakespearean play, A Farewell to Arms is not broken into by any comic episode, a knocking at the door of the incipient tragedy. The best that Hemingway (with Frederic as his narrator) can achieve is a scene of nostalgic and gentle warming, either among Henry and his Italian soldiers or—more often—between Henry and Catherine as they enjoy each other's love. The euphoria that might suffuse a love story unclouded by war, the sheer vitality of finding a great love and then having it reciprocated, never colors this narrative.

Yet the novel qualifies as a fine love story. As Hemingway wrote to Max Perkins after the first amazing sales of the novel, another way to advertise the book would be to use this copy:

There's more than
War in

A Farewell to Arms
It is
The Great Modern Love Story[3]

The manuscript drafts of the novel show how skillfully Hemingway worked to contrive a structure that began with an emphasis on war and then shifted to make the love story central. As to which kind of novel— war or love—is more likely to attain a vast readership, Hemingway took precautions to avoid choosing: for instance, a likely ending would have given the reader some sense of Frederic Henry's punishment for his desertion. (The reader who thinks of the book as a war novel might speculate that Henry is retelling his story of loss from the prison where he has been incarcerated after his capture. Since this is not the case, since Frederic is kept completely sympathetic throughout the book, the plot of war must gradually be erased.) Another would have been a return to the comradeship of both the priest and Rinaldi, the two figures besides Catherine who are closest to Frederic. But the book does not make that return. Instead, Frederic is left visibly, and empathetically, alone.

Other kinds of information included in the "Introduction" are the types of fiction being written during the immediate postwar period, particularly during the 1920s, both in the United States and in other countries; discussions of other significant war novels from the twentieth century; and a brief analysis of reasons for the popularity of *A Farewell to Arms*.

Chapter 1 focuses on the narrative content of the novel. Its usefulness as a summary of plot and character interaction is intended to clarify some of the parts of the book that have provoked controversy, as well as the novel's general course of action. Some of the scenes singled out for close attention are those of Frederic Henry's wounding, his relationship with Catherine, and Catherine's death. Hemingway's careful alternation in the book between sections of "war novel" and "romance" (both treated in surprisingly sexual language) comprises much of the discussion of structure. The main characters of this novel are then related to those of Hemingway's earlier *The Sun Also Rises*.

The next chapter is devoted to an explanation of the genesis of the novel. For Hemingway, who had achieved a kind of fame (though not bestsellerdom) from his sparse and somewhat cynical presentation of a postwar expatriate—and elite—culture, turning to a relatively old-fashioned novel of romantic appeal marked a definite change in his aesthetic and in his intentions. *A Farewell to Arms* was his attempt to write a blockbuster, a book that would sell to Hollywood. The fact that one of his original pieces of fiction—probably lost in the theft of Hadley's luggage on the train to Austria[4]—was also a war novel shows that the theme of war and love had been important to him for the entire decade of the 1920s. It also suggests that he had learned enough through his writing of shorter pieces about the war (the vignettes of *In Our Time*, the stories "Soldier's Home" and "Big Two-Hearted River" from that collection and "In Another Country" and "Now I Lay Me" from *Men Without Women*) to shape this novel in ways that were much more contrived than any simple elaboration of an autobiographical narrative would have been. Ironically, since the pattern Hemingway chooses is that Frederic's telling of his story *is* meant to seem autobiographical, he carefully avoids using the structure and method of autobiography. *A Farewell to Arms* is not told chronologically, and it does not have any quality of randomness, of groping for memories. It is a cleverly told story, its parts arranged in precision order, with a concluding impact that only a master craftsman of modernism could have achieved.

The third chapter explores in detail the literary context for *A Farewell to Arms*. It comments about the important United States World War I texts: John Dos Passos's *One Man's Initiation* and *Three Soldiers*, e.e. cummings' *The Enormous Room*, Thomas Boyd's *Through the Wheat*, Willa Cather's *One of Ours*, Edith Wharton's *A Son at the Front*, (as well as Wharton's nonfiction, considered along with Mildred Aldrich's writing about the war and Gertrude Stein's poems about it), and one British writer's novels, Virginia Woolf's *Jacob's Room* and the later *Mrs. Dalloway*. It also surveys the great war novels of world literature: the Russian, the French, the English. It devotes much attention to the newly current theories of memory, in relation to the war's most invidious effect on its participants—post-traumatic behavior. In an investigation of the long-term psychological effects of trauma, whether trauma be actual wounding or the anguish of fear, this chapter brings to the reading of this literature of World War I a more current understanding of such a conflict's possibilities for damage.

In a fourth chapter, the study analyzes in a more comprehensive way the twin intellectual themes of war and survivorship (with its emphasis on killing others, saving one's own life even if that aim means deserting, and saving the lives of others) and a sometimes unconscious emphasis in the book on the paradigm of increasingly gendered lives during wartime. By employing both Rinaldi and the young priest as comparative figures for Frederic Henry, Hemingway creates a panorama of attitudes toward male power, male pleasure (in all its sexualized dimension), and male condescension. Because the love story of the novel is a heterosexual one, Catherine Barkley is cast into a highly visible gendered role: brave as she might be, foolhardy in the same ways that Rinaldi and Henry are shown to be, Catherine cannot act other than as a female in the context of this dilemma of war and conflict. Accordingly, her biological trap—to become pregnant and then to die in childbirth—must be feminine. War takes away choice: it constructs lives so that battle is at the heart of all human effort. By emphasizing his dual stories of war and love, Hemingway creates a world in which androgyny does not exist. The man partakes of soldiering; the woman bears children, the soldier's children. Even as Hemingway undercuts this pattern—by having Frederic and Catherine fail to marry, giving them no sanction for their coupling, and then keeping them on the run so they can never find the space or opportunity to legitimate their liaison—he reinforces it. The two play at being married. People refer to Catherine as Frederic's "wife" and he assumes the conventional role of father in the hospital. But the morality that undergirds all the risk-taking the couple subject themselves to is only a facade. One of the themes A Farewell to Arms interrogates is the power of society to make judgments, best illustrated in the novel when Catherine feels like a whore in the hotel room.

A fifth chapter focuses on the narrative art Hemingway employs in the novel. As a gauge of his maturity as a writer, the complex—and complexly balanced—novel shows much more conventional structuring than had his 1926 book, The Sun Also Rises. In that work, narrative was established in a day-by-day journey format; Hemingway's chief task was to keep the characters in the same place so that they could meet frequently. But in A Farewell to Arms, the cast of characters is huge: armies, opposing forces, townspeople, friends (and enemies) of both Frederic and Catherine, as well as the silent and unfaced majority that judges the two lovers/deserters and provides a kind of moral chorus for the reader. Hemingway's structural format reflects that difference. He makes use of seemingly separate, and usually tidy, scenes. The aesthetic of his arranging these scenes as if they were mosaics in a panoramic tile floor is one of the ways Hemingway grows. He did not know how to handle the wide view, and, in A Farewell to Arms, he has learned that.

The penultimate chapter discusses the critical reception of the novel, from writers contemporary with its publication as well as from the established critics. Ford Madox Ford's introduction to a 1932 printing of the novel is read as a reliable guide to Hemingway's reputation at the time;

other critics since the early 1930s are then discussed so that the oeuvre of this critical reception provides an ever-changing tapestry of readers' views on a novel as problematic as *A Farewell to Arms*. With the advent of feminist criticism, the character of Catherine Barkley has been read as seriously flawed; but in the 1990s, objections to her characterization have been ameliorated to some extent. This chapter surveys those attitudes. It also makes connections between *A Farewell to Arms*, and its character Catherine, and Hemingway's most controversial posthumously published novel, *The Garden of Eden*, which has its own somewhat differently drawn Catherine.

The last section of this reference guide comments on a number of the most important books and essays that treat *A Farewell to Arms*. There are several hundred, but the bibliographic narrative limits those discussed to some that can more easily be found (in anthologies of criticism or in widely circulated journals). Elsewhere, at intervals throughout this guide, reference will be made to particularly seminal readings that have proved to be highly influential.

NOTES

1. Hemingway coined this now-famous phrase in his *In Our Time* vignette, Chapter VI, in which the wounded young soldier, Nick, reflects on the fact that he and his companion, a seriously wounded man named Rinaldi, have made this peace. He also insists, "sweatily," that they are not "patriots." The implication is that each of them is nearing death, p. 63. Ernest Hemingway, *In Our Time* (New York: Scribner, 1925).

2. Scott Donaldson provides this and other details in his *Hemingway vs. Fitzgerald: The Rise and Fall of a Literary Friendship*, (Woodstock, NY: Overlook Press, 1999), pp. 146–148.

3. Quoted in Donaldson, p. 148.

4. The best and fullest discussion of Hemingway's production of *A Farewell to Arms*—and his apprenticeship before and during the writing of it—remains Michael S. Reynolds' *Hemingway's First War*, (Princeton, N.J.: Princeton University Press, 1976).

1 Introduction

Ernest Hemingway's *A Farewell to Arms* has become, once again, the classic American war novel. The novel, first published to critical acclaim and near best-seller status in 1929, has endured that most significant test, the test of time. It has become a critical commonplace to say that Shakespeare's plays last because their themes are ageless, timeless. King Richard's greed, Macbeth's demand for power, Lear's trust in his daughters—and his eventual bereavement, Prospero's trust in the right—today's audience understands the emotional crux of such literature. So too with Hemingway's novel: the bewilderment and fear any soldier experiences, the conflict between military training and humane impulse, the desire to live as well as to love and procreate. These timeless themes mark the true greatness of a work now over seventy years old, a novel that might have been set aside as one remnant of early twentiet- century conflict, a World War I novel, not a literary classic. As Ray B. West, Jr., one of the ablest of Hemingway's early critics, wrote in 1949, Hemingway made his mark by writing—in various ways— about "the condition of man in a society upset by the violence of war. . . . [T]he setting for *A Farewell to Arms* is the war itself, and the romance of Frederic Henry and Catherine Barkley, their attempt to escape the war and its resulting chaos, is a parable of twentieth-century man's disgust and disillusionment at the failure of civilization to achieve the ideas it had been promising throughout the nineteenth century."[1]

In the following reference guide, *A Farewell to Arms* will be assessed first as a novel of World War I. The various theaters of the conflict, to which Hemingway refers, will be described, as will the military aspects of Frederic Henry's behavior. How does an officer treat the soldiers serving under him? What does it mean to execute a fellow soldier? What does it mean to be a deserter? What would be the penalty or punishment for the desertion that both Frederic and Catherine are guilty of? As his writing throughout his lifetime showed, Hemingway was fascinated by the narrative possibilities of war, the military, and the male ego faced with both fear and the opportunity for power. As Hemingway said years after writing *A Farewell to Arms*, "I am interested in the goddam [*sic*] sad science of war."[2]

In a similar vein, what did physicians and psychiatrists at the time of World War I know about shell shock and war trauma? While it is plausible that Frederic Henry is experiencing some of these post-traumatic effects as he recovers from his badly wounded leg in the Milan hospital, it is more likely that Hemingway's intention was to portray Catherine Barkley as a victim of war trauma. Catherine—as we first meet her in the nurses' quarters—is erratic, moody, and confused. It is clear that her friend, Helen Ferguson, feels the need to look after her. While the nurses have already met Rinaldi, and Catherine might be pictured as interested in the young Italian doctor, she seems to think that her newest acquaintance, Frederic Henry, is her fiancé who has recently been killed in action. Her dialogue as Hemingway creates it shows that—despite her medical training—she was as innocent about the carnage of war as the naïve patriotic civilians at home who urged their sons and husbands to fight the Hun, to make the world safe for democracy.

It is partly the character of Catherine Barkley that signals readers that Hemingway was using events from his own life in the creation of *A Farewell to Arms*. Not that he had fathered a child who died, or that the child's mother, his great love from his hospitalization during those months of World War I, had herself died—but that Hemingway's purposefully veiled references to his love, coupled with his acknowledgment of the truly traumatic effects of his own war injuries and lengthy recuperation, initiated the stories that he seldom contradicted.

BRIEF BIOGRAPHY OF HEMINGWAY, FROM 1899 THROUGH 1929

Born July 21, 1899, Ernest Miller Hemingway was the second child and first son of Clarence and Grace Hall-Hemingway. Ambitious for themselves and their children (who would number six before the family was complete), the parents were outstanding—and upstanding—citizens of the modestly wealthy, but eminently moral, Chicago suburb of Oak Park, Illinois. Grace was a singer who also wrote music and gave prestigious piano and voice lessons in her home; she claimed that she could have been on the opera circuit had she not married her physician-husband. Prominent in part because of her father's wealth, Grace was a hard-driving woman who saw no reason to choose among life's paths.[3] Even at the turn into the twentieth century, Grace Hall-Hemingway wanted it all.

Living for several years with Ernest Hall, Grace's father, the Hemingway family in 1899 bought property on Walloon Lake, realizing as so many Chicagoans had that the natural air-conditioning of the pine forests and lakes in central Michigan would make summers bearable. Before he turned one year old, Ernest began spending his summers at the cottage Grace had named "Windemere," and the small Walloon Lake became his adventure site. With his father, he learned to swim, fish, row a boat, and camp; by himself or with Marcelline, his older sister, he did those things—and others—without supervision. By the time he was five, he was a member of his father's Oak Park Agassiz group, studying the natural world in both Illinois and Michigan (and the richly provocative museums of Chicago).[4]

The family was inherently musical; each of the children had an instrument to practice. They subscribed to, and read, magazines for children and made frequent trips to the public library. They attended the Third Congregational Church on Sundays, did the appropriate charitable activities, and saw themselves as pillars of the blatantly Republican, conservative Oak Park society. After Ernest started first grade in 1905, with Grace's inheritance from her father Ernest Hall, the family planned and built their own large house at 600 North Kenilworth Avenue in Oak Park. The house included a thirty-foot-square music studio and recital hall, where Grace's many students performed. It was during these early elementary school years that Grace arranged for Marcelline and Ernest to be in the same grade, so the fact that she dressed them alike could be taken to indicate that they were twins. It is a biographical detail made much of by some critics.[5]

Ernest attended Oak Park High School between 1913 and 1917, and, even though he wrote for the school literary magazine (*Tabula*) and the newspaper (*The Trapeze*), he was hardly a polished writer. In fact, his tastes ran toward heavy-handed (adolescent) humor, and the coverage of sports events. As a gawky teenager, Ernest tried to run cross-country track and played lightweight football, finally making the varsity squad during his senior year.[6] But he was, consistently, a reader. As Mark Spilka and Hemingway's biographers have shown, Hemingway was steeped in Victorian moralists and novelists: reading, like all education early in the twentieth century, had the wholesome responsibility to instruct.[7]

Too young to enlist in the U.S. armed forces in the summer of 1917, following his graduation from high school, Hemingway spent a few months at Lake Walloon and then was hired (thanks to Missouri relatives) as a cub reporter on the *Kansas City Star*. While this work surely honed his prose style, and taught him a lot that he hadn't had the opportunity to learn about life (especially life away from Oak Park), he was eager to get into World War I. So, in late spring, he volunteered to drive ambulances for the American Red Cross in Italy. After two weeks of limited action at Schio, he asked to handle a rolling canteen on the Piave River front. It was there, on the night of July 8, 1918, scarcely a month after he had come to Italy, that he was badly wounded by an Austrian trench mortar shell.

Convalescing in Italian hospitals for the next six months, Hemingway heard stories about the war he had scarcely seen. He learned some Italian, he had a good ear; fell in love with Agnes von Kurowsky, the American nurse eight years his senior; and tried to learn to get over the trauma of his multiple wounds, more than 200 shrapnel pieces in his legs and groin. Because his near-death experience had occurred at night, nights were bad for him—he had trouble sleeping, he experienced nightmares, and he was to need to leave a light on through much of his adult life. After he returned to the States in January of 1919, he lived at home in Oak Park and in a rented room in Petoskey, Michigan, trying to become a serious writer. Agnes von Kurowsky had ended their relationship during the spring (the correspondence between them has been published in book form, and became one of the bases for the film *In Love and War*).[8] Difficulties with his mother over the issue of Hemingway's taking responsibility, getting a job, and leaving home—despite his injuries—led to his moving to Chicago.

In Chicago, Hemingway met Hadley Richardson, a woman eight years his senior, visiting from St. Louis. They carried on their romance through letters. Hadley, a well-read pianist who had lived at home in order to care for her ailing parents—now dead, gave Hemingway a number of novels to read; their letters are a kind of bookish instructional dialogue.[9] In September of 1920, they were married at Horton Bay in Michigan. They lived in Chicago for a time, where they met Sherwood Anderson. As soon as they could, a little over a year later, they arranged to leave the

States, and, equipped with letters of introduction from Anderson, trav-eled to Paris for a glimpse of the new literary scene. Hemingway wrote columns for the *Toronto Star*, and they supplemented his earnings from Hadley's then-substantial trust fund.

In January of 1922, Ernest and Hadley moved into a fourth-floor walk-up apartment in the Latin Quarter of Paris. Over the next year and a half, Hemingway filed eighty-eight stories for the *Star*, including important coverage of the Genoa Economic Conference, the Greco-Turkish war, and the Lausanne Peace Conference. He interviewed Benito Mussolini, and, as Michael Reynolds said, "These events began Hemingway's serious political education, giving him a privileged view of the postwar political leaders setting Europe's agenda: Clemenceau, Tchitcherin, Barthou, Lloyd George, and Mussolini. He wrote about anarchists, anti-Semitism, fascism, power politics, disarmament, German inflation, Paris nightlife, Spanish bullfights, and German trout fishing."[10] From it all, Hemingway emerged a widely educated man.

His efforts to become a writer—aside from the weighty investment in journalism—brought him to the feet of the influential American poet Ezra Pound and, more practically, Gertrude Stein. It was Stein who told him to give up his Toronto *Star* reporting, because he needed time to think about what he *wanted* to be writing. By 1923, when his first slim book appeared, until 1926, when *The Sun Also Rises* was published by Scribner's, Hemingway immersed himself in contemporary writing. He borrowed books from Sylvia Beach's lending library at Shakespeare and Company; he talked books with Pound, Stein, T. S. Eliot, James Joyce, F. Scott Fitzgerald, Harold Loeb, John Dos Passos, and Ford Madox Ford (for whom he worked at the *transatlantic review*); he sent out his stories (usually rejected by magazine editors who called them "vignettes" or "sketches," not stories), poems, and prose poems—but with little success. Meanwhile, he and Hadley had traveled back to the States in order for their child to be born. They soon returned to Paris but the stresses of tak-ing care of an infant in the exciting city led, in part, to Hemingway's affair with Pauline Pfeiffer, a fashion magazine editor who was a friend of both Ernest and Hadley.

By the time Hemingway was returning to his "war novel," and there is evidence that he had earlier, well before writing *The Sun Also Rises*, begun his story of World War I, his life was in complicated ruins. He loved Hadley and their son Bumby, but he also loved Pauline. Hadley had lost much of her money through her investment manager's bad choices; Pauline was from a wealthy St. Louis family. Hadley had also, through no fault of her own, lost all of Hemingway's short-story manuscripts (and their carbons) when she was traveling to join him in Switzerland; Pauline cheered him on with every word he wrote, including the adolescent *The Torrents of Spring*. The "war" that Hemingway was describing in the text for his new novel had metaphoric overtones as well as literal and—some would say—autobiographical events: it was all too easy for Hemingway to find the reflection of his own confused marital state—not to mention the debacle of his parents' miserable marriage—in his current work.

Divorced from Hadley and married to Pauline during the spring of 1927, he saw his second important story collection, *Men Without Women*, published that same year. In the spring of 1928 he began writing the war story that would become *A Farewell to Arms*. The difficult birth of Patrick, his first child with Pauline, interrupted Hemingway's writing, and the family's life in tropical Key West—far from, and different from, Paris—meant more emotional adjustment. During 1928, however, once in Key West and once in Chicago, Ernest got to see his father, Clarence. His sense of personal disaster peaked when he received news of his father's suicide by gun in December of that year. Written on the outside fold of the manuscript of *A Farewell to Arms* is Hemingway's chronology of events that—his handwritten note suggests—contributed to the final version of the novel:

> Begun winter of 1928 in Paris. . . . [T]hat fall went to Chicago—saw my father—Drove to Key West with Sunny [who had offered to type the novel]—she told me about my father—went to NY to get Bumby—wrote father on train—informed of death in station— went to Chicago then to KW to rewrite.[11]

The great sense of loss that permeates the ending chapters of *A Farewell to Arms* may well have been Hemingway's own unresolved grief at the unexpected, and sudden, death of Clarence. As he wrote to his friend John Dos Passos on September 4, 1929: "Old Hem ruined by his father shooting himself."[12]

THE NOVEL OF WAR AND/OR LOVE

Whether to consider *A Farewell to Arms* primarily a novel about war, or a book about the wages of passionate sexual love, has been a critical dilemma for the past fifty years. For readers who regard its strength as its emotional impact, its emphasis on romance allows for the inclusion of the death of a beloved, not necessarily a lover: in this case, the death of Clarence Hemingway. Loss is loss, and Hemingway's creation of that tone of somber relinquishment marks the book from its beginning. From the first page, readers know that this is no "happy-ending" narrative.

As Frederic Svoboda has recently pointed out, in every Hemingway novel, "it is the loss of love, and often the memory of its loss, that is a core element in the appeal to a reader. War often provides a parallel and resonance to these tales of the loss of love. Revolutions mark *In Our Time* (1925) and *To Have and Have Not.* . . . [and it] is in *A Farewell to Arms* that the First World War is most directly treated, and the loss of love through Catherine Barkley's death in childbirth is not merely paralleled by the war. In the novel the many losses of the war become nearly equal in dramatic force to the loss of love." Svoboda contends that the book "convincingly entertwines their [the lovers'] fate with the war. . . . Images of war, disease, and death are set in counterpoint against the passing seasons in the mountain landscape of northern Italy."[13]

A Farewell to Arms was, of course, marketed—and received—as a novel of World War I. Such influential reviewers as Malcolm Cowley (using as title the militaristic "Not Yet Demobilized"), Fanny Butcher, Clifton P. Fadiman, and Henry S. Canby (with his war-related title "Story of the Brave")[14] did not try to finesse the fact that the book was about World War I; they were not bothered by its publication date of 1929. (Years later, critic Millicent Bell would comment that "as a war novel, it is curiously late"; she accordingly would read it as the expression of Hemingway's "inner being, his secret life.")[15] Most of the American novels about the First World War had appeared throughout the 1920s, and 1929 also saw the publication of Erich Maria Remarque's *All Quiet on the Western Front*, a book considered more important than Hemingway's.

The academic critics, too, who did the first serious scholarly writing on Hemingway read *A Farewell to Arms* as a novel of war: Earl Rovit, Philip Young, Carlos Baker, Sheridan Baker, Arthur Waldhorn, and others[16] wrote so well and carefully about this way of reading *A Farewell to Arms* as to necessitate different emphases in subsequent analyses. For Stanley Cooperman, writing in his *World War One and the American Novel*, the book becomes a lynchpin of the definition of fiction of war.[17] Clearly, too, Michael S. Reynolds' 1976 study of the novel underscores its narrative type: he titles his book *Hemingway's First War: The Making of* A Farewell to Arms.[18]

As other comments in this reference guide have suggested, the novel has in the past twenty-five years become something of a cauldron for highly gendered interpretations of the characters Catherine Barkley and Frederic Henry.[19] Were the novel read consistently as a "war novel," attention would still fall on Frederic Henry but it might be more often focused on the other male military figures (Rinaldi, the young priest, the ambulance drivers) rather than on Catherine. Still, the spring of 2000 brought at least one important return to the definition of the book as war novel.

Matthew C. Stewart's "Ernest Hemingway and World War I: Combatting Recent Psychobiographical Reassessments, Restoring the War" claims that *A Farewell to Arms* was the logical culmination of what can, in retrospect, be seen as Hemingway's pervasive reliance on war and its devastation in his writing up to 1929. He cites the author's early uses of the war, and of his wounding in the *In Our Time* vignettes and stories, in his many poems, and in some of his "finest stories—'In Another Country,' 'Now I Lay Me,' and 'A Way You'll Never Be.'" Stewart also points out that "many of Hemingway's protagonists—including those in his earliest stories—are men wounded in war: Nick Adams, Jake Barnes, Frederic Henry, Robert Jordan."[20]

Stewart's main point, however, is that it is Hemingway's probing the "dark dimension" of his personal war—his wounding—that dominates the writing. (He turns to family accounts of Hemingway's behavior after he returned from Italy—staying in bed for long periods, withdrawing from the family and its activities, drinking surreptitiously—for explanations of some of his fictional themes.) He also describes Hemingway's "recurrent battle nightmares," running to at least five years after his wounding. As proof, Stewart quotes from an unpublished early manuscript of a "fictionalized version of his [Hemingway's] wounding":

> Writing longhand on Milan Red Cross stationery, Hemingway sketches the downfall of Nick Grainger of Petoskey, Michigan. Like Hemingway, Nick has been struck in the legs by a mortar on the Italian front. Yet, his case is worse than Hemingway's in that he apparently has lost both his legs and his left arm to amputation. . . . Nick bitterly fingers his medals. . . . The sketch ends before he swallows the poisonous bichloride solution he has filched for the clear purpose of committing suicide.[21]

With emphasis on the maiming of the so-called glorious activity of war, Hemingway here writes about the most obvious kinds of wounding. (He may be responding in part to William Faulkner's 1926 novel about the war, *Soldiers' Pay*.) But in *A Farewell to Arms*, Frederic Henry's wounds are as much psychological as they are physical. The novel's structure, and the development of the romance plot, makes him more vulnerable to the loss of Catherine than to the loss of any war.

Hemingway's focus has shifted—perhaps aided by his own decade of separation from the shelling that led to his wounding and perhaps in his search for topics that would interest his readers in 1929. Always self-conscious about the work he had chosen to do, and how well that writing was being received, Hemingway told Lillian Ross that the much later novel, *Across the River and into the Trees*, was a better book than *A Farewell to Arms* because the former didn't have "the youth and the ignorance."[22]

Thinking about the tragedy, and the political travesty, of any war, Hemingway in his introduction to *Men at War*, his 1942 anthology of war fiction, wrote clearly about military theorists like Clausewitz (and himself, filled with what he saw as his own knowledge about battle):

> The editor of this anthology [himself], who took part and was wounded in the last war to end war, hates war and hates all the politicians whose mismanagement, gullibility, cupidity, selfishness and ambitions brought on this present war and made it inevitable. But once we have a war there is only one thing to do. It must be won. For defeat brings worse things than any that can ever happen in a war.[23]

Even at the height of World War II patriotism, Hemingway speaks harshly about the unreasonableness of war. Despite his denunciation, his closing sentiments are qualified. One is reminded of his prolegomenon about patriotism (or, rather, anti-patriotism) which serves as a narrative centerpiece in *A Farewell to Arms*. The now-famous paragraph occurs in the midst of a fairly technical discussion about military strategy that Frederic Henry has with Gino, one of the Italian ambulance drivers. The discussion moves from fighting in the mountains,[24] to the military history of Austria and France, to food shortages in wartime. It is in answer to Gino's statement that "We won't talk about losing. There is enough talk about losing. What has been done this summer cannot have been done in vain" that Hemingway creates Henry's stream-of-conscious soliloquy:

> I did not say anything. I was always embarrassed by the words sacred, glorious and sacrifice and the expression in vain. We had heard them, sometimes standing in the rain almost out of earshot, so that

only the shouted words came through, and had read them, on proclamations that were slapped up by billposters over other procla- mations, now for a long time, and I had seen nothing sacred, and the things that were glorious had no glory and the sacrifices were like the stockyards at Chicago if nothing was done with the meat except to bury it. There were many words that you could not stand to hear and finally only the names of places had dignity. Certain numbers were the same way and certain dates and these with the names of the places were all you could say and have them mean any- thing. Abstract words such as glory, honor, courage or hallow were obscene beside the concrete names of villages, the numbers of roads, the names of rivers, the numbers of regiments and the dates. (184–85)[25]

Coming relatively late in the novel, this passage typifies Frederic Henry's growing realization that the stories of war are fiction, that the reason he wanted to serve in the military has been itself fictionalized, that the least educated Italian soldier knows as much about the nature of war—its causes and its natural outcome—as the young American whose studies have been undertaken with the blindness of the belief in valor. The novel progresses through levels of Henry's disillusion; it does not begin with that attitude.

An apparent and conventional war story, *A Farewell to Arms* sets the stage with several early chapters describing the activities of soldiers and of officers during battle. The first, a brief two-page chapter, is descriptive: it provides for readers the soldiers, the rain, the endless marching. The sec- ond chapter, however, takes place later and in it Hemingway announces to the reader that the circumstances of the soldiers' placement had changed and "The war was changed too" (6). Rather than the summer green of the lush forest surrounding their town, "now there were the stumps and the broken trunks and the ground torn up." Worse, with the swiftness of a yellow cloud, "everything was gray and the sky was covered and the cloud came on down the mountain and suddenly we were in it and it was snow. The snow slanted across the wind, the bare ground was covered, the stumps of trees projected, there was snow on the guns and there were paths in the snow going back to the latrines behind trenches" (6). Nature conspires with enemy shelling to devastate the pleasant countryside: the war turns earnest. As Henry notes, "Up the river the mountains had not been taken; none of the mountains beyond the river had been taken. That was all left for next year" (6). Only ominous, Hemingway's depiction of the natural world foreshadows the impossibility of winning this war—or any war.

As the writer of journalistic sketches and people-filled narratives that he had become, Hemingway does not long resist turning to characterization. The physician Rinaldi, the unnamed young Italian priest, the officers' mess participants become foci for the reader and even though these people are set in the midst of the action of war, Hemingway draws their personalities through the interplay among them—discourse about sexual prowess, about hunting, about peacetime contrasted with military service. In fact, as we are introduced to the characters of Frederic Henry's military life, there is little mention of the war. Even in these initial chapters, the plot presented to the reader takes on the quality of a narrative of romance. It is the men's sexual activity—or lack of it—that becomes the basis for their acceptance into or rejection from the male camaraderie. The first sample of the men's conversation is the captain's baiting the priest about his amours with the Italian girls: "Priest to-day with girls" and, to the young man's blushes, the repetition, "To-day I see priest with girls" followed by the ribald exaggeration: "Priest every night five against one," complete with gestures that run throughout the rest of the scene (7). It is in the midst of the sexual hilarity that the men shout about their plans for leaves, conversation interrupted by the priest's serious suggestion to Henry: "I would like you to go to Abruzzi. . . . There is good hunting. You would like the people and though it is cold it is clear and dry. You could stay with my family. My father is a famous hunter" (9). The immediate juxtaposition of the captain's urging everyone to "go whorehouse before it shuts" closes down the intimacy of the priest's offering Henry his family hospitality, and contrasts the adolescent lust with the suggested solitary purity of Abruzzi. Frederic Henry never makes that visit.

Hemingway's third brief chapter continues the sexual odyssey: Henry returns from a long leave and a tour of most of Italy's cities, to be interrogated by Rinaldi about his sexual conquests in those places. Within a few thousand words, Miss Barkley is introduced. Rinaldi admires her, lusts after her, suggests that Henry meet her. The novel, only a few pages after it begins, has become a recognizable romance in the terms that John Cawelti defines so clearly: "[I]ts organizing action is the development of a love relationship, usually between a man and a woman." If there is adventure or war, "the dangers function as a means of challenging and then cementing the love relationship." Further, the intense focus on the love affair, in effect, supports what Cawelti calls the "moral fantasy" that love is all anyone needs in life. Both the structure of the work and all narrative conventions reinforce this premise. "Though the usual outcome is a permanently happy marriage, more sophisticated types of love story sometimes end in the death of one or both of the lovers, but always in such a way as to suggest that the love relation has been of lasting and permanent impact." It goes without saying that in this plot, both writer and reader have accepted traditional gender roles, that male characters are the aggressors (and the heroes) and that women characters play the conventional role of female love object.[26]

Once Frederic Henry meets Catherine, he almost immediately begins a courtship of seduction. As the introspective lines in the novel suggest, she is preferable to—and physically safer than—his going to a whorehouse. This troubling introduction to what will become a conventional "all for love" plot shows that Hemingway was ambivalent about both the narrative romance structure and the character he was envisioning for Frederic Henry. For instance, on the couple's first meeting, Henry learned that she was recovering from the death of her fiancé in the Somme ("a ghastly show," Henry agrees). Catherine carries that man's rattan stick, an omnipresent reminder of his death, but the conversation on her part is not so much flirtatious as blunt: rather than war being "picturesque," she describes her fiancé's death—"He didn't have a sabre cut. They blew him all to bits" (20). Yet when Henry compliments her on her beautiful hair, she tells him that she had wanted to cut it all off when her "boy" was killed:

> "I wanted to do something for him. You see I didn't care about the other thing and he could have had it all. He could have had anything he wanted if I would have known. I would have married him or anything. I know all about it now. But then he wanted to go to war and I didn't know. . . . I didn't know about anything then. I thought it would be worse for him. I thought perhaps he couldn't stand it and then of course he was killed and that was the end of it." (19)

Her sexual candor surprises Henry. It would have surprised any man at the time, especially since she had earlier informed him that she had been properly brought up. And the suggestion of recent sexual experience—"I know all about it now"—also serves as a forthright revelation, the "it" used with Hemingway's characteristic meaningful ambivalence. (Does Catherine mean death? loss? sex? the relative unimportance of sexual intercourse in the life-and-death dailiness of war?)

The minutes-long conversation also includes Catherine's tersely revealing comment that "Anybody may crack." She here argues with Henry when he contends (from his inexperienced point of view—he is, after all, a soldier who is only an ambulance driver; and one who has seen no action, at that) that the French will not crack. Catherine thinks differently: "We'll crack. We'll crack in France. They can't go on doing things like the Somme and not crack" (20). Catherine implies that she has broken herself, that her misunderstanding of what death could mean—and what love might have meant—has cost her some elements of her personal control.

Hemingway uses the second scene between Frederic and Catherine to reinforce these tentative suggestions. Chapter V begins directly: "The next afternoon I went to call on Miss Barkley." Because she is on duty, however, Catherine cannot see him. He returns that evening. Again, minutes after he arrives, they are aware of their sexual attraction. He places his arm around her, under her arm, and she slaps him. The conventional skirmishes have begun. But within a page, the two are kissing deeply and she is calling him "darling," clearly returning to memories of embraces with her dead lover. "'What the hell,' Henry thought." For him, as Hemingway makes clear, courting Catherine is a game, "seeing it all ahead like the moves in a chess game" (26–27).

By the next encounter, the romance is settled: Catherine is his. At her request, he tells her he loves her; they speak reassurances; he realizes that "I thought she was probably a little crazy. It was all right if she was. I did not care what I was getting into. This was better than going every evening to the house for officers where the girls climbed all over you. . . . I knew I did not love Catherine Barkley nor had any idea of loving her. This was a game, like bridge, in which you said things instead of playing cards. Like bridge you had to pretend you were playing for money or playing for some stakes. Nobody had mentioned what the stakes were" (30–31).

Hemingway has arranged these four scenes to alternate with accounts of Henry's activities within the war context. These reminders of what the lovers' lives exist within are useful, but the reader's attention is less fixed on the bivouac than on the nurses' quarters. Each section builds to the romantic encounters; each supposedly tough comment by Frederic Henry (or Rinaldi) is undercut by the sensual description Hemingway provides—not only of the Henry–Catherine plot but of the accounts of the military. The most often-described scene, the first glimpse of the soldiers in their capes, looking as if they were "six months gone with child," (4) for instance, has been termed by critic George Montiero a "psalm" because of its dense and repetitious texture, as well as its resemblance to the Twenty-third Psalm.[27] Even this initial descriptive scene is set in a context of "we" characters—never named—living in an intimacy that allows such lines as "Sometimes in the dark we heard the troops . . ." (3) Sometimes events connected with the military are given an overt sexual implication—for instance, Hemingway's lengthy description of Henry's attempts to "master the jerk of the ridiculous short barrel" of his Astra 7.65 caliber, concluding that, with such a weapon, "there was no question of hitting anything" (29).

More significantly, many of the apparent "war" passages also have a sexual—or at least sensual—texture and, accordingly, effect. In the scene when Hemingway is trying to think about what hunting in the high country of the Abruzzi would be like, his mind returns (in another very long passage) to,

> [T]he smoke of the cafes and nights when the room whirled and you needed to look at the wall to make it stop, nights in bed, drunk, when you knew that that was all there was, and the strange excitement of waking and not knowing who it was with you, and the world all unreal in the dark and so exciting that you must resume again unknowing and not caring in the night, sure that this was all and all and all and not caring. Suddenly to care very much and everything sharp and hard and clear and sometimes a dispute about the cost. (13)

The young character's condescending line toward the end of the next lengthy section of this passage makes clear that he is describing the physical satisfaction of even random sex: "I cannot tell it now. But if you have had it you know" (13). One of the reasons he "cannot tell it now" is the likelihood of the book's being unpublishable, but another reason is that Hemingway is using this undercurrent of sexuality to prompt his reader to follow the romance narrative.

By the time Hemingway has finished writing his World War I novel, *A Farewell to Arms* has become the bleak narrative that conveys its author's knowledge about both the Great War and his first great love. As Hemingway had written to his older sister Marcelline in November of 1917, when he was planning to join the Canadian Army, "I will go not because of any love of gold braid glory etc. but because I couldn't face any body after the war and not have been in it."[28]

But even as he wrote it, still steeped in both his reading and United States propaganda, Hemingway did not believe that war would not be something to treasure. It is his letter from one year later, November of 1918, that shows how changed the young Oak Park man was. He writes to her this time from Milano:

Child, I'm going to stay over here till my girl [Agnes von Kurowsky] goes home and then I'll go up north or get rested before I have to go to work in the fall. The doc says that I'm all shot to pieces, figuratively as well as literally you see. My internal arrangements were all battered up and he says I won't be any good for a year. So I want to kill as much time as I can over here. If I was at home I'd either have to work or live at the folks. And, I can't work. I'm too shot up and my nerves are all jagged. . . . You won't know me. I'm about 100 years older and I'm not bashful and I'm all medalled up and shot up.[29]

It is the still vivid memory of his glimpses of World War I that fuels Hemingway to conceive, and to complete, the book that was less autobiographical than he gave readers to believe. But it was a book that had what he considered to be great truths, and great sorrow, in it.

NOTES

1. Ray B. West, Jr. "The Unadulterated Sensibility" from his *The Art of Modern Fiction* (New York: Holt, Rinehart & Winston, 1949), p. 139.

2. Ernest Hemingway as quoted in the Lillian Ross profile, "How Do You Like It Now, Gentlemen?" *New Yorker* 16 (May 13, 1950), p. 60.

3. See Jamie Barlowe's "Hemingway's Gender Training" in my *A Historical Guide to Ernest Hemingway* (New York: Oxford University Press, 2000), pp. 117–154.

4. The best description of Hemingway's important education in the natural world is Susan F. Beegel's "Eye and Heart: Hemingway's Education as a Naturalist," *A Historical Guide to Ernest Hemingway* (New York: Oxford University Press, 2000), pp. 53–92.

5. See Kenneth S. Lynn, *Hemingway* (New York: Simon & Schuster, 1987), Jeffrey Meyers, *Hemingway: A Biography* (New York: Crown, 1985), and Max Westbrook, "Grace under Pressure: Hemingway and the Summer of 1920," in my *Ernest Hemingway: Six Decades of Criticism* (E. Lansing: Michigan State University Press, 1987), pp. 19–40.

6. See for these early years, both Michael S. Reynolds, *The Young Hemingway* (New York: Basil Blackwell, 1986) and Peter Griffin, *Along with Youth: Hemingway, the Early Years* (New York: Oxford University Press, 1985).

7. Mark Spilka, *Hemingway's Quarrel with Androgyny* (Lincoln: University of Nebraska Press, 1990) includes many of his earlier essays about the influence of Kipling and such writers on Hemingway's psyche.

8. See Henry S. Villard and James Nagel, eds., *Hemingway in Love and War: The Lost Diary of Agnes von Kurowsky, Her Letters and Correspondence of Ernest Hemingway* (Boston: Northeastern University Press, 1989) and Gioia Diliberto, *Hadley* (New York: Ticknor, 1992).

9. The correspondence between Hadley and Hemingway is available, as is so much else, in the Ernest Hemingway Collection in the John F. Kennedy Library, Boston.

10. See Michael S. Reynolds, "Ernest Hemingway, 1899–1961: A Brief Biography" in *A Historical Guide to Ernest Hemingway* (New York: Oxford University Press, 2000), pp. 24–25.

11. Holograph note on outside of *A Farewell to Arms* manuscript, Hemingway Collection, John F. Kennedy Library. At another place in the manuscript, Hemingway had written, "I loved my father. Very much."

12. Hemingway to Dos Passos, September 4, 1929, in *Ernest Hemingway: Selected Letters, 1917–1961*, ed. Carlos Baker (New York: Scribner's, 1980), p. 304.

13. Frederic J. Svoboda, "The Great Themes in Hemingway," *A Historical Guide to Ernest Hemingway* (New York: Oxford University Press, 2000), pp. 159–161.

14. Malcolm Cowley, *New York Herald Tribune Books* (October 6, 1929); Fanny Butcher, "Review of *A Farewell to Arms*," *Chicago Tribune* (September 28, 1929), reprinted in the Paris *Tribune* (October 20, 1929); Clifton P. Fadiman, "A Fine American Novel," *The Nation* (October 30, 1929), pp. 497–498; Henry S. Canby, *Saturday Review of Literature* (October 12, 1929), pp. 231–232.

15. Millicent Bell, "Pseudoautobiography and Personal Metaphor," *Modern Critical Interpretations: Ernest Hemingway's* A Farewell to Arms, ed. Harold Bloom (New York: Chelsea House, 1987), p. 123.

16. Earlier readings of the novel did not question its being a novel of war: see Philip Young, *Ernest Hemingway* (New York: Rinehart, 1952) and *Ernest Hemingway: A Reconsideration* (University Park: Pennsylvania State University Press, 1966); Carlos Baker, *Hemingway: The Writer as Artist* (Princeton, NJ: Princeton University Press, 1952) and *Ernest Hemingway: A Life Story* (New York: Scribner's, 1969); Earl Rovit, *Ernest Hemingway* (New York: Twayne, 1963); Sheridan Baker, *Ernest Hemingway: An Introduction and Interpretation* (New York: Holt, Rinehart, 1967); and Arthur Waldhorn, *A Reader's Guide to Ernest Hemingway* (New York: Farrar, Straus and Giroux, 1972).

17. Stanley Cooperman, *World War One and the American Novel* (Baltimore: Johns Hopkins University Press, 1967).

18. Michael S. Reynolds, *Hemingway's First War* (Princeton, NJ: Princeton University Press, 1976).

19. One of the best-known critiques is Judith Fetterley's *The Resisting Reader: A Feminist Approach to American Fiction* (Bloomington: Indiana University Press, 1978); a great many other critics have weighed into the gender discussion: see also Alan Holder, "The Other Hemingway," *Twentieth Century Literature* (1963), pp. 153–157, reprinted in *Ernest Hemingway: Five Decades of Criticism*, ed. Linda W. Wagner (E. Lansing: Michigan State University Press, 1974); Linda W. Wagner, "'Proud and friendly and gently': Women in Hemingway's Early Fiction," *College Literature* 7 (1980), pp. 239–247; Joyce Wexler, "E.R.A. for Hemingway: A Feminist Defense of *A Farewell to Arms*," *Georgia Review* 35 (1981), pp. 111–123; Charles J. Nolan, Jr., "Hemingway's Women's Movement," *Hemingway Review* 3 (Spring 1984), pp. 14–22; James Nagel, "Catherine Barkley and Retrospective Narration in *A Farewell to Arms*," in *Ernest Hemingway: Six Decades of Criticism*, ed. Linda Wagner-Martin (E. Lansing: Michigan State University Press, 1987), pp. 187–194; Sandra Whipple Spanier, "Catherine Barkley and the Hemingway Code: Ritual and Survival in *A Farewell to Arms*," *Modern Critical Interpretations of Ernest Hemingway's* A Farewell to Arms, ed. Harold Bloom (New York: Chelsea House, 1987), pp. 131–148; Jamie Barlowe-Kayes, "Re-Reading Women: The Example of Catherine Barkley," in *Hemingway: Seven Decades of Criticism*, ed. Linda Wagner-Martin (E. Lansing: Michigan State University Press, 1999), pp. 171–184; Marilyn Elkins, "The Fashion of *Machismo*," *A Historical Guide to Ernest Hemingway* (New York: Oxford University Press, 2000), pp. 93–115; and, among other more recent treatments, Debra A. Moddelmog, *Reading Desire: In Pursuit of Ernest Hemingway* (Ithaca, NY: Cornell University Press, 1999).

20. Matthew C. Stewart, "Ernest Hemingway and World War I: Combatting Recent Psychobiographical Reassessments, Restoring the War," *Papers in Language and Literature* 36 (Spring 2000), pp. 198–217; this section 204, 213, 208.

21. Ibid., pp. 202–203.

22. Ross, *New Yorker* profile, p. 43.

23. Ernest Hemingway, "Introduction," *Men at War* (New York: Crown, 1942), p. 12.

24. One of the more relevant discussions about war strategy occurs here, and—like much of the seemingly random description of the novel—foreshadows battle conditions in the mountainous area of Caporetto. This is Henry's apparently informed answer to Gino's comment about fighting at San Gabriele: " 'that was a special case because it was a fortress rather than a mountain, anyway. The Austrians had been fortifying it for years.' I meant tactically speaking in a war where there was some movement a succession of mountains were nothing to hold as a line because it was too easy to turn them. You should have possible mobility and a mountain is not very mobile. Also, people always over-shoot downhill. If the flank were turned, the best men would be left on the highest mountains. I did not believe in a war in mountains. I had thought about it a lot, I said. You pinched off one mountain and they pinched off another but when something really started every one had to get down off the mountains."

It is in this discourse, too, that Gino describes the way the shells come, as if "directly for you. There is the boom, then instantly the shriek and burst." The two men also examine a shell fragment, "a smoothly jagged piece of metal over a foot long." Ernest Hemingway, *A Farewell to Arms* (New York: Scribner's, 1929), pp. 182–183; hereafter cited in text.

25. See my essay "The Intertextual Hemingway" for comparisons between this passage and the same content in other novels of war (*A Historical Guide to Ernest Hemingway* [New York: Oxford University Press, 2000], pp. 184–187).

26. John G. Cawelti, *Adventure, Mystery, and Romance: Formula Stories as Art and Popular Culture* (Chicago: University of Chicago Press, 1976), pp. 39–42.

27. George Montiero, "Ernest Hemingway, Psalmist," *Hemingway: Seven Decades of Criticism* (E. Lansing: Michigan State University Press, 1999), pp. 126–130.

28. Ernest to Marcelline, in Marcelline Hemingway Sanford, *At the Hemingways (with 50 years of correspondence between Ernest and Marcelline Hemingway)* (Moscow: University of Idaho Press, 1999), p. 271.

29. Ibid., p. 297.

2 Content

The trauma of war in its various ramifications colors much of Hemingway's writing during his first decade of publication, from the short stories and vignettes of *in our time* (1924) and *In Our Time* (1925) through *The Sun Also Rises* (1926), the second major story collection in 1928, *Men Without Women* (a title that draws the reader back to the theme of war, where women would be largely absent), and the work which is most clearly war-connected, *A Farewell to Arms* in 1929. In fact, it could be said that Hemingway's novel of World War I was his protest against all war, all conflict that resulted in such immense loss of life (estimates place the dead at over ten million, and the wounded at twice that figure).

Like a grim black-and-white photo, the opening scene of Hemingway's *A Farewell to Arms* depicts soldiers, muffled and misshapen in their bulky rain gear, marching across a bleak, rain-drenched landscape. The narrator's voice adds to the tone of unhappiness as it comments that with winter would come the cholera, of which "only seven thousand died" among the troops (4).

Hemingway's "warscape" continues in the next chapter. It is a year later, and the Allies have had some victories. Frederic Henry, the American protagonist who has volunteered to command Italian ambulances, sits at the officers' mess. His Italian companions there are a young Catholic priest, the captain who teases the priest about his imaginary sexual encounters with women, the major, and Lieutenant Rinaldi, the surgeon who is Henry's roommate.

When Frederic Henry returns from a leave during which he sees many of Italy's cities (and has a number of sexual experiences), Rinaldi introduces him to the British V.A.D., Catherine Barkley. She is mourning for the death of her fiancé who was killed at the Somme; she seems confused, and tells Henry there is no need to play the usual games of romance. After several meetings, she becomes Henry's girlfriend. When he goes out on post or to manage ambulances for an attack upriver, she gives him a Saint Anthony medal to keep him safe.

Hemingway has forced the reader to imagine what the soldiers and the Italian ambulance drivers are like through their conversations as they await the battle. Their task then is to drive the wounded or dead to the various hospitals or battleground aid stations. Several chapters provide good detail. But then as Frederic Henry and Passini, one of the drivers, and several others sit in a shallow dugout eating cold macaroni and cheese, a trench mortar shell hits them. Passini is killed; Henry—badly wounded—is carried to the post aid station by two of the other drivers.

The next chapters describe Henry's wounds, the surgery, and his recuperation, first at the field hospital—where both Rinaldi and the young priest manage to visit him—and then in a Milan facility, where Catherine comes to work. In the better equipped city hospital, Henry is given mechano-therapy; there too, he and Catherine become lovers: she consistently volunteers for the night shift. Even though the other hospital personnel are suspicious, she and Henry spend the nights in his bed. (His behavior is also frowned upon because—against doctors' orders—he drinks a quantity of wine and brandy; later he develops jaundice.)

The summer passes. As Henry improves, he is allowed to leave the hospital—for his treatments and so that he and Catherine can take in the sights, chief among them the horse races. Catherine becomes increasingly content with their isolation; as Henry gets ready to have a leave, she tells him she is three months pregnant. His jaundice cancels his leave, but his inability to be happy about her pregnancy has already begun to undermine the intimacy between them. For all their protestations about being married and not needing any ceremony, Hemingway suggests that a love originating in the circumstances of war may not be very stable.

Before Henry returns to his unit and to the front, the couple goes to a cheap hotel to make love. It is then that Catherine tells him that, in those surroundings, she feels like a whore.

Frederic Henry returns to the front to find his Italian friends discouraged and depressed. They are losing the war. Hundreds of men have been slaughtered. Rinaldi believes he has syphilis. The next day the ambulances start out, heading generally for Caporetto. The mountainous terrain, filled with both Italians in retreat and Germans infiltrating, is dangerous. Henry and his ambulance crew don't know when to be seen and when to hide: fifteen divisions of Germans have broken through the lines. The rain is mixed with snow. Roads are filled with fleeing Italians.

For this action, Henry has a different group of Italian ambulance drivers; Hemingway makes the reader care about each of them—Bonello, Aymo, and Piani. As they travel in caravan, one driver picks up two young Italian sisters, frightened virgins; another gives a lift to two Italian sergeants of engineers. The latter will not accept orders from Henry so he shoots one, and Bonello finishes the execution. In the disarray of the retreat, their ambulances mired in mud, Henry and his drivers try to escape. Aymo is killed, probably by Italians; Bonello deserts; Piani stays with Henry as they reach the group of Italian officers who are questioning—and then executing—fellow Italian officers at a checkpoint on the Tagliamento River.

Henry sees that he too will be shot so he dives into the river and escapes the bullets falling around him as he swims underwater. He crosses the Venetian plain and escapes by rail, hiding in a flatcar, until he reaches Milan. Loyal acquaintances there help him with papers and clothes, and he follows Catherine and her friend Helen to Stresa, where they have gone for a holiday. Reunited, he and Catherine stay at Stresa until they are warned that military police know of Henry's location; in the middle of the night, Henry rows them across the lake into Switzerland. They satisfy the border police and—miraculously—spend the next several months in the ski areas of Switzerland.

Despite Catherine's pregnancy—and her prescient images of death in the rain—these months are the idyll (the "separate peace" of Hemingway's earlier war stories) of a great love affair, the couple in love isolated from all harm, creating their own universe. As he has done frequently, Hemingway alternates the moods of hope and security with those of fear and dread: what happens as the novel ends leaves Frederic Henry, the story's narrator, a broken and disillusioned man. A *Farewell to Arms* is Henry's story told from the distance of a decade, a purging of the greatest grief this character has experienced: the loss of not only his son, a child born dead, but of his beloved Catherine, who dies in the aftermath of the Caesarean delivery of that child.

Despite the fact that the novel is a war novel, and that much reader interest focuses on the romance between Henry and Catherine, the novel is crafted to belong to Frederic Henry. Reproducing that character's wounded psyche was one of the chief narrative aims of Hemingway's book. Always an admirer of the work of Henry James, despite his protests against fiction in which nothing happened, Hemingway knew that fiction, like poetry, was fueled by emotional conflict. In *A Farewell to Arms*, Frederic Henry's conflict comes from wanting to be a part of the war activity, even to joining the American Red Cross in Italy, and yet wanting to escape the dangers—and the horrors—of such conflict. That millions of men died in World War I meant that nobody connected with the slaughter in any way escaped unchanged.

It was not only that Hemingway had been seriously and painfully wounded in the war; he also was a voracious reader of great novels about war.[1] And not unlike Stephen Crane's Henry Fleming, similarly conflicted in *The Red Badge of Courage*—a novel Hemingway called the epitome of war story—[2] Hemingway's Frederic Henry suppressed his fear until he had amassed so much evidence that events in war had no logic that he could then desert. To avoid the chance of being erroneously, or randomly, killed made even more sense in the context of his being able to choose to live in some private world, apart from national identities or bellicose allegiances, a world he could create with his beloved Catherine and, eventually, with their child.

Hemingway's moral thrust throughout *A Farewell to Arms* is not, however, limited to some prescriptive (and/or patriotic) maxim. The reader understands that Hemingway is not saying, "Frederic Henry deserted and therefore he is punished by being left alone, still a deserter, Catherine and their baby dead, leaving him with an almost unbearable grief." Rather, Hemingway's novel suggests that moral values are continuously fluid. Deserting was one plausible way for Henry to try to find that "other country" where he and Catherine could exist—happily—without the constraints of militarily imposed rules. The reader sympathizes with Frederic Henry, the man, and is willing to lose sight almost completely—as the book does—of Frederic Henry, the soldier.

THE STRUCTURE OF THE PLOT

In the Hemingway Collection at the John F. Kennedy Library is a single sheet of paper on which Hemingway has copied out, from the *New York Times* for March 2, 1915, a paragraph of conversation between Preston Lockwood and Henry James:

One finds it hard in the midst of all this to apply one's words as to endure one's thoughts. The war has used up words; they have weakened, they have deteriorated like motor car tires; . . . and we are now confronted with a depreciation of all our terms, or, otherwise speaking, with a loss of expression through increase of limpness, that may well make us wonder what ghosts may be left to walk.[3]

We have seen Hemingway's recasting of this sentiment in the passage about *sacred, glorious,* and *sacrifice* already quoted; we have seen the way *A Farewell to Arms* makes even the prowar reader question such conflict. Hemingway's problem remained, as he had learned in his arduous efforts during the writing of *The Sun Also Rises,* how to convey such immense conflict—and its layers of ambiguity—to a reader, without simply stating it as a problem.

In his understanding of the way to create dramatic structures, which would in turn keep readers reading, Hemingway found that in order to tell both a war story and a love story, he needed to alternate suspenseful segments of each narrative. While critics of the book did not uniformly mention its clearly defined, and almost predictable, organization, Ray B. West, Jr., notes that "the sequence of events in *A Farewell to Arms* is ordered and logical to an extreme which (outside of Henry James) is the exception in the American novel."[4] West points out that the book's structure is that of a drama: "It is composed of five separate books, each composed by a series of scenes, and each scene broken into sections which might be likened to stage direction and dialogue."[5]

Accordingly, then, *A Farewell to Arms* opens with the war, but the war is tamed into a journalistic description of soldiers marching through the rain-sodden countryside, as miserable as they are vulnerable. In the metaphor of pregnancy, Hemingway makes the segue into the realm of the romance: readers will return to this image of the soldiers' capes extended over their gear, as though they are six months gone with child, when they learn about Catherine Barkley's pregnancy and her similarly vulnerable state. Unmarried, alien, traveling on a passport that will not hold up once she—like Frederic Henry—deserts her military role, her vulnerability is that of both physical frailty and inadequate medical science at the turn of the twentieth century.

In the first of the novel's five books, more attention is paid to the war theme, but because Catherine Barkley is introduced early in the fourth chapter of Book I, her presence dominates the rest of the book (through Chapter 12). Book I is a "war" section, however, and the climax of the action—which consists largely of conversation among the ambulance drivers—occurs in Frederic Henry's wounding. Chapter 9 is the stream-of-consciousness account of the shattering blow, and the remaining chapters of Book I chart Henry's rescue, operations, and hospitalization. The book closes with separate visits to Henry in his hospital room—one from Rinaldi, the other from the young priest; Hemingway can thereby create a repetition of the effect of each man and his friendship upon Frederic Henry. Rinaldi's ribald and sexualized camaraderie is set against the priest's tranquil and calming sense of a safe haven. The war as a total entity, however, has been personalized so that it becomes one man's wounding.

Book II continues the focus on Frederic Henry; it begins with Henry's transfer to the more sophisticated hospital in Milan. The discomfort of the move and his adversarial relationship with the two nurses in charge occupy the first chapter of this book, but the long section immediately becomes the story of his romance with Catherine. She appears soon after the second chapter of the book opens. From then on for more than six chapters, the larger war disappears into Henry's somewhat adolescent musings about (1) the condition of his leg and his self and (2) the sex he is having with Catherine. Rather than drama about the war, Hemingway's drama in these chapters is the diagnosis of Frederic Henry's injury, and whether or not he and Catherine will get caught in their frequent night-time love making. The author is not subtle about the connection between Catherine's availability and Frederic Henry's "love" for her: as he describes the wounded man's recognition of the lovely V.A.D. upon her arrival,

> "Hello, darling," she said. She looked fresh and young and very beautiful. I thought I had never seen any one so beautiful.
> "Hello," I said. When I saw her I was in love with her (91).

Two pages later, Hemingway clarifies the suddenness of Henry's feelings: "God knows I had not wanted to fall in love with her. I had not wanted to fall in love with any one" (93).

Within those intervening two pages, Henry and Catherine have intercourse—barely five minutes after her arrival. In keeping with the high percentage of dialogue that is fixated on sexual activity, such behavior seems less flamboyant than—according to hospital procedures and military protocol—it was. Again, Hemingway's interpretation of what love might mean to people in war can be said to be somewhat sensationalized.

Subsequent chapters, again, fail to mention war. Chapter 18, for example, opens "We had a lovely time that summer" (112) and the next chapter continues that placid mood: "The summer went that way" (117). During this chapter, however, and continuing through the next several—to the end of Book II—the tone darkens. Catherine fears the rain, and has visions of either herself or Henry dead in it. In Chapter 21, the war reappears—and the news is bad: "The fighting at the front went very badly and they could not take San Gabriele" (133). On the home front, Catherine has to admit to Frederic that she is pregnant, and has been for three months. In a scene striking for its shame and irony (her shame and his irony about "her" condition), Hemingway undercuts what one had taken to be the theme of Book II—Catherine's and Frederic's great love. The last two chapters describe Henry's jaundice, his preparations to return to his unit, and the couple's last love-making, in the hotel room that makes Catherine feel like a whore. Book II, which has been given almost entirely over to the love story, ends with a clearly ominous tone. Frederic's and Catherine's romance, complicated by absence and pregnancy, seems to be running parallel with the unsuccessful military effort.

Book III begins with Henry's return, and the by-now anticipated encounters with both Rinaldi and the priest. Cordoned off from his real life, that with Catherine, Frederic Henry the military man has the chance to choose between two ways of living. One is the sensual; the other is the religious. Because Rinaldi's discourse fits so well with the reader's anticipations of a return to the romance plot, his scenes with Frederic are more memorable. They too, however, are tinged with the sorrow of waste: fearing that he has syphilis, drinking himself into oblivion, worried about the outcome of the war and—daily, hourly—faced with dying men that, for all his skill, he cannot save, Rinaldi is nearing despair. He gives up his drunkenly brave chatter to speak, "You can't do it. You can't do it. I say you can't do it. You're dry and you're empty and there's nothing else. There's nothing else I tell you. Not a damned thing. I know, when I stop working" (174).

In contrast, the priest offers his acceptance of defeat gently, telling Henry, "It has been a terrible summer" (177). As the reader compares his weary account ("You cannot believe how it has been. Except that you have been there and you know how it can be. Many people have realized the war this summer," [178]) with the "lovely" summer Henry and Catherine have been experiencing, the idyllic sense that love can conquer all begins to diminish. Book III leads the reader into what will be Hemingway's full treatment of military conflict—the battles, the retreat and its resulting losses of life and courage, Henry's own impoverished sense of self, and his final desertion. Book III illustrates the disgust evident in the "sacred, glorious, and sacrifice" paragraph. That somber disgust lasts for all seven chapters of the book, and the reader is returned to the romance narrative only at the very end of Chapter 32. Saved from being either shot or drowned, Frederic Henry lives through a stream-of-consciousness revelation that shows him he must return to Catherine. "Anger was washed away in the river along with any obligation. . . . I was not made to think. I was made to eat. My God, yes. Eat and drink and sleep with Catherine. To-night maybe. No that was impossible. But to-morrow night, and a good meal and sheets and never going away again except together. . . . She would go. I knew she would go" (232–233).

The last two books, IV and V, move quickly. They comprise scarcely a hundred pages of the 330-page novel. Except for the fact that Henry and Catherine are deserters, the war is seldom mentioned. *A Farewell to Arms* becomes almost entirely the romance narrative. Hidden away, Frederic and Catherine seem oblivious to the danger they are in; their life together is interrupted only once, by Count Greffi's wish to play billiards with Henry. It is in that cameo appearance of the very old man that Hemingway sets the philosophic tone for the last chapters. The Count disclaims that age brings wisdom; he says "[men] do not grow wise. They grow careful" (262). He also instructs Frederic in cynicism, and in the fact that loving another person is a kind of religion.

In the atmosphere of having created a separate peace, of leaving the war in order to live their own lives, Catherine and Frederic seem surprised when they have been discovered, and are ordered to flee. Book IV ends with the lovers making their escape to Switzerland, a flight which culminates in the grueling thirty-five-kilometer row across the lake at night—an episode equal in drama to Henry's wounding. They land, are arrested, and move to what appears to be a safe location, again creating their own country. Their arrival in Switzerland ends Book IV.

Book V consists of only four chapters. In the first, their days are placid, withdrawn, self-consumed. While the tone of Hemingway's description of their weeks in this other country is pleasant, the reader cannot dismiss the war as easily as Frederic seems to have dismissed it. He has apparently relegated it to distant memory. Subliminally, Hemingway's hints of disaster—whether it be in the repetition of the rain or in Catherine's biting commentary about her sense of the future—make the reader sensitive to the somewhat ironic picture of lovers' bliss. The second chapter of the four opens as if to echo the first scene of the novel:

By the middle of January I had a beard and the winter had settled into bright cold days and hard cold nights. We could walk on the roads again. The snow was packed hard and smooth by the hay-sleds and wood-sledges and the logs that were hauled down the mountain. The snow lay over all the country, down almost to Montreux. The mountains on the other side of the lake were all white and the plain of the Rhone Valley was covered. We took long walks on the other side of the mountain. . . . Catherine wore hobnailed boots and a cape and carried a stick with a sharp steel point. She did not look big with the cape and we would not walk too fast. (302)

Hemingway's emphasis on the hardness of the road, the snow, the whiteness creates an image of stark winter. The scene is not entirely pleasant, but neither is it frightening—unless one recalls the earlier dialogue about the difficulty of fighting in the mountains. Clearly, Catherine and Frederic are now surrounded by mountains, and, in her labor, which is approaching, one characteristic word to describe that process is *hard*. What the scene emphasizes is how objectively a person's existence can be described, and, toward the end, with the mention of Catherine's *cape*, the reader is returned to the military capes described in the initial scene. Her sharp-pointed *stick* also recalls the stick she carried in memory of her dead lover.

The rains begin in the third of the last four chapters. By the time Catherine's birth pains occur at the beginning of the fourth chapter, the reader feels only dread. Hemingway's manuscripts show how carefully he had built Book V and the ending of the novel.[6] In the immense amount of material that is given the reader in that single concluding chapter, it is difficult to sort through which set of scenes is most important: the progression of Catherine's labor, the birth of the dead son, and throughout, the shocked comprehension on Frederic's part that his wife is going to die, followed—almost too quickly—by Catherine's death.

The impassioned grieving that marks Frederic's last glimpse of Catherine is shaded off to the mournful yet somehow tranquil memory that closes the novel. War has been absorbed into its surrogate narrative, the death of Catherine Barkley.

One of the ways Hemingway was able to bring the story to its end so quickly—and relentlessly—is that he had been writing about Catherine's death throughout other parts of the novel. Just as the description of the snowy roads above recasts the opening scene, and invested a natural description with the threat of harm, so Hemingway was preparing the reader throughout for the bloodshed of Catherine's childbirth and its aftermath. For instance, philosophically, Frederic Henry explains that he has no fear for his own death in the coming conflict: "I knew I would not be killed. Not in this war. It did not have anything to do with me. It seemed no more dangerous to me myself than war in the movies" (37).

In the most often quoted scene from the novel, that of Frederic's wounding, readers are given a description evocative of sexual intercourse, particularly with his use of the words *dead* and *died*. As Hemingway writes this passage, he makes a move into a kind of advance description of Catherine's death—of hemorrhage after childbirth. All the descriptions of Henry's wounding, care, and bloodletting anticipate her difficulty breathing, her pain, and of course her death, of which there is almost no description. Here is the central image of Henry's wounding, which begins this compelling sequence:

> [O]n and on in a rushing wind. I tried to breathe but my breath would not come and I felt myself rush bodily out of myself and out and out and out and all the time bodily in the wind. I went out swiftly, all of myself, and I knew I was dead and that it had all been a mistake to think you just died. Then I floated, and instead of going on I felt myself slide back. I breathed and I was back. (54)[7]

Henry's wounding is necessary, so far as the narrative goes, because Hemingway wants to give the reader the hospital scene, the full import of death and the frustration of medical knowledge (anticipated by Rinaldi's disillusion) that cannot save lives; and to create the mood of inexorable death, complete with its blood, relentless blood, the blood that readers who focus on the white purity of snow, chastity, innocence, and military honor would like to deny. The reader cannot avoid the recognition of blood as Hemingway describes Passini's dreadful death—after the futile tourniquet attempt, and Henry's own "warm and wet," repeated as "wet and warm," wounds, and his careful planting of the word *hemorrhage* ("there was so much dirt blown into the wound that there had not been much hemorrhage" [57]). Once Henry is on the operating table, we are told again, with careful repetition, about the blood, this time the "sweet smell of blood." And after the cleaning and suturing, the doctor closes his cynical and distant monologue with the comment, "Your blood coagulates beautifully."

There are many ways to describe wounds and operating rooms. With all the skill Hemingway had acquired in his writing by 1929, his use of scenes and words and images that would both foreshadow and ironically comment on Catherine's later hospital scene seems more than accidental. He is, for example, careful to avoid describing Henry's wounds as *leg* wounds so that the reader can think of all the dark wounding that passion can bring to the mortal body. And the doctor's flippant inquiry almost contributes to extending Henry's experience into Catherine's. The doctor asks, "How did you run into this thing anyway? What were you trying to do? Commit suicide?" (59). The reader later thinks, what was Catherine trying to do? To procreate, to give life, to allow the great passion she had experienced with Frederic to come to fruition. But her blood, the reader assumes, did not coagulate beautifully.

Hemingway uses carefully ambiguous language throughout the operating scene that *is* described, the surgery on Frederic's leg: "The captain, doing things that hurt sharply and severing tissue. . . . Me—trying to lie still and feeling my stomach flutter when the flesh was cut. . . . Captain doctor—(interested in something he was finding). . . . Sweat ran all over me. 'Good Christ!' I said. . . . The pain . . . had started and all that was happening was without interest or relation" (58–60). By the end of the novel, Hemingway provides very little description of Catherine's ordeal, but the reader has already experienced it. And his description here continues with the pain and agony, but with complete suppression of the word *blood*. But later, as Henry is being transported by ambulance, his stretcher is placed under that of another wounded man. Again, the words *hemorrhage, warm, dead*.

As the ambulance climbed along the road, it was slow in the traffic, sometimes it stopped, sometimes it backed on a turn, then finally it climbed quite fast. *I felt something dripping. At first it dropped slowly and regularly, then it pattered into a stream.* I shouted to the driver. He stopped the car and looked in through the hole behind his seat.

"What is it?"

"The man on the stretcher over me has a hemorrhage."

"We're not far from the top. I wouldn't be able to get the stretcher out alone." He started the car. *The stream kept on. In the dark I could not see where it came from the canvas overhead. I tried to move sideways so that it did not fall on me. Where it had run down under my shirt it was warm and sticky.* I was cold and my leg hurt so that it made me sick. *After a while the stream from the stretcher above lessened and started to drop again* and I heard and felt the canvas above move as the man on the stretcher settled more comfortably.

"How is he?" the Englishman called back. "We're almost up."

"He's dead I think," I said.

The drops fell very slowly, as they fall from an icicle after the sun has gone. It was cold in the car in the night as the road climbed. At the post on the top they took the stretcher out and put another in and we went on (my emphasis, 61).

The complete absence of the word *blood*—in its place, *something, the stream, the drops*, and particularly the innocent *it*—achieves terrible force.

As an isolated scene, coming to close the one episode of war wounding that Frederic Henry experiences, this passage is remarkably powerful; but as a foreshadowing of the romance denouement, the proof of medical inability to save life, the randomness of hemorrhage and death, the scene is superb. Hemingway's art of omission here, and in his treatment of the actual intercourse between Catherine and Frederic, also feeds into the romance tradition. It is almost possible for the reader to believe that this great love is, somehow, pure and chaste.

Metaphorically, Hemingway brings together the themes of war and love—even if both narratives end in a kind of death. For Catherine, death is actual. For Frederic, at least in the years after her death, his life becomes immersed in mourning. But the fact that he is telling the story, that his sensibility of loss evokes so beautifully the love that they had, can be seen as a kind of survival. Allowing himself to write his farewell to whatever commitments war and love had obligated him to may have been a strategy that saved Frederic. Or so this novel would have its readers believe.

THE CHARACTERS OF THE NOVEL

Robert W. Lewis, Jr., sees what he calls the key to A *Farewell to Arms* in its "first-person narration. . . . [Catherine's] death is really only the end of a beginning so far as Frederic Henry is concerned."[8] Because the novel is told by Henry, and because the reader is aware that he as the protagonist has recovered from the incomprehensibly sorrowful blow of Catherine's death, the narrative is, finally, a more positive story than the events that occur during it would suggest.

Much of the critical attention to the novel has focused, accordingly, on the character of Frederic Henry. In most readings (at least up to the last twenty years, when feminist influences created a less hospitable reception for the bereaved lover), Henry is seen to grow throughout his relationship with Catherine. Toughened by her personal losses in the war, Catherine is early on the character who understands the code. Through his intimacy with her, Henry comes to realize how wise she is.[9] But much of the tone of the novel comes from our response to Frederic Henry's despair at both her death and at his realization of the corruption of war itself: this is one of the reasons that Henry as character must stay at the center of Hemingway's book. As Daniel J. Schneider said early in the critical history of the novel, "The dominant emotion or state of mind behind the events of *A Farewell to Arms* is seldom stated explicitly. It is always there, informing every scene of the novel. . . . a bitterness, a disgust, a desolation of soul, a remorse of such depth and durance that it can be held in check only by dint of the severest, most unremitting self-control." He uses the often-quoted passage from Frederic's thinking to illustrate this remorse:

> If people bring so much courage to this world the world has to kill them to break them, so of course it kills them. The world breaks every one and afterward many are strong at the broken places. But those that will not break it kills. It kills the very good and the very gentle and the very brave impartially. If you are none of these you can be sure it will kill you too but there will be no special hurry.

Schneider emphasizes, "The world's malevolence is taken for granted in Hemingway's novels."[10] And here Henry is the vehicle for the expression of this malaise.

Robert Merrill concurs, describing Frederic's philosophy as a kind of nihilism. His reading of the book, however, depends on the structure Hemingway has chosen—that of tragedy. "As in all tragedies, the power of *A Farewell to Arms* derives from the tension between what we desire for its hero and what we know will be his fate. Hemingway establishes his fictional world as more or less what Frederic thinks it to be (a world which breaks and kills indiscriminately, where nothing is sacred)."[11] For Scott Donaldson, however, Henry's personality is marked by inordinate self-pity. As part of his argument, Donaldson critiques Maxwell Perkins' letter that criticizes the novel, written May 17, 1929, to Owen Wister, as being shortsighted: "'The serious flaw in the book' [Perkins writes] 'is that the two great elements you named—one of which would make it a picture of war, and the other of which would make it a duo of love and passion—do not fully combine. It begins as one thing wholly, and ends up wholly as the other thing.' But Perkins and Wister missed the point. The subject of the novel is not love and war, in whatever combination, but Frederic Henry."[12]

Denying that Henry is autobiographical, Donaldson sees in Hemingway's changes from what might have been an autobiographical rendering of the substantial—and not always admirable—self of the novel's protagonist. To this critic, Frederic Henry's "pose of passivity cannot hide the guilt underneath, nor can he dissipate the guilt by play-acting or by writing about it. Hemingway's untrustworthy narrator remains a principal agent of both his farewells—to war as to love."[13]

While Henry was often seen as the bereaved hero of the book, most critics did little with the character of Catherine—besides to place her as the romantic love object who adds to the tragedy of Henry's life by dying in childbirth. Yet it is clear throughout the early segments of the book that Catherine is a victim of the war. Her fragmentary conversation shows that she mourns not only her fiancé's death, but the fact that she had not given herself to him sexually before he went to battle. Her guilt as a virginal woman is the primary motive in her flirtation with Henry; in fact, the word *flirtation* is misleading. What Hemingway shows, with poignant accuracy, is Catherine's complete *transference* of her emotion. As she purposely misidentifies Frederic Henry with her dead fiancé, she shows how distraught she is over the latter's death. Then, once she has instructed Henry to say "I've come back to Catherine in the night," the reader can see how important the detail of her carrying her lover's walking stick is to her postwar identity.

Catherine Barkley is the woman bereaved to near-madness, and her acute disorientation is one reason for her friend Fergie's oversight of her. It can be said that Helen Ferguson can barely stand for Catherine to be out of her vision. While a few recent critics have read Fergie's motive as sexual interest, identifying her as a lesbian,[14] it makes more sense in the context of Hemingway's working hard to show Catherine as a badly damaged victim of the war to see Fergie as her protective friend.

A Farewell to Arms makes clear that Catherine needs friends, lovers, and good luck. She doesn't have much of the latter. As Frederic Svoboda recently pointed out, "Chance has ruled Frederic's life—in his meeting with Catherine, in his wounding, in sending him back to the front at an inopportune moment, in the accident of obstetrics that hemorrhages away Catherine's life and chokes their son in her womb—and the war has conditioned all these chances. Losses build and interrelate."[15] Circumstances for Catherine are even worse. At the end of the novel, for all her supposed cynicism, Catherine Barkley is filled with hope for her life with Frederic Henry and their child. She is Henry's reassurance, his panacea, his good luck. Her relinquishment at the end of the birth scene shows that she has played that role throughout their relationship, as she—although barely able to speak—tries to comfort him:

"Poor darling," Catherine said very softly. She looked gray.

"You're all right, Cat," I said. "You're going to be all right."

"I'm going to die," she said; then waited and said, "I hate it." I took her hand.

"Don't touch me," she said. I let go of her hand. She smiled. "Poor darling. You touch me all you want."

"You'll be all right, Cat. I know you'll be all right."

"I meant to write you a letter to have if anything happened, but I didn't do it."

"Do you want me to get a priest or any one to come and see you?"

"Just you," she said. Then a little later, "I'm not afraid. I just hate it." . . .

"Please go out of the room," the doctor said. "You cannot talk." Catherine winked at me, her face gray. "I'll be right outside," I said.

"Don't worry, darling," Catherine said. "I'm not a bit afraid. It's just a dirty trick." (330–331)

Although Catherine herself does not express all the anguish of Frederic Henry's realization, his stream-of-consciousness sections—several before this scene, and one after it—complete the reader's experience. As Henry comes to understand that Catherine will die, so too does the reader. By the time he enters her room for the scene above, Henry is crying.

Hemingway's reliance on the most elemental of passions—grief, love, bravery, fear—makes A Farewell to Arms a novel of power and endurance. What he has learned to do by the late 1920s, even though he had declared himself a writer only six or seven years earlier, was to distill the thousands of words in English into a few memorable scenes and phrases, quiet places in his prose that the attentive reader will remember whenever the novel is mentioned.

NOTES

1. See Robert O. Stephens, "Hemingway and Stendhal: The Matrix of A Farewell to Arms," PMLA 88 (March 1973), pp. 271–280; Paul W. Miller, "Hemingway vs. Stendhal or Papa's Last Fight with a Dead Writer," Hemingway Review 19 (Fall 1999), pp. 127–140; Carolina Donadio Lawson, "Hemingway, Stendhal, and War," Hemingway Notes 6 (1981), pp. 28–33; Daniel Fuchs, "Ernest Hemingway, Literary Critic," Ernest Hemingway: Five Decades of Criticism, ed. Linda W. Wagner (E. Lansing: Michigan State University Press, 1974), pp. 39–56; Edward Engelberg, "Hemingway's 'True Penelope': Flaubert's L'Education Sentimentale

and *A Farewell to Arms,*" *Comparative Literature Studies* 16 (1979), pp. 189–206; John McCormick, "The Anachronous Hero: Hemingway and Motherland" in his *Fiction as Knowledge: The Modern Post-Romantic Novel* (New Brunswick, NJ: Rutgers University Press, 1975), pp. 109–131; Michael Garraty, "Love and War: R. H. Mottram, *The Spanish Farm Trilogy,* and Ernest Hemingway's *A Farewell to Arms*" in *The First World War in Fiction: A Collection of Critical Essays,* ed. Holger Klein (London: Macmillan, 1976), pp. 10–22; Zhang Yidong, "Hemingway's and Sholokhov's Viewpoints on War," *International Fiction Review* 14 (Summer 1987), pp. 75–78; my "The Intertextual Hemingway" for commentary on Henri Barbusse's *Le Feu,* Blasco Ibáñez's *The Four Horsemen of the Apocalypse,* Hugh Walpole's *The Young Enchanted,* and Ford Madox Ford's *The Good Soldier* in *A Historical Guide to Ernest Hemingway* (New York: Oxford University Press, 2000), pp. 173–194; Jeffrey Walsh, "Two Modernist War Novels" pairs Cummings' *The Enormous Room* with *A Farewell to Arms* in his *American War Literature, 1914 to Vietnam* (New York: St. Martin's, 1982), pp. 41–58; Biyot Kesh Tripathy, "Into the Labyrinth: Crane, Hemingway, Mailer, Jones" in *Osiris N: The Victim and the American Novel* (Amsterdam: B. R. Gruner, 1985), pp. 171–226; and appropriate entries from Charles M. Oliver, *Ernest Hemingway A to Z: The Essential Reference to His Life and Works* (New York: Facts on File, 1999).

2. Hemingway's introduction to *Men at War* (New York: Crown, 1942) praises the fact that Crane "wrote that great boy's dream of war that was to be truer to how war is than any war the boy who wrote it would ever live to see," p. xvii. Michael Reynolds emphasizes that, like Crane, Hemingway learned much about war by "reading histories, talking to veterans, and looking at pictures" (*Hemingway's First War* [Princeton, NJ: Princeton University Press, 1976], p. 13).

3. Unnumbered sheet with *A Farewell to Arms* manuscripts, Hemingway Collection, John F. Kennedy Library.

4. Ray B. West, Jr., "The Unadulterated Sensibility," *The Art of Modern Fiction* (New York: Holt, Rinehart & Winston, 1949), p. 15.

5. Ibid.

6. See the appendix of Sheldon N. Grebstein's *Hemingway's Craft* (Carbondale: Southern Illinois University Press, 1973) for his work with the novel's manuscripts; Bernard Oldsey's *Hemingway's Hidden Craft: The Writing of A Farewell to Arms* (University Park: Pennsylvania State University Press, 1979); Alex Vernon's doctoral dissertation, "War Theory and Literary Practice: Hemingway, Salter, and O'Brien," for his interpretation of the writers' work from the perspective of "war theory" (University of North Carolina-Chapel Hill, 2001) and Jennifer Anne Haytock's doctoral dissertation, "At Home, At War: American Domestic Literature and the First World War," (University of North Carolina-Chapel Hill, 2000).

7. As Henri Barbusse described a similar wounding, "The earth has opened in front of me. I feel myself lifted and hurled aside—doubled up, choked, and half

blinded by this lightning and thunder. But still my recollection is clear; and in that moment when I looked wildly and desperately for my comrade-in-arms, I saw his body go up, erect and black, both his arms outstretched to their limit, and a flame in the place of his head!" (173) Barbusse uses this paragraph to close a chapter. He also frequently uses imagery of blood, as on p. 49, "The smell of fresh blood was enough to bring your heart up" (*Le Feu, Under Fire: The Story of a Squad*, trans. Fitzwater Wray [New York: E. P. Dutton, 1917]).

8. Robert W. Lewis, Jr., *Hemingway on Love*, (Austin: U of Texas P, 1965), p. 39.

9. Among critics who see Catherine as Frederic Henry's tutor are Sheldon N. Grebstein, *Hemingway's Craft*; Mark Spilka, *Hemingway's Quarrel with Androgyny* (Lincoln: U of Nebraska P, 1999); Sandra Whipple Spanier, "Catherine Barkley and the Hemingway Code" (see below); James Nagel, "Catherine Barkley and Retrospective Narration in *A Farewell to Arms*"; in *Ernest Hemingway: Six Decades of Criticism*, ed. Linda W. Wager (E. Lansing: Michigan State University Press, 1987) pp. 171–185, Roger Whitlow, *Cassandra's Daughters: The Women in Hemingway* (Westport: Greenwood, 1984); and Joyce Wexler, "E.R.A. for Hemingway: A Feminist Defense of *A Farewell to Arms*," *Georgia Review* 35, no. 1 (1981), pp. 111–123.

10. Daniel J. Schneider, "The Novel as Pure Poetry," *Ernest Hemingway: Five Decades of Criticism*, ed. Linda W. Wagner (E. Lansing: Michigan State University Press, 1974), p. 253.

11. Robert Merrill, "Tragic Form in *A Farewell to Arms*," *Modern Critical Interpretations of Ernest Hemingway's* A Farewell to Arms (New York: Chelsea Hause, 1987), p. 31.

12. Ibid.

13. Ibid., p. 112.

14. Among the recent critics who have suggested lesbianism are Valerie Rohy, *Impossible Women, Lesbian Figures & American Literature* (Ithaca, NY: Cornell University Press, 2000) and, by implication, Debra A. Moddelmog, *Reading Desire: In Pursuit of Ernest Hemingway* (Ithaca, NY: Cornell University Press, 1999). Initial discussion stemmed from Sandra R. Spanier, "Catherine Barkley and the Hemingway Code: Ritual and Survival in *A Farewell to Arms*," *Modern Critical Interpretations of Ernest Hemingway's* A Farewell to Arms (New York: Chelsea House, 1987), pp. 131–148; Nancy Comley and Robert Scholes, *Hemingway's Genders: Rereading the Hemingway Text* (New Haven, CT: Yale University Press, 1994). Charles J. Nolan, Jr., sees the women—both Scottish—as possible old friends ("Catherine Barkley: Hemingway's Scottish Heroine," *Hemingway Review* 7 [Fall 1987], pp. 43–44).

15. Frederic J. Svoboda, "Great Themes in Hemingway," *A Historical Guide to Ernest Hemingway* (New York: Oxford University Press, 2000), p. 162.

3   Texts

Because Charles Scribner's publishing house recognized how crucial it was to keep its authors' books on its own list, once an author began publishing with Scribner's, the firm usually managed to keep that writer in its stable. With the exception of Edith Wharton, who kept a sharp eye out for the best price, Scribner's authors were loyal. For that reason, so long as copyright law protects the Scribner's claim to *A Farewell to Arms*, the novel will be published by that company, and will be issued in what has become the authorized version—that very little changed from the 1929 version. The purpose of this section of the reference guide is to assess different versions, but once the novel appeared as novel, changes were nonexistent. The writing of *A Farewell to Arms*, and that first publication, deserves our notice.

The story of Hemingway's writing his World War I novel has frequently been told. As Carlos Baker, one of Hemingway's earliest critics—as well as his first biographer—recounted: there was probably a start on a World War I novel among the manuscripts Hadley lost as she was bringing Hemingway's writing to him in Switzerland.[1] But the years between that loss and his starting to write, in 1928, the book that would become *A Farewell to Arms* were filled with furious activity.

During those years, Hemingway had come into his own as a writer. Once *In Our Time* had appeared to fine—if few—reviews, the young American could see how publishing might work for him. His careful planning so that Charles Scribner's would be the publisher for *The Sun Also*

Rises, in late 1926, showed that he had mastered the art of networking, of asking friends for favors and reviews, and of being cavalier if necessary about favors he himself might have promised others. Hemingway worked hard to meet the right people: if he wasn't reading in Sylvia Beach's book-shop and lending library Shakespeare and Company or sitting at an out-side cafe table or in the Luxembourg Gardens, he was spending time at Gertrude Stein's and Alice Toklas's apartment.[2] At Ezra Pound's sugges-tion, Hemingway also worked (without pay) as an assistant editor for Ford Madox Ford's journal, transatlantic review. Wherever the young Heming-way spent his time, he was meeting important figures in the Paris renais-sance of the arts, painters and musicians as well as writers and editors. The circles he invested himself in were international ones, and the charming young American—who managed to speak some French, Span-ish, and Italian, thanks to what must have been a good ear and his equally charming wife Hadley's tutelage—was considered an asset.

In Leonard Leff's view, Hemingway found the 1920s cultural emphasis on advertising and the popularization of the arts in a commercial venue a fascinating spectacle: he worked hard at creating an image of himself as the serious (but appealing and eager to learn) American who was fast becoming one of the country's most talented writers. Not above planning his encounters, Hemingway may also have manipulated the biographical events that have become so memorable—telling others about Zelda Fitzgerald's hostility toward him (given that F. Scott was one of the key players in Hemingway's plan to become a Scribner's property), teaching Ezra Pound how to box, taking his acquaintances to Pamplona for the bullfights. Leff characterizes most of the efforts of advertising during the 1920s as "bold, and noisy, and professionalized." He claims that Heming-way was a man "acutely aware of audience" who wrote as he lived—to be observed; and much of his attention to the exotic, and the sensational, may have been a part of that "being noticed" campaign.[3] Leff also points out that to help Scribner's promote his novels, Hemingway—always con-scious of the physical image—supplied the publisher with "retouched stu-dio portraits shot by Helen Breaker."[4]

Leff speculates that one of the reasons for Hemingway's going abroad may have been the incipient glamour, and newsworthiness, of the expa-triate life. Because The Sun Also Rises certainly drew on the allure of for-eign cultures, Leff sees that novel as "market wise." Its characters were "fashionably indecent" but its style was moderate, making no attempt to mimic the difficult and allusive modernism of James Joyce or T. S. Eliot.[5] So far as the indecent or sensational, Leff notes that this novel plays into the 1920s appetite for the racy in song, popular fiction, and movies. Indeed, Max Perkins had written to Fitzgerald that *The Sun Also Rises* was "almost unpublishable"; getting the book out, and to a receptive audience, was a challenge for everyone involved with it.[6]

Leff's work has only resituated accounts from John Raeburn's 1984 *Fame Became of Him: Hemingway as Public Writer*. Raeburn, too, saw Hemingway's early career years as the crucial foundation for what was to become the Hemingway myth; in fact, Raeburn says that by the time *Death in the Afternoon* was published in 1932, the iconic Hemingway was already in place. Hemingway was no longer the good-looking middle-class Illinois boy, with no college education; he was the archetypal American sportsman, world traveler, war veteran, and tormented artist.[7] The notion that Hemingway was a masterful publicist is not new; what is new is Leff's aligning the Hemingway motive with a wider cultural atmosphere.

In line with the writer-as-commodity, the book-as-product atmosphere of the monied 1920s, Marilyn Elkins has studied the dress Hemingway chose to wear throughout his public years, once he had decided to work to attain his celebrity status. She too sees a consciousness that goes beyond nattiness, and beyond self-consciousness: Hemingway was clearly making himself into a style-setter. That he had succeeded by 1934 is clear: Elkins reports that in that year "*Vanity Fair* published an article that offered costumes representing various aspects of his public persona; readers could cut them out and place them on a Hemingway paper doll. They included 'Ernie, the Neanderthal Man' (a loincloth and a rabbit for one hand and a club for the other); 'Ernie as the Lost Generation' (turtleneck, beret, and a cafe table covered with empty bottles as a prop); 'Ernie as Isaac Walton' (fisherman's attire and gear and a boat loaded with fish as background); 'Ernie as Don Jose, the Toreador' (a matador's outfit and a dead bull as a prop); and 'Ernie the Unknown Soldier' (a military uniform, crutches, and a bloody battle scene as backdrop)."[8]

In the advertisement for himself that his clothing helped create, Hemingway associated costume with gendered characteristics as soon as he had joined the American Red Cross. Few people realized that Hemingway had not been a soldier. It would have been hard to tell that he was only a volunteer ambulance driver, a youth from the States who was a Red Cross employee rather than a member of any military unit. When he returned to the States after his wounding and convalescence, he wore "a *Spagnoli* uniform that he had specially tailored and that was rightfullly reserved for officers of the Italian army—not for Red Cross Volunteers," complete with a "black Italian cape with silver clasp."[9] Years later, Elkins points out, Hemingway often wore the trenchcoat and khakis that returned veterans adopted, and throughout much of his life, sported a vest rather than a jacket. Stripped down, unquestionably masculine, ready for action, the Hemingway style was frequently derived from the military.

When Hemingway began to write the novel that would become A Farewell to Arms, however, he was not thinking only of World War I. His attention had been usurped for the past year and a half by his personal war—whether or not to leave Hadley and Bumby, both of whom he loved deeply; whether or not to marry Pauline Pfeiffer, who—as a practicing Catholic—would not live with him unless they married. In the spring of 1927, Hadley had divorced Hemingway so that he would be free to marry Pauline, which he did a month later.

In March of 1928, he began writing what he "thought was only a story," he told Max Perkins, but in another two weeks, still working on it, he "suddenly [got] a great kick out of the war and all the things and places and it has been going very well." As Robert Lewis recounts in his study of the novel, a month later Hemingway and Pauline had moved from Paris to Key West, where they lived in a small fishing village. A few months later, in Piggott, Arkansas, for the delivery of their first child, which was by Caesarean delivery, Hemingway continued writing, telling Perkins "Am now on page 486 . . . am going out to Wyoming. . . . Will finish the book there."[10] The first draft of A Farewell to Arms was done in August of 1928.

From the first, Hemingway had reserved some months for a rewrite. Perkins understood that a draft was not a finished work and knew better than to put pressure on the young writer for a book that might have been completed earlier. In the fall, returning to Key West, Hemingway started revising. His sister Sunny went to Key West in November of 1928 to type the final manuscript, which took two months.[11] (Pauline, despite the new baby, also helped.) While the processes of both writing and revising are innately mysterious, known not even to the writer in many cases, biographer Michael Reynolds points to one of the questions that still remains about this particular novel: how did Hemingway, who had never been in the parts of Italy that he was writing about, know enough to get the descriptions right? As Reynolds says, for a craftsman as meticulous as Hemingway was about people and places,

> [I]t is difficult to balance his lack of firsthand knowledge of the Italian front of 1915–1917. He had not seen the Tagliamento river when he wrote A Farewell to Arms; he had not walked the Venetian plain between Codroipo and Latisana. It was not until 1948 that he saw

Udine. He may never have seen Gorizia, the Isonzo river, Plava, or the Bainsizza plateau; he certainly had not seen them when he wrote the novel. His return trip to Fossalta di Piave in 1922 and his skiing trip at Cortina d'Ampezza in 1923 did not take him to the terrain of the novel. His 1927 trip to Italy with Guy Hickock did not cover the war zone of 1915–1917. Not only had Hemingway not experienced the military engagements in which Frederic Henry takes part, but he had not seen the terrain of Books One and Three of A *Farewell to Arms*. Yet the geography is perfectly accurate and done with the clarity that made its author famous for his decriptions of place.[12]

Reynolds includes a map of Italy to show that the action Hemingway saw with the Red Cross was around Schio at the far west of Italy, whereas the military front in A *Farewell to Arms* was located in the extreme east of the country.

Reynolds also sees A *Farewell to Arms* as a kind of fiction entirely different from *The Sun Also Rises*, where Hemingway's knowledge of the people who were, at base, the models for many of the characters in the 1926 book took over the narrative. Difficulties with publication, difficulties with reviewers and friends who objected to those real models, difficulties within his personal life made Hemingway wary of the real. While he knew he would have problems with Perkins and Scribner's publishing house over A *Farewell to Arms*, it would be because of the soldiers' language, the deeply offensive (if realistic) speech that Hemingway felt had to appear in the book. There would also be problems about the battle scenes and their bloodshed. And there might be some censorship necessary in the Catherine-Frederic relationship.

Scott Donaldson recounts some of the censorship issues. He notes that F. Scott Fitzgerald had warned Hemingway about the language well before the book's publication,

"I think if you use the word cocksuckers here [during the retreat, in two places] the book will be suppressed & confiscated within two days of publication." This was a problem Perkins immediately anticipated upon reading the manuscript in Key West, early in February. "BOOK VERY FINE BUT DIFFICULT IN SPOTS" he wired New York. Later, in a letter to Charles Scribner (who held strict views about what should or should not be printed), he expanded on the point. "It is Hemingway's principle both in life and literature never to flinch from facts, and it is in that sense only, that the book is difficult. It isn't at all erotic, although love is represented as having a very large physical element." Perkins was playing the role of middleman here, trying to reassure his boss (Scribner) that the novel was publishable and to keep Hemingway from erupting in anger when he heard about the emendations that, Max knew, would have to be made.[13]

Before *A Farewell to Arms* was published as a book, Perkins arranged for it to be serialized in *Scribner's Magazine*—a strategy both useful and provocative, because readers of the serial were sure to buy the book; and both the journal and the publishing house were owned by Charles Scribner's. Such established best-selling novelists as Edith Wharton were often published in serial form before a book appearance; the wider readership created an interest that frequently led as well to movie sales. For the serial alone, *Scribner's Magazine* paid Hemingway sixteen thousand dollars. Given that his check from Scribner's publishers in August of 1928 had been only $3,718.66 (for *The Sun Also Rises*, the story collection *Men Without Women*, and *The Torrents of Spring*), this amount seemed to predict that Scribner had hopes for a best-seller from Hemingway.

Divided into six segments, *A Farewell to Arms* had passed muster with its first installment. But upon the publication of the second part, Boston police chief Michael H. Crowley banned *Scribner's* Magazine on June 20, 1929. According to Scott Donaldson, "The ruling banned distribution of the magazine by Boston bookstores and newsstands for the run of the serial over the next four months. It did not hurt overall circulation figures of the magazine, and undoubtedly stimulated sales of the book when it was published on September 27."[14]

But in the matter of language, the banning of the novel was helpful to Perkins and Scribner's. For serialization (because *Scribner's* Magazine might be read by younger readers), the words Hemingway wanted left in the novel and Scribner's wanted out had been replaced by blank spaces. Even though Hemingway wanted the words—*shit, fuck, balls, cocksuckers*—replaced in the novel, he was afraid *A Farewell to Arms* might be suppressed,[15] so he told Perkins to leave out any objectionable word, rather than risk nonpublication. (Other words that had been removed from the serialization were replaced for the novel: *son of a bitch, whore, whorehound,* and *Jesus Christ*. Words that had already appeared in the serial version were *damn, God, goddamn, bastard,* and *good Christ*.)[16] Because he had received no advance, Hemingway knew the novel had to be published, advertised, and well reviewed in order for him to continue to make money on it. And obviously, a published book was the only way to get a contract for movie rights.

Reviewers—alerted perhaps by the Boston banning—were divided in their responses to *A Farewell to Arms*. Few were as vituperative as Robert Herrick, writing in *Bookman* under the title "What Is Dirt?" Unfortunately, he compared Hemingway's novel to that of Remarque, *All Quiet on the Western Front*, calling the latter a work of art and *A Farewell to Arms* "unpleasant garbage" and "mere dirt."[17] Unfortunately, too, some subscribers to *Scribner's Magazine* had canceled their subscriptions and even though history provides the perspective to show that many works of modernist writers seemed offensive at the time, it seems strange that Hemingway's war novel would have prompted such outrage.

For the most part, reviewers were excited to find another good Hemingway novel, this one different from the first collection of stories, *In Our Time*, and the second, *Men Without Women*, as well as the first serious novel, *The Sun Also Rises*. Clifton Fadiman's "A Fine American Novel" rehearsed some of the writing history; Henry S. Canby, writing in *Saturday Review of Literature*, defended both the erotic story and Hemingway's frank language and in "Chronicle and Comment" took a more retrospective view of *A Farewell to Arms'* initial reception; and Malcolm Cowley took a stand for the book's greatness. One reviewer, "A.C." who wrote in the *Boston Transcript*, praised the characterization of Catherine Barkley, an emphasis usually lost in the interest in modern war and its aftermath.[18]

Whether despite or because of the reviews, *A Farewell to Arms* was selling more quickly than its publishers had ever imagined. Even after the stock market crash, sales continued. Maxwell Perkins was ecstatic. He wired Hemingway often with sales reports. Less than a month after publication, the book had sold 28,000 copies and Scribner's had printed 50,000. By October 22, sales reached 33,000. By November 21, sales passed the 50,000 mark and the publisher had printed another 20,000 copies, making the total 70,000 in all. By January 8, 1930, all 70,000 copies were sold. (Reynolds points out that by 1961, nearly a million and a half copies of *A Farewell to Arms* had sold.)[19]

The income from this novel was enough to change Hemingway's life. A large share of the previous three years' royalties were from sales of *The Sun Also Rises*, so those dollars belonged to Hadley and Bumby, as arranged in the Hemingways' divorce settlement. In contrast, the income from *A Farewell to Arms* would belong to Hemingway. It had been difficult for him to accept financial help from Pauline's uncle, G. A. Pfeiffer, as he had been forced to while at work on his novel. The book's dedication to G. A. Pfeiffer no doubt signals his gratitude.

Even with the success of *A Farewell to Arms*, Hemingway was still in desperate need of money. He was trying to establish a $50,000 trust fund for his mother (who had little substantial income since Clarence Hemingway's suicide the previous winter), for the care of herself and the younger Hemingway children. Along with various kinds of financial support for Ernest, Pauline, and their child, it seems that Pfeiffer had offered to contribute $30,000 to the Grace Hall-Hemingway trust.[20] With Hemingway's royalties and fees from German, French, and other publishers for the rights to translate the novel, Hemingway would be able to provide once and for all for Grace.

Rumors were that Hemingway might try to find another publisher, one who would give him a higher percentage of royalties. In order to increase Hemingway's royalties, so that his were equal to the contracts Scribner's had with F. Scott Fitzgerald, Perkins in December of 1929 asked Charles Scribner to give Hemingway a 17.5 percent rate once 25,000 copies had been sold, and a 20 percent rate once sales had moved past 45,000 copies. Scribner said there would be one rate, the 20 percent, and it would go into effect after 25,000 copies.[21]

Hemingway stayed with Scribner's. All editions of *A Farewell to Arms* today are in either a Scribner's or a Scribner's imprint format, and pages are numbered as they were many years ago. The copyright date of 1929 is still in effect, especially with the Bono copyright extension. When Hemingway was writing little, and had not had a best-selling novel for more than seven years, in 1947 Scribner's revived his reputation by reissuing *The Sun Also Rises, A Farewell to Arms*, and *For Whom the Bell Tolls* in a boxed set with matched binding. They saw to it that Jonathan Cape, Hemingway's British publisher, kept his titles in print and that there was a college edition of *A Farewell to Arms* with an introduction by Robert Penn Warren, available for classroom use.[22] At a low point in his life, before he had won the Pulitzer Prize for fiction or the Nobel Prize for literature, Scribner's featured Hemingway's books so that he could continue to think of himself as a success.

Another way Hemingway made money from *A Farewell to Arms*, as well as increasing his personal visibility, was through his sale of screen rights for the novel to Paramount Pictures. By 1932 the novel was a movie starring Gary Cooper as Frederic Henry, Helen Hayes as Catherine Barkley, and Adolphe Menjou as Rinaldi. While Hemingway did the wrong thing in selling his novel outright to the studio, so that subsequent movies made from *A Farewell to Arms* brought him no income,[23] he saw the income of $80,000 from the sale of the book as a godsend, a way out of the seemingly endless financial problems that faced him, as well as his family.[24] Alongside this, the fact that Lawrence Stallings was directing a stage version that was about to open for what turned out to be a short run on Broadway scarcely piqued his interest, though Stallings' play provided the basis for the film script.

Hemingway's disappointments with the film were partly a reflection of the Motion Picture Code that dominated film production in the 1930s. Despite good footage of battle, the film was cast as a romantic story. To avoid censure, Catherine and Henry were married early in the film, in a bedside ceremony after Henry had been wounded. The film was advertised to theaters with two endings available—the one in which Catherine dies, the second in which Catherine, resting in Henry's arms, manages to be revived: the audience could determine whether or not she lived as the film ended. Most theaters chose to show the former ending, since it followed the novel; but Hemingway was upset that the two endings existed. Although only eighty minutes in length, A Farewell to Arms was nominated for Best Picture, which it did not win, though it did win Oscars for cinematography and sound recording. According to film historian Gene Phillips, the movie was "the biggest grosser of its year."[25]

Phillips makes the point that Hollywood remained attracted by A Farewell to Arms.[26] In such subsequent Hemingway movies as The Snows of Kilimanjaro, The Sun Also Rises, and Hemingway's Adventures of a Young Man, "material from this novel was borrowed to fill out plot details" (29). To this comment one must add that a quantity of material from A Farewell to Arms also worked its way into the 1996 Richard Attenborough film, In Love and War. Supposedly based on the diaries of Agnes von Kurowsky, the film bore enough similarity to parts of Hemingway's war novel to confuse an audience that knew little about either source. As Frederic Svoboda points out, even though Chris O'Donnell and Sandra Bullock were not the right choices for the lovers, "the film did a decent business, and viewers paid attention. On the Internet Movie Data Base, a standard electronic resource, viewers polled it at 7.8 on a ten-point scale, only three-tenths less than The English Patient, with its nine Oscars."[27]

Hemingway's fascination with film—and especially with the income a writer could garner from a sale to the movie industry—had motivated much of his fiction throughout the 1920s. Once he and Hadley were living abroad, they were as interested in American film as they had been when they lived in Chicago, and they were not atypical: the world was watching movies. I have written in several places about Hemingway's admiration for the Spanish-Argentinian novelist Blasco Ibáñez. His best-sellers The Four Horsemen of the Apocalypse (a 1919 war novel) and Blood *and Sand* in 1922 were both made into films starring Rudolph Valentino. Rights to *The Four Horsemen* sold for $200,000.[28]

Interested as well in celebrity status, Hemingway was surely attracted to the movie personnel, particularly the actors and actresses he came to know. Reynolds writes somewhat nostalgically about the friendship between Hemingway and Gary Cooper, who played the lead actor in both *A Farewell to Arms* and the later *For Whom the Bell Tolls*. Reynolds describes their time together during the 1930s:

> Hunting frequently with Gary Cooper, who was more a Montana cowboy than a Hollywood movie star, Ernest posed for countless pictures, holding the day's bag. Cooper, he found, was a better rifle shot; Ernest was best wing-shooting with his over-and-under shotgun. Both men had come of age in an America so abundant with game that bag limits seemed onerous, and predators were to be eliminated. On his 1933–34 African safari, Hemingway had amused himself shooting hyenas; Cooper did the same with hawks on telephone poles and coyotes in the field. The two were both artists and outdoorsmen, fitting comfortably together in the field and at supper. . . . both men knew and admired each other's work.[29]

Whatever the avenue, if Ernest Hemingway could find admiration and friendship, he thought himself successful. To add in what to most writers of the modernist mode appeared to be a small fortune—well over $100,000 in screen rights, royalties, stage adaptations—was to realize heights that the young Midwesterner had only dreamed of. *A Farewell to Arms* had been a means of opening doors to experiences, to acquaintances, to opportunities, that seemed in themselves like something from a novel. And besides that, *A Farewell to Arms* was a great book. Hemingway could not believe he had been so lucky.

NOTES

1. Carlos Baker, *Ernest Hemingway* (New York: Scribner's, 1969), pp. 20–56 and see "Carlos Baker on Ernest Hemingway," *Talks with Authors*, ed. Charles F. Madden (Carbondale: Southern Illinois University Press, 1968), p. 75.

2. See Scott Donaldson's *Hemingway vs. Fitzgerald: The Rise and Fall of a Literary Friendship* (Woodstock, NY: OverLook, 1999); Linda Wagner-Martin's *"Favored Strangers": Gertrude Stein and Her Family* (New Brunswick, NJ: Rutgers University Press, 1995); Shari Benstock's *Women of the Left Bank, Paris*

1910–1940 (Austin: University of Texas Press, 1987); and Michael Reynolds' first two volumes of the Hemingway biography, *The Young Hemingway* and *Hemingway: The Paris Years* (both Cambridge, MA: Basil Blackwell, 1986, 1989).

3. Leonard J. Leff, *Hemingway and His Conspirators: Hollywood, Scribner's, and the Making of American Celebrity Culture* (New York: Rowman & Littlefield, 1997), p. xii.

4. Ibid., p. xvi.

5. Ibid., p. 44.

6. Ibid., p. 37; quotes from Perkins to Fitzgerald, May 29, 1926, John F. Kennedy Library.

7. John Raeburn, *Fame Became of Him: Hemingway as Public Writer* (Bloomington: Indiana University Press, 1984). Raeburn also connects Hemingway's expertise with creating celebrity from his association with two such self-created figures, Ezra Pound and Gertrude Stein. See also Leo Braudy, *The Frenzy of Renown: Fame and Its History* (New York: Oxford University Press, 1986).

8. Marilyn Elkins, "The Fashion of Machismo," *A Historical Guide to Ernest Hemingway* (New York: Oxford University Press, 2000), pp. 93–116; quote from p. 103.

9. Ibid., p. 98.

10. Robert W. Lewis, *A Farewell to Arms: The War of the Words* (New York: Twayne, 1992), pp. 16–18; letters quoted by Lewis.

11. Bernice Kert, *The Hemingway Women* (New York: W. W. Norton, 1983), p. 217.

12. Michael S. Reynolds, *Hemingway's First War* (Princeton, NJ: Princeton University Press, 1976), p. 5.

13. Scott Donaldson, *Hemingway vs. Fitzgerald* (Overlook, 1998), pp. 132–134.

14. Ibid., p. 133.

15. Ibid. Donaldson recounts the story that Fitzgerald was able to get an advance copy of Erich Maria Remarque's *All Quiet on the Western Front*, a war novel already published in both Germany and England, with a United States edition about to be printed. Remarque had used most of the words Hemingway wanted to include, so Fitzgerald thought Hemingway could use this book as a lever to get Scribner to do as he wanted.

16. Reynolds, *Hemingway's First War*, p. 72.

17. Robert Herrick, "What Is Dirt?" *Bookman* 70 (November 1929), pp. 258–262. See also Donald Davidson, "Review of *A Farewell to Arms*," *Nashville Tennessean* (November 3, 1929), p. 7; Henry Hazlitt, "Take Hemingway," *New York Sun* (September 28, 1929), p. 38; and Percy Hutchinson, "Love and War in the Pages of Mr. Hemingway." *New York Times Book Review* (September 29, 1929), p. 5.

18. Clifton Fadiman, "A Fine American Novel," *The Nation* 129 (October 30, 1929), pp. 497–498; Henry S. Canby, "Story of the Brave," *Saturday Review of Literature* (October 12, 1929), pp. 231–232 and "Chronicle and Comment,"

Bookman 70 (February 1939), p. 644; Malcolm Cowley, "Not Yet Demobilized," *New York Herald Tribune Books* (October 6, 1929), pp. 1, 6; A. C., "Review of *A Farewell to Arms*," *Boston Transcript* (October 19, 1929), p. 2. See also Agnes W. Smith, "Mr. Hemingway Does It Again," *New Yorker* 5 (October 12, 1929), p. 120 and T. S. Matthews, "Nothing Ever Happens to the Brave," *New Republic* 60 (October 9, 1929), pp. 208–210.

19. Reynolds, *Hemingway's First War*, pp. 80–81.

20. Donaldson, *Hemingway vs. Fitzgerald*, pp. 147–148; Donaldson says the benefactor was "probably" Gus Pfeiffer.

21. Ibid.

22. Michael Reynolds, *Hemingway: The Final Years* (New York: Norton, 1999), p. 154.

23. Ibid., p. 293. Reynolds comments on the 1957 version, with Rock Hudson and Jennifer Jones acting in a script that David Selznick had rewritten so that the story was "more believable" (p. 303). Hemingway also had given up script authority.

24. Michael Reynolds, *Hemingway: The Thirties* (New York: Norton, 1997), p. 52.

25. Gene D. Phillips, *Hemingway and Film* (New York: Frederick Ungar, 1980), pp. 22–23.

26. The 2001 film *Pearl Harbor* testifies to the pervasive influence of Hemingway's film. *Pearl Harbor* creates not one but two Frederic Henry characters— Danny and his older friend, Rafe, who both taught him to fly and fell in love first with Evelyn, the nurse who bore Danny's son, also named Danny. For all the emphasis on the movie as a recounting of the "infamous" attack on Pearl Harbor, which brought the United States into World War II, the war narrative takes second place to the romance.

The character of Rafe, however, parallels that of Frederic Henry in that Rafe volunteers to fly for the British, when he could have remained in comparative safety; his being shot down by German planes precipitates the romance between Evelyn and Danny.

27. Frederic J. Svoboda, "Great Themes in Hemingway," *A Historical Guide to Ernest Hemingway* (New York: Oxford University Press, 2000), p. 156.

28. See my "The Secrecies of the Public Hemingway," *Hemingway: Up in Michigan Perspectives*, ed. Frederic J. Svoboda and Joseph J. Waldmeir (E. Lansing: Michigan State University Press, 1995), pp. 149–156 (summarized in "The Intertextual Hemingway" in *A Historical Guide to Ernest Hemingway*) and Susan Beegel, "'The Undefeated' and *Sangre y Arena*: Hemingway's Mano a Mano with Blasco Ibáñez," *Hemingway Repossessed*, ed. Kenneth Rosen (Westport, CT: Praeger, 1994), pp. 71–85.

29. Michael Reynolds, *Hemingway: The Final Years* (New York: Norton 1999), p. 35.

4 Contexts

It is important to recognize that Hemingway's *A Farewell to Arms* is not simply a war novel; rather, it is a *modernist* war novel. Had Hemingway lived even twenty years earlier, he would have been less firmly entrenched in the belief that traditions were ineffectual, that change was a necessity, and that the old was poised to give way to the innovative (as, in his hometown of Oak Park, Illinois, his neighbor Frank Lloyd Wright was creating structures unlike any previously known).

But, born as he was in 1899, by the time Hemingway was a literate and reasonably questing person, he was being bombarded with ideas about freedom—freedom to believe, to love, to write—as well as questions about the sanctity of religion, the efficacy of science, the problems of speaking only one language, and the difficulty of living within a single culture. The prideful United States of America was beginning to lose some of its confidence. Yes, it still believed in "the American dream" of success—personal and material—and so did the thousands of immigrants that tried to come into the States to live. But there were almost omnipresent interrogations of beliefs: Was it true that one should follow in parental footsteps? Was it wrong to drink alcohol? Was the censure of racy ideas, books, films, radio programs a right or an imposition?

Modernism is usually defined as the period from 1910 (or perhaps 1914) through the 1920s and into the 1930s. It brackets World War I and the changes that came in that debacle's aftermath. It also benefits from the great prosperity of the 1920s. People had the funds to live their lives as they wished; their dependence on family was considerably lessened by that financial autonomy. But whatever the dates chosen, most observers of historical periods recognize that cultural contexts are amazingly complex. In the case of modernism, one might say it was an attitude more than a stylistic emphasis or a historical period. In the search for stability, which resulted from the devastation of belief after scientism and was then intensified by the First World War, writers and artists privileged their dedication to craft over traditional beliefs. They became philosophical skeptics. The role of literature (and other arts) became less the established one of confirming social vision than of questioning it. The shape of literature changed to reflect its purpose: instead of predictable structures and rhythms, modern writing was sometimes chaotic, its structures both ironic and whimsical.

In the absence of deep religious conviction, the artist and writer in modernism took on the role of philosophical authority. Early in the twentieth century, Ezra Pound, T. S. Eliot, Amy Lowell, and Ford Madox Ford, who were writing hundreds of essays and reviews for the new media outlets, created the figure of the artist-god, and accordingly made literature supreme. Experiments were valued; neither was modernist literature prescriptive about genre distinctions. A number of writers wrote in all possible forms—poetry, short story, prose poem, novel, memoir, drama—and sometimes in composites of several. To be different, to be attempting the different, was the aim. Writers as distinct as Gertrude Stein, William Carlos Williams, e.e. cummings, Anita Loos, Djuna Barnes, John Dos Passos, and Langston Hughes congregated at readings, rallies, salons: membership in the avant-garde depended on one's authenticity.

Rather than fight the status quo of self-satisfied United States culture, which was always quick to criticize the innovative, a great many modernist artists and writers moved away. Expatriation became the heart of modernism: either hiding out in Greenwich Village or Harlem or Provincetown, or making the actual move to London or Paris or Berlin. Through the catalytic salons of Edith Wharton, Natalie Barney, and Gertrude Stein; the influence of Sylvia Beach's Paris bookshop; and the power of such little magazines as *Poetry, Crisis, Double Dealer, Broom, The Dial, transatlantic review, American Caravan,* and *Opportunity* modernism attempted to break through convention in every direction. But in general, the modernist aesthetic was to awaken readers to new insights, new understandings: to bring literature (and art) back to a central position in life so that reading would be a means of gaining wisdom. There would be no simple parroting of agreed-upon morals; the reader would, like the writer, set out on a journey through a sometimes difficult medium to find a truth personal as well as universal.[1]

Michael North, in his recent study *Reading 1922: A Return to the Scene of the Modern*, emphasizes the fascination in the public mind with the study of thought: "the enthusiasm for things psychological was so extreme, both in the United States and in Great Britain, that it might quite reasonably have seemed a psychological symptom itself."[2] From the time of Williams James' two-volume handbook on the field he christened "psychology" through the translation into English of a number of Sigmund Freud's studies, interest was supported with published work by A. A. Brill, Smith Ely Jeliffe, James Strachey—and implicated in the studies by linguist Ludwig Wittgenstein and anthropologist Bronislaw Malinowski. Partly because of people's interest in the war-damaged psyche, the study of psychology became politicized. "Even as early as 1922," states North, "the practice of psychology was influential enough and the habit of psychological self-consciousness pervasive enough to influence public policy and inspire public controversy. Implicit within these controversies were two questions the new public sphere was inherently ill-equipped to answer: of what value is intellectual attainment and distinction if reason has little influence in public affairs, and how can the liberal values of tolerance and fairness be upheld once prejudice is considered to be both universal and inescapable?"[3] In short, partly because the nineteenth-century values and morals were seen as unstable, people were turning for answers to fields of study that had not existed prior to the twentieth century.

Part of the uneasy quest, according to Quentin Anderson, lay in the fact that "publicly recognized authority lost legitimacy, while the arts took on more and more of the job of defining the human horizon. The challenge they posed to church and state was less direct, but rather more effective in the long run than that of anarchists and social revolutionaries. Such movements as expressionism produced paintings and plays that startled their audiences, music that provoked riots. These outbursts testify to a lively awareness among the public that cherished conventions were threatened."[4]

As these critics make clear, part of the problem with considering modernism as a movement is that so much of its energy grew out of nineteenth-century thought. Even as it seemed as though outward regulation had given way to inner, personal choice—especially since religious belief seemed to have been eclipsed—such philosophies drew from those of Nietzsche, Hobbes, Hegel, Marx, Darwin, T. E. Hulme, F. H. Bradley, Henri Bergson, and, of course, William James and Sigmund Freud.

What such immense philosophical change meant for literature was that both subject matter and form became obviously "new." Edmund Wilson recalled that writers who were his contemporaries wanted to create "something in which every word, every cadence, every detail, should perform a definite function in producing an intense effect."[5] Gorham Munson reminisced about the division between the new writers and the older at a party given for Edgar Lee Masters: "The younger people were as usual discussing the everlasting topic of form, the older people aired their views on anti-religion."[6] In their attempt to make something entirely new, these modernist writers created works such as *Tender Buttons* (Gertrude Stein), *The Sound and the Fury* and *As I Lay Dying* (William Faulkner), and *Manhattan Transfer* and *U.S.A.* (John Dos Passos).

Modernism was both self-conscious and formalist. It used control of craft and methods to reach readers, methods that included violence and shock. Many of the techniques used in the literature were borrowed from visual art, film, and poetry and signaled those other arts to the reader. In the modernists' view, literature was to be suggestive, not didactic. It was to work on the reader through indirection. It might even pretend to be *un*literary, using colloquial speech rather than poetic diction or literary or educated language.

Similarly, to rid their work of the smell of the lamp (and the library), modernists chose to write about common people as characters. Their aim in writing about them was to achieve psychological accuracy: characters were interesting not so much for what they did but for their motivation. F. Scott Fitzgerald's Gatsby is surely a failure, but his reasons for the life choices he made render him memorable. Willa Cather's Ántonia lives a remarkably placid, hard-working life, but in the eyes of the novel's narrator, her life seems romantic and fulfilling. Faulkner's Temple Drake interests the reader not for anything she does but because his portrayal of her character is an incredibly prescient depiction of rape trauma. And because characters were to appear as live, they were presented in interaction with others, and were drawn through dialogue and scene. Therefore, the role of the author as storyteller changed dramatically: in modernist writing, there was little obvious authorial opinion or intervention. The author shaped the narrative through selection of detail and scene, through choice of character, but he or she did not appear in the text itself. If an author's presence was noticeable, his or her voice was in the reportorial objective mode, distanced into irony. Readers were supposed to find the clues to how they should feel about the characters through the densely designed structure and writing of the text.

The icon of American modernism was T. S. Eliot's long poem *The Waste Land* (1922), a work that described the twentieth-century culture through an apparently impersonal collage of character, scene, dialogue, and allusion to other works of Western history and literature. The poem was structured as a montage of separate scenes (the speaker in the poem says near its end, "These fragments I have shored against my ruin," explaining the method as if it were his theme), and it evoked the sense of a journey or quest. Using archetypes and myth throughout, *The Waste Land* echoed what was to be known as the mythic method, which was explored to the fullest extent in James Joyce's novel *Ulysses* (also 1922, but published in serial form—in part—earlier). Much literature of the time traced a journey, drew on life-giving water or sunlight and darkness, and made clear the importance of Freud, Jung, Frazer, and other accounts of both myth and archetype.

In Eliot's *The Waste Land*, the character of the Fisher King attempted to save his country from drought, searching for water to transform the wasted land into a fruitful one. It was not a happy poem, nor did its ending claim to be positive. Modern writing itself was almost completely, sometimes overwhelmingly, serious. Angst at the ultimate recognition— the meaninglessness of human life, learned either through the failure of religion or the destruction of war—pervaded most writing from the time of the Great War through the 1920s and into the 1930s. With the end of peace and the onset of a second world war even more destructive than the first, readers' temperaments changed, and they searched increasingly for humor. There had been little of that in modernist writing.

Because the literature of modernism struggled to meet so many caveats, a great many themes were never attempted. War—complete with violence and brutality—seemed appropriate. That subject could be treated with realistic detail or with irony. It could be viewed seriously, or it could become the ground for experimental techniques; writers as diverse as John Dos Passos, e.e. cummings, William Faulkner, Willa Cather, Thomas Boyd, Sinclair Lewis, Edith Wharton, and Ernest Hemingway wrote well about its waste. And because male characters were likely to occur in writings about war, the classic *bildungsroman* pattern (the novel of a male character's education) was often seen, complete with depictions of the modern American culture with its capitalistic economic and personal ideals.

Partly because modernist writing in the United States seemed to be so male-dominated, recent critics have challenged its prominence in literary history. Such critics as Andrew Ross and Sandra M. Gilbert and Susan

Gubar have criticized the writing of this period because it failed to present a range of human emotions and experience germane to all readers, regardless of education, gender, race, or religious or political persuasion. It has been called both elitist and reductive.[7] It has also been called a product of academic readers who failed to find interest in so-called domestic fiction, literature about women's lives, even during the height of politically disturbed gender relations because of the visibility of the "New Woman."[8]

THE PLACE OF HEMINGWAY'S WRITING IN MODERNISM

Because of his willingness to experiment, Hemingway moved quickly into prominence among his fellow writers. Championed by Ezra Pound, an influential United States poet who served as "foreign editor" for many American little magazines, the young Hemingway was first seen as "a poet from Chicago" when his work appeared in Harriet Monroe's journal, *Poetry*. Pound said that Hemingway's writing was "the best prose he had read in forty years,"[9] and he persisted in thinking that the prose poem interchapters of Hemingway's *in our time* and the later *In Our Time* were among his best work. As Pound wrote, Hemingway's style was "Imagist" because he had accepted "the principles of good writing that had been contained in the earlier imagist document and [had applied] the stricture against superfluous words to his prose, polishing, repolishing, and eliminating, as can be seen in the clean hard paragraphs of the first brief *In Our Time*, in *They All Made Peace*, in *The Torrents of Spring*, and in the best pages of his later novels."[10]

To transfer the obvious effects of an Imagist poem into prose was Hemingway's chief labor during the mid-1920s. Most easily seen in the juxtaposition of vignette and story in his collection *In Our Time*, Hemingway understood the montage effects of abstract painting. He would allow his readers to see the threads of connection between a story about a boy's watching the disintegration of his parents' marriage and a vignette about a soldier's coming to understand that people die in battle. The author's role was not to make the connection: his role was to describe an event so vividly, and so realistically, that the reader—despite his or her own experience—could discern the pattern. When Hemingway was first sending out his stories for publication, editors would sometimes reject them on the basis that "nothing happened" in them. That subtlety was a part of the understated, poetic modernist method. Ezra Pound would have approved.

By the time Hemingway was writing *A Farewell to Arms*, Pound had moved to Italy and there was no correspondence between them. That Hemingway always thought kindly of the generous, if sometimes misguided, older poet became clear during the 1950s, when he helped to get Pound released from St. Elizabeth's mental hospital in Washington, D.C., and when he sent him a large check after he had been awarded the Nobel Prize for Literature.

The other great influence on Hemingway's writing was a composite of all the reading he did during his Paris years, and before, judging from the correspondence between Hadley Richardson, soon to become the first Mrs. Hemingway, and the young Hemingway. It was often pointed out that Hemingway read a book a day, or approximately that (following on the heels of another of his mentors, Gertrude Stein). The point to be made is that modernists were readers. They were observers of art in all its forms; they prided themselves on being conversant with everything that was happening in the world of art and literature, and they diligently learned from whatever was happening.

To say that Hemingway learned a great deal about writing the war novel from his friends John Dos Passos and, through him, e. e. cummings, is not to detract from Hemingway's accomplishment in *A Farewell to Arms*. Dos Passos was one of the first friends Hemingway made after he arrived in Paris. He knew his work because *One Man's Initiation: 1917* had been published in 1920, with the better-known *Three Soldiers* appearing in 1922. Just as he would seek an introduction to F. Scott Fitzgerald a few years later, Hemingway wanted to become friends with people who were already well published. Dos Passos had published yet another book before his more important *Manhattan Transfer* came out in 1925. Knowing the young Harvardite, who had also driven ambulances during World War I, was a way for Hemingway to understand the cultures of both the Ivy League-educated and commercially published young writers. In the case of e. e. cummings, who had been at Harvard with Dos Passos and published poems in the same collection as he had, Gertrude Stein much admired his war memoir/novel, *The Enormous Room*, fluidly expressed in both French and English and published by Liveright in 1922.

Given Hemingway's interest in poetry, he probably preferred Dos Passos' *One Man's Initiation* to the more realistic prose of *Three Soldiers*. In the first novel, written in 1917 though not published until 1920, Dos Passos moved between outright poetry to prose that had the heavy markings of a poem, and then into more conventional prose. Sections were juxtaposed, forcing the reader to adjust his or her expectations about what form the writing would next take, and what effect that writing would create.

All of the sections are unified in that they are filled with factual detail presented concretely, with a painter's reliance on light and color. White handkerchiefs and yellow crates are shaded with the brown light of the wharf as the novel opens; soon "the rosy yellow and drab purple" buildings of the New York skyline pass the ship. Into the whirl of colors Dos Passos interjects the relatively stark dialogue of the young soldiers:

"This your first time across?"

"Yes. . . . Yours?"

"Yes. . . . I never used to think that at nineteen I'd be crossing the Atlantic to go to war in France." The boy caught himself up suddenly and blushed.

Then swallowing a lump in his throat he said, "It ought to be time to eat."

God help Kaiser Bill!

O-o-o old Uncle Sam.

He's got the cavalry,

He's got the infantry,

He's got the artillery;

And then by God we'll all go to Germany!

God help Kaiser Bill!

The iron covers are clamped on the smoking room windows, for no lights must show. So the air is dense with tobacco smoke and the reek of beer and champagne. In one corner they are playing poker with their coats off. . . . [11]

Dos Passos' alternating glimpses of bravado and nervousness (the drinking, playing poker in very informal attire, smoking), set against the young untraveled man who swallows a lump in his throat, take the narrative quickly from the early pastiche to the stolid irony of the body of the book. Throughout *One Man's Initiation*, Dos Passos sets the unrelieved horror of physical battle against the propagandist version of that war, with snatches of popular (and usually war-themed) songs serving as punctuation.

One of the recurring motifs of the novel is the young Martin Howe's realization of the horror of physical disfigurement. Usually contextualized in the flowers of the French countryside, or of the city streets, his visualization of the damaged soldier is repeated at intervals: "Between the pale-brown frightened eyes, where the nose should have been, was a triangular black patch that ended in some mechanical contrivance with shiny little black metal rods that took the place of the jaw" (p. 54). Shocking as this sight is for Howe, Dos Passos hammers home the irony of the image by setting against it the old woman who sells bouquets—roses for luck, daisies for love.

Each chapter of the book adds another dimension to the repulsion Howe feels, added in to his anger that these men have been lured to war in the guise of patriotic fervor. Dos Passos shows the destruction of a venerable abbey, the slow deaths of ambulance patients (many from the blood streaming down onto the patient below them), and the wounding of people so that the reader is given to see "a depression, a hollow pool of blood lying where the middle of a man had been," and the utter destruction of a soldier when he is shattered by an exploding grenade.

As Hemingway's own early poems showed, he too saw the war as a good topic for art. Some of the more effective poems concern the military: "Ultimately," "The Age Demanded," "Captives," "Champs D'Honneur," "Mitraigliatrice," and "Riparto D'Assalto." The latter poem begins with a detailed description of soldiers riding in a cold truck:

Damned cold, bitter, rotten ride,
Winding road up the Grappa side.[12]

It is only after another fairly long passage of factual detail that, in the last line, Hemingway the poet tells of the men's deaths ("where the truckload died"). Set in the location of his own short-lived ambulance service, his poem is not meant to be artistic or patriotic. It is rather a realistic, if imagistic, record of the group of naïve men who had no choices about their own lives or deaths.

As Hemingway moved from the terse poems he wrote early in his life in Paris to the short pieces of prose—whether the prose poem vignettes or the comparatively short stories like "My Old Man," "Indian Camp," and "The Doctor and the Doctor's Wife" (his stories from the mid-1930s, for example, would be three and four times as long as these first attempts)—he kept reading. Although some of the records of his borrowings from Sylvia Beach's lending library are lost, those from most years show extensive borrowing, and that he kept some books for months rather than weeks. When Hemingway kept a book for a long time, one can infer that he was studying it as well as reading it.

Among his reading were the novels (and travel literature) of Edith Wharton and Willa Cather. One could not be interested in American literature in the 1920s and not have read those authors—Wharton had won the first Pulitzer Prize for fiction (in 1921, for *The Age of Innocence,* a novel that had an independent and foreign-married woman in Ellen Olensky who might have been one model for Hemingway's Brett Ashley in *The Sun Also Rises*). Perhaps more important for Hemingway, nearly all Wharton's novels were filmed. (One of her slightest, *The Glimpses of the Moon* in 1922 became a movie after F. Scott Fitzgerald had done the screenplay from it.)[13] As a Scribner's author from the turn of the century, when *The House of Mirth* had been a best-seller in 1905, Wharton published regularly, a novel or a collection of stories or a memoir of travel nearly every year. Many of her novels were first serialized in *Scribner's Magazine.* In achieving the kind of Scribner's success that *A Farewell to Arms* did, in fact, Hemingway was copying Wharton's usual pattern.

Wharton was one of those influential writers that Hemingway would never have acknowledged any respect for. As an older woman, an elite and wealthy member of the New York "400" and the Paris international set (a group that did not include Gertrude Stein for reasons of both anti-Semitism and antibohemianism), Wharton was exactly the kind of privileged writer the modernists were trying to replace. Heavily influenced by the best Continental and Russian fiction, immensely well-read and -educated (though never in schools), Wharton—like Ellen Glasgow, whose novels were also consistent best-sellers, and Willa Cather, whose middle-class background saved her to some extent from the class suspicion that the avant-garde surrealists, Dadaists, and various kinds of modernists manifested—wrote with an almost overwhelming erudition, not to mention control of craft.

Wharton was also one of the few American authors who wrote extensively about World War I. While much of her publishing during the conflict was in the form of essays, to parallel her extensive war work with the American Hostels for Refugees in France, particularly to aid orphaned children, she also published books. In 1915, Scribner's brought out *Fighting France, from Dunkerque to Belfort* and in 1916, her edited collection, *The Book of the Homeless (Le Livre des Sans-Foyer).* According to Alan Price—whose *The End of the Age of Innocence: Edith Wharton and the First World* War is the definitive study of the war years—both of these books sold widely and were as useful as propaganda as they were informative about the European theater of war.[14] *The Book of the Homeless* was conceived, with Scribner's cooperation, as a money-raising project; all proceeds went into the war relief efforts Wharton sponsored.

Wharton also wrote two novels, *The Marne* in 1918 and the longer *A Son at the Front* that was published in 1923. This war novel concerns a young man somewhat estranged from his biological father, a painter who lives abroad. It is his mother's second husband, his stepfather, who pulls strings to enable George Campton to avoid being on the front lines, but eventually the soldier goes into battle despite his parents' efforts and is killed. The almost homoerotic treatment of the father-son relationship marked the book as being light years ahead of the times.[15]

It was Willa Cather, rather than Wharton, who won the prize for her war fiction. *One of Ours*, published in 1922, was awarded the Pulitzer Prize for fiction. Even as F. Scott Fitzgerald frequently acknowledged his admiration for both Wharton and Cather, and most readers found little wrong with the women's portrayals of twentieth-century life, Ernest Hemingway decided to teach Cather a lesson about gender. His vituperative comment about *One of Ours* has become notorious: as he wrote to Edmund Wilson (and Wilson later published his comments in *The Shores of Light*),

> Look at *One of Ours*. . . . Prize, big sale, people taking it seriously. You were in the war weren't you? Wasn't that last scene in the lines wonderful? Do you know where it came from? The battle scene in *Birth of a Nation*. I identified episode after episode, Catherized. Poor woman, she had to get her war experience somewhere.[16]

The sexualization of her method, reeking of the bullyingly adolescent insult, serves to divide the successful woman novelist—Cather, and by implication Wharton and Glasgow—from the male writer who (apparently) had had firsthand experience with wars. The irony of Hemingway's comment was that his knowledge of war was itself limited. As Michael Reynolds and others have proved, Hemingway drew his information for much of *A Farewell to Arms* from secondary written sources. (It was Edith Wharton who literally "saw" the most warfare.)

Michael North, along with Jo Ann Middleton and other Cather scholars, defends Cather's 1922 World War I novel in terms of its incipient modernist style (a great many omissions, scenes juxtaposed, characterization left purposefully incomplete). He finds the reason for many male critics' dismissal of the book to be largely gendered.

> The reception of *One of Ours* thus seems a classic instance of the way in which literary modernism was defined negatively by distin-

guishing it from a popular literature associated primarily with women. Whether this modern literature was to be toughly realistic or aesthetically experimental, it could define itself in contradistinction to a passive, sentimental, and essentially conformist female art. And yet, drawing the lines in this way is to accept without much probing both *One of Ours* and the male response to it, which need not have been quite so fierce if Cather really were, as Hemingway pretends, merely an object to be pitied. It may be that the massive condescension of the younger male writers to their older female colleague masks another reaction, that distinction is insisted on, as it so often is, precisely because the resemblance is too close. (179)

Into this bracket one might also place Hemingway's unfriendly reaction to Virginia Woolf's novel of World War I, *Jacob's Room* (despite his naming the protagonist in *The Sun Also Rises* for the Woolf character, Jacob Flanders—"Jacob" as a "Flemish" name),[17] and his consistent criticism of Ford Madox Ford, with whom he had worked on *transatlantic review*.

As the author of one of the best-received war novels, *The Good Soldier*, Ford was one of Hemingway's most attacked subjects in his posthumous *A Moveable Feast*, and (as the character Braddocks) targeted as well for ridicule in *The Sun Also Rises*. The subtitle of Ford's *The Good Soldier* was "A Tale of Passion," and in the manuscript version of his 1926 novel, Hemingway writes,

> In Braddock's novels there was always a great deal of passion but it took sometimes two and three volumes for anyone to sleep with anyone else. In actual life it seemed there was a great deal of sleeping about among good people[,] much more sleeping about than passion. . . . Who knew anything about anybody? You didn't know a woman because you slept with her any more than you knew a horse because you'd ridden him once. . . . Besides you learned a lot about a woman by not sleeping with her.[18]

In Ford's novel, as in *A Farewell to Arms*, the themes of war and love are carefully, if ironically, intertwined. In Ford's *The Good Soldier* occurs one version of the famous passage about the language of war, just as in that novel the man who loves too much kills himself rather than endure life without his beloved. Ford's character Edward Ashburnham stoically kills himself with "quite a small penknife," not in a field of battle but in his own stable yard. Ford's original title for the novel, "The Saddest Story," captured the various kinds of bereavements that the war-damaged characters experienced. *The Good Soldier* was a clear tragedy. In Hemingway's competitive nature, his attempt to write an even more melancholy story for Frederic Henry led to his giving Catherine and her child the sacrificial role.

PARIS AS THE SITE OF MODERNISM

The concept of expatriation has become synonymous with modernism, and several excellent studies attempt to locate the way exotic geography influenced both the themes and styles of American modernist fiction. J. Gerald Kennedy relies on a broad sweep of cultural information to use as both background and foreground for his analyses of the writing being done there during postwar years.[19] But he would agree with other critics who write about these places and times, that the dimensions of postwar Paris (Paris in the 1920s and early 1930s) are more mythic than actual. As he and Donald Pizer hypothesize in their respective books, Paris of that time has endured at least in part because of its imaginative creation, and re-creation, in the literary and artistic works shaped both within it and about it. While Kennedy sees those years in Paris as a definable culture, Pizer sees even the actuality of Paris as an imaginary state. As he writes in his prologue,

> Reduced to its most fundamental level, the expatriate or self-exile state of mind is compounded out of the interrelated conditions of the rejection of a homeland and the desire for and acceptance of an alternate place. The world one has been bred in is perceived to suffer from intolerable inadequacies and limitations; another world seems to be free of these failings and to offer a more fruitful way of life.[20]

Pizer's assessment of the qualities of postwar France, in what he calls "the Paris moment," includes "the freedom of thought and action possible within the Paris scene and nourished as well in body and spirit by the richness of Paris life" (141). As a result of being in such an "Edenic" location, the artist or writer finds a rebirth of "the spirit and its attendant capacity to speak through art" (142). Pizer notes too that the freedoms are sexual and personal as well as aesthetic.

George Wickes, who has long studied the Paris of these years, adds in the amazingly low cost of living as he summarizes some of the reasons young Americans needed the location of Paris as "an escape from the puritanism and provincialism of postwar America, of which Prohibition was simply the most conspicuous manifestation—the America of Harding and Coolidge, of William Jennings Bryan and Wayne B. Wheeler. Paris was where you could go on a moral holiday without fear of reproach, where the natives did not confuse pleasure with sin."[21]

No need, perhaps, for the somewhat hyperbolic praise of Gertrude Stein (who hedged her bets by claiming her roots in the United States even as she spent the last forty years of her life in France: "America is my country but Paris is my home town"[22]). For Stein, "Paris was where the twentieth century was. . . . Paris was the place that suited those of us that were to create the twentieth-century art and literature, naturally enough."[23]

Kennedy, in a more recent essay that brings F. Scott Fitzgerald together with Hemingway, reaffirms the importance of Paris as refuge:

> Fitzgerald and Hemingway initially reveled in their uprooting. Freed from American mores and family influences, inhabiting a culture more tolerant of vice and pleasure than our own, both writers indulged in "secrets, taboos, and delights," revolted against middle-class conventions, and managed to smash apart their personal lives. With palpable regret, both belatedly recognized (and dramatized in fiction) the results of their recklessness. Far from their native shores, released from any attachment to "region or tradition," they explored in Paris the beguiling possibilities of an expatriate life predicated on the desire—the ineluctable "hunger" metaphorized in Hemingway's memoir—that always culminates in the present moment.[24]

As American as the drive for exploration of the frontier, the myth that man can conquer whatever land is before him, the expatriate search for self—and art—in Paris did not, finally, remove people from those roots they were running to escape. But, as Kennedy goes on to point out, "in that foreign place, neither writer could escape the weight of time, the inevitability of consequence, or the burden of memory." For both writers, Paris had only seemed magical. As "Hemingway later perceived, Paris was also 'a very old city' where everything was 'more complicated' than it first appeared, and where young American writers hell-bent on fame could succumb to their own illusions of greatness and indestructibility, make irreversible mistakes, and lose the very things they cared about most."[25]

For Michael Reynolds, postwar Paris was never freed from the memory of World War I—and he contends that for Hemingway, too, the war had marked both the city and its people irrevocably. In Reynolds' description, "The war merely put a period on the end of a sentence that had been twenty years in the writing. The stable values of 1900 had eroded beneath the feet of this generation: Home, family, church, and country no longer gave the moral support that Hemingway's generation grew up with. . . . If his characters seemed degenerate, if their values appeared shallow, so did the world appear, at home and abroad, in those postwar years."[26] Reynolds quotes an unpublished note written by Hemingway in conjunction with the concept of the "lost generation," which he was to use as one of the epigraphs to his 1926 novel, *The Sun Also Rises*. In that note, Hemingway says,

> There will be more entanglements, there will be more complica-
> tions, there will be successes and failures. . . . My generation in
> France for example in two years sought salvation in first the
> Catholic Church, second DaDaism, third the movies, fourth Royal-
> ism, fifth the Catholic Church again. There may be another and
> better war. But none of it will matter particularly to this generation
> because to them the things that are given to people to happen have
> already happened.[27]

As all readers and critics know, the life of any piece of literature depends in large part on the culture of its reception—both the culture immediately contemporary with its publication and its initial response, and the culture of the present-day readers. Marc Dolan has read the works of postwar Paris, by "lost generation" writers, as a kind of self-designed cultural moment. His book intends to place the troublesome phrase into a large frame, one that hinges in part on modernism and in another part on the geographic location of Paris. As he says, most literary history creates a "narrativized perception of the decade [by giving it] a clear protagonist (the generation of the 1890s), a clear beginning (the enthusiastic days just after 'The War'), and a very clear end (the more resigned time just after 'The Crash')."[28] But he also insists that

> [W]hat may be most significant about early-twentieth-century
> American cultural history is neither the appearance of purely mod-
> ernist discourses nor the appearance of purely modernizing ones nor
> even the increasingly shared assumption of modernity but rather the
> logical coincidence of all three modes. . . . [T]he declaration of
> modernity hinged on a "recognition" that the individual's experi-

ence of modern life was more "disorganized" than s/he expected. Modernism and modernization most frequently functioned as strategies for "organizing" modernity, so that it would cohere into more comprehensible patterns, by asserting either the "individual" over the "corporate" or the "corporate" over the "individual." (37)

This more sociological stance toward the aesthetics of modernism makes the reader conscious of how many different aims the writers usually considered the Paris expatriates were juggling. It supports George Wickes' comment that "Fitzgerald was catering to the popular expectations of *Saturday Evening Post* readers, while Hemingway was creating a personal legend in describing the squalor of his humble beginnings as a writer. And after all, disillusioned realism was his trademark, just as lyricism was Fitzgerald's. A *Moveable Feast* gives a clear picture of what Paris meant to Hemingway to the end of his life: the scene of his early struggles to master his craft."[29]

THE WAR AND MODERNISM

"Every war is ironic because every war is worse than expected," writes Paul Fussell in his *The Great War and Modern Memory*.[30] Just by repeating the ghastly figure—8,000,000 people dead, the *million* ringing in a consciousness that had never even written such a large number—Fussell sets up the marker for the carnage of not only trench warfare but land mines, poison gas, airplane strafing and bombing, and myriad other methods of dying. The brutality of hand-to-hand combat was in World War I enhanced by various inventions of modern technology.

The commonplace trench system hardly brought to mind the horror it should have evoked. Fussell describes the three lines of trenches that comprised the usual British design:

The front-line trench was anywhere from fifty yards or so to a mile from its enemy counterpart. Several hundred yards behind it was the support trench line. And several hundred yards behind that was the reserve line. There were three kinds of trenches: firing trenches, like these; communication trenches, running roughly perpendicular to the line and connecting the three lines; and "saps," shallower ditches thrust out into No Man's Land, providing access to forward observation posts, listening posts, grenade-throwing posts, and machine gun positions. The end of a sap was usually not manned all the time: night was the favorite time for going out. Coming up from the rear, one reached the trenches by following a communication trench sometimes a mile or more long. It often began in a town and gradually deepened. By the time pedestrians reached the reserve line, they were well below ground level. (41)

To intensify his description, the author points out that the *daily* losses in dead and wounded ran to 7,000 British officers and men—"'Wastage' the Staff called it" (41).

Robert Lewis summarizes the carnage of World War I in both its physical and its ideological dimensions,

When the Great War began in this era of transition, such old-fashioned military tactics as cavalry charges met the modern world and its technology. What died were not simply the millions scythed down by machine-gun bullets and high explosives but also many of the ideals that had brought the world's leading nations to the great debacle. Such concepts as the chivalric code of battle died too, but not easily. The Machine Age that it was hoped would make life easier and more productive also ushered in the machine gun; advanced, highly destructive artillery; barbed wire; the airplane; the submarine; poison gas; and the tank—all first used extensively in World War I. The concept of the tank derived from its benign birth in American Caterpillar tractors for agricultural and engineering use. Covered with armor plate and studded with cannon and machine guns, it became the Jekyll-Hyde instrument of doom for the lightly-armed, old-fashioned individual soldier, now also vulnerable from the air and sea as well. Little wonder that the bloodied French army, led by generals adhering to outmoded tactics, revolted or that the literature of the war written by those who were in the trenches describes a world gone mad, a world in which sudden death could be a relief from mental and physical anguish.[31]

It is also no surprise that the antiwar novels and poems took more than a decade, in some cases, to appear. The stunning impact of World War I—on the world at large—took time to be recognized, much less digested.

One of the more interesting sets of writings about the European conflict, for example, appeared from the pen of American drama critic and producer, Mildred Aldrich. As a close friend of Gertrude Stein and Alice Toklas, Aldrich knew Hemingway well; during the 1920s he sometimes went along on picnics to Aldrich's country home. Unfortunately, that country home was on a hill that overlooked the bloody battle of the Marne (in which thousands of men were killed during one attack). Aldrich's *A Hilltop on the Marne*, published in 1915 after excerpts had appeared in the *Atlantic Monthly*, was followed by several other volumes of her war observations; while Aldrich's prose was genteel, drawn in some cases from her letters to Stein and other friends, she did not flinch from describing the soldiers' bodies, "long lines of grain-sacks," strewn across her fields. When the bodies were set on fire, they "stood like a procession of huge torches across my beloved panorama." Aldrich became famous for the fact that she had served tea on her lawn to British officers during one of the bloodiest encounters of the battle. American readers were hungry for news of the war: her book sold out seventeen printings.

While Hemingway did not emphasize battles on the Somme or the Marne, or trench warfare per se (partly because *A Farewell to Arms* recounted the Italian front, which was a problem with mountains and valleys rather than the flat-land strategies), he worked through several battles, as well as the fearful retreat from Caporetto. Metaphorically, however, the tone of sorrow, and even of doom, throughout the novel is achieved in part through the descriptions of the helpless: the two sisters at the mercy of the ambulance drivers in their escape from their occupied village, wounded soldiers dying despite medical aid at either the front lines or the hospital, Rinaldo's despair at the fact that he cannot save most of the men, and perhaps he will not be able to save himself, and—near the book's end—the account of ants burning out of the log Frederic Henry had put on his camp fire. Hemingway positions the metaphoric portrait of the innocent caught by chance just after the nurse has told Henry that the baby was born dead, and just before he is called into Catherine's room ("So now I sat out in the hall and waited to hear how Catherine was").

> Once in camp I put a log on top of the fire and it was full of ants. As it commenced to burn, the ants swarmed out and went first toward the centre where the fire was; then turned back and ran toward the end. When there were enough on the end they fell off into the fire. Some got out, their bodies burnt and flattened, and went off not knowing where they were going. But most of them went toward the fire and then back toward the end and swarmed on the cool end and finally fell off into the fire. I remember thinking at the time that it was the end of the world and a splendid chance to be a messiah and

lift the log off the fire and throw it out where the ants could get off onto the ground. But I did not do anything but throw a tin cup of water on the log, so that I would have the cup empty to put whiskey in before I added water to it. I think the cup of water on the burning log only steamed the ants. (328)

In his best objective writing, the protagonist whom Hemingway had created is using restraint, terribly compressed emotions, to counter the outburst he has just (silently, also compressed, known only to himself) voiced. One of Hemingway's few stream-of-consciousness paragraphs occurs immediately before the description of the ants. That meditation is not controlled: it is the grim commentary on people's deaths—in life as well as in war.

So that was it. The baby was dead. That was why the doctor looked so tired. But why had they acted the way they did in the room with him? They supposed he would come around and start breathing probably. I had no religion but I knew he ought to have been baptized. But what if he never breathed at all. He hadn't. He had never been alive. . . . Maybe he was choked all the time. Poor little kid. I wished the hell I'd been choked like that. No I didn't. Still there would not be all this dying to go through. Now Catherine would die. That was what you did. You died. You did not know what it was about. You never had time to learn. They threw you in and told you the rules and the first time they caught you off base they killed you. (327)

Like manuscript drafts of other sections of the novel, this almost inchoate passage tries to take the reader into Frederic Henry's mind. At the time of this passage, he has no idea that Catherine is in danger. Yet his intuition is such that he sees her death as possible. In relation to that, if he were dead himself, "there would not be all this dying to go through."

In an unpublished stream-of-consciousness section, Hemingway writes in long, sprawling sentences, but the import is the same:

They say the only way you can keep a thing is to lose it and this may be but I do not admire it. The only thing I know is that if you love anything enough they take it away from you. This may be done in infinite wisdom but whoever does it is not my friend. I am afraid of god at night but I would have admired him more if he would have stopped the war.[32]

The omnipresence of war in Hemingway's/Frederic Henry's thinking is indisputable. Similarly, in a draft for Hemingway's introduction to the collection of war fiction, *Men at War*, he writes a passage that sounds like an echo of *A Farewell to Arms*:

> This book will not tell you how to die. The cheer-leaders of war who head the variously initialled departments in Washington will probably eventually issue a pamphlet which will tell the best way to go through that small but necessary business at the end.[33]

A number of unpublished passages in the Hemingway Collection, fragmentary though they are, suggest that Michael Reynolds' assessment is correct. As he summarized in *Hemingway: The Final Years*, no matter what period in his writing history, Hemingway was "unable ever to dissociate love and war."[34] Using Catherine's death—the metaphor for the death of love—to transcribe and reflect Frederic Henry's feelings of both loss and fear fuses the separate themes into one. It is that thematic blending that lies at the heart of the power readers feel as they learn to read *A Farewell to Arms*.

THE NOVEL IN ITS CONTEXTS

Michael Reynolds devotes several chapters in his 1976 study, *Hemingway's First War*, to the sources of various kinds that he has unearthed in his intensive work on *A Farewell to Arms*. Both in "The Retreat from Caporetto" and the more didactically named "Sources for the Fiction," Reynolds mentions a variety of books—including collections of maps of World War I engagements—that would have been accessible to Hemingway during the 1920s. He also values the people Hemingway had met and, in some cases, become friends with—among those, Ted Brumback, Chink Dorman Smith, and the Italians Hemingway had known both during his volunteer service and, more extensively, during his stays in Italian hospitals. There are also what the critic describes as Hemingway's "picture books. While he was in Italy he collected postcard photographs of the battle zones. Sometime after he returned to Oak Park, he pasted these into a scrap book that included other war mementos, including his Italian medals. This scrap book was with him in Paris when he began the novel and was very likely with him when he finished it."[35]

Among the key sources Reynolds found are illustrated German war books and a great many magazines with articles about the war, many with maps and photographs, *Baedeker's Guide to Italy*, Hugh Dalton's *With British Guns in Italy*, the *Report by the Joint War Commission of the British Red Cross*, Stendhal's *The Charterhouse of Parma*,[36] Charles Bakewell's *The Story of the American Red Cross in Italy*, and the five-volume *Great Events of the Great War* (complete with essays by writers who had themselves taken part in the retreat beyond the Tagliamento), these latter two published in 1920.[37] As Hemingway worked toward perfecting his writing skills and began focusing on his own greatest adventure—the war and his wounding in it—whatever books were published, whatever articles appeared in the press, became information he collected. Not unlike a magpie, Ernest Hemingway was preparing himself for what would be one of his greatest works—when the time came.

To Reynolds' exhaustive discussion, I would like to add the short stories of American writer Ambrose Bierce. Hemingway himself several times disclosed his debt to Stephen Crane's novella, *The Red Badge of Courage*. That he said much less about Ambrose Bierce, whose story "An Occurrence at Owl Creek Bridge" he had read at least by 1928, if not earlier,[38] is typical of Hemingway's practices when he has found and used what he considers an invaluable source. Like Crane, Bierce wrote about the Civil War; but unlike Crane, Bierce wrote detailed, graphic, almost unreadable stories.[39] (Bierce had himself been in a number of the bloodiest war battles, and earned for himself the name of Bitter Bierce after his stories began to see publication. Many, for obvious reasons, were not published during his lifetime.)

The Owl Creek Bridge story is one of the more palatable of Bierce's war stories. Its heavy irony leads to the death of the southern gentleman who falls for the misinformation a spy feeds him. Thinking he can destroy a crucial bridge, Peyton Farquhar is captured during his attempt—and the story begins as he awaits his execution atop the railroad bridge itself. What Bierce does in the story is to give Peyton an imaginary escape (diving into the water below, swimming to safety despite bullets falling all about him) only to bring the reader up short with the jerk of the rope that breaks the protagonist's neck. The fantasy sequence shares elements of description with Frederic Henry's plunge under water as he swims to save his life from the Italian military police.

> Suddenly he heard a sharp report and something struck the water smartly within a few inches of his head, spattering his face with spray. He heard a second report, and saw one of the sentinels with his rifle at his shoulder, a light cloud of blue smoke rising from the

muzzle. . . . Farquhar dived—dived as deeply as he could. The water roared in his ears like the voice of Niagara, yet he heard the dulled thunder of the volley and, rising again toward the surface, met shining bits of metal, singularly flattened, oscillating slowly downward . . .

As he rose to the surface, gasping for breath, he saw that he had been a long time under water; he was perceptibly farther down stream—nearer to safety. (16–17)

Remarkably detailed, precise in their geographic descriptions, such Bierce stories as this and "Chickamauga," "A Horseman in the Sky," and "One of the Missing" gain their escalating effect through the author's careful assemblage of visual information. In the latter, the portrait of the young scout Jerome Searing, "with his extraordinary daring, his woodcraft, his sharp eyes, and truthful tongue" (32), puts the reader into the trapped man's mind as he tries to survive his erstwhile burial under a shelled building. Scouting for Sherman's army near Kennesaw Mountain, Georgia, Searing thought himself a seasoned scout; unfortunately, he decided to kill a few of the retreating Confederate soldiers, since (Bierce writes ironicallly) "it is the business of a soldier to kill. It is also his habit if he is a good soldier" (34). That Searing's own death results from his unsoldierly fear during his entrapment is another of Bierce's manifestations of irony.

The course Hemingway chose in the creation of his own tales of soldiers and civilians was to make his "soldier," Frederic Henry, a "civilian" and therefore a protagonist who might observe battle—and its mandate that a soldier kill—rather than participate in it.

NOTES

1. Among my writings about modernism are *The Modern American Novel, 1914–1945* (New York: Twayne, 1989) and "Modernism" in *The Oxford Companion to Women's Writing in the United States* (New York: Oxford University Press, 1995), coedited with Cathy N. Davidson.

2. Michael North, *Reading 1922: A Return to the Scene of the Modern* (New York: Oxford University Press, 1999), p. 66.

3. Ibid., p. 86.

4. Quentin Anderson, "The Emergence of Modernism" in *The Columbia Literary History of the United States*, ed. Emory Elliott (New York: Columbia University Press, 1988), pp. 695–714; this citation from pp. 695–696.

5. Edmund Wilson, *The Shores of Light* (New York: Farrar, Straus and Young, 1952), p. 15.

6. Gorham Munson, "A Comedy of Exiles," *Literary Review* 12, no. 1 (Autumn 1968), p. 47.

7. Andrew Ross, *The Failure of Modernism: Symptoms of American Poetry* (New York: Columbia University Press, 1986; see also Alan Wilde, *Horizons of Assent: Modernism, Postmodernism, and the Ironic Imagination* (Baltimore: Johns Hopkins University Press, 1981) and Morton P. Levitt, *Modernist Survivors* (Columbus: Ohio State University Press, 1987).

8. Sandra M. Gilbert and Susan Gubar, *No Man's Land: The Place of the Woman Writer in the Twentieth Century* (New Haven, CT: Yale University Press, 1988), I, pp. 75–76, 99–100.

9. Quoted in Morley Callaghan, *That Summer in Paris* (New York: Coward-McCann, 1963), p. 30.

10. Ezra Pound, "Small Magazines," *English Journal*, 19, no. 9 (November 1930), p. 700.

11. John Dos Passos, *One Man's Initiation: 1917* (London: Allen & Unwin, 1920); rpt. as *First Encounter* (New York: Philosophical Library, 1945), pp. 44–45. Some critics kept noting that Dos Passos wrote out of his World War I experiences for several decades. What is more likely is that his involvement in the war crystallized his philosophy and attitudes, and gave him an alternate canvas to set against that of his relatively secluded years at Choate and Harvard. Other page references cited in text.

12. *The Collected Poems of Ernest Hemingway* (New York: Haskell House, 1960), p. 22. One of the works Pound mentioned in his praise (above) is more strident, less of an imagist treatment. "They All Made Peace—What Is Peace" is available in Louis Zukofsky's "Comment, Program: 'Objectivists,' 1931," *Poetry* 37 (February 1931), pp. 270–271. A few lines from this satire follow:

Lord Curzon likes young boys.

So does Chicherin.

So does Mustapha Kemal. He is good looking too. His eyes

Are too close together but he makes war. That is the way he is . . .

13. Drawing from a notation in F. Scott Fitzgerald's ledger, Robert A. Martin thinks the work Fitzgerald did toward the film was providing titles ("The Salons of Wharton's Fiction," Martin and Linda Wagner-Martin in *Wretched Exotic: Essays on Edith Wharton in Europe*, ed. Katherine Joslin and Alan Price (New York: Peter Lang, 1993], p. 100); a more interesting comparison is set forth in Helen Killoran's "An Unnoticed Source for *The Great Gatsby*: The Influence of Edith Wharton's *The Glimpses of the Moon*," *Canadian Review of American Studies* 21 (Spring 1991), pp. 223–224. While Killoran sees the Wharton novel's influence within the achievement of Fitzgerald's *Gatsby*, one might also connect that 1925 novel with Willa Cather's 1922 *A Lost Lady*.

14. Alan Price, *The End of the Age of Innocence: Edith Wharton and the First World War* (New York: St. Martin's, 1996), pp. 77–78 and ff. See also Jean Gallagher, *The World Wars Through the Female Gaze* (Carbondale: Southern Illinois University Press, 1998).

15. The fact that Ernest Hemingway frequently did not acknowledge the very writers who were most helpful to him makes the critic wonder how disclosive he was being about Wharton. In his personal library in Cuba, according to James D. Brasch and Joseph Sigman (*Hemingway's Library: A Composite Record* [New York: Garland, 1981]), Hemingway had six of her books, including *French Ways and Their Meaning*, 1919, as well as the more famous novels and her autobiography, *A Backward Glance*. Michael S. Reynolds confirms the presence of the novels and short stories (*Hemingway's Reading, 1910–1940: An Inventory* [Princeton, NJ: Princeton University Press, 1981]). Critic Adeline R. Tintner recounts the connection between Wharton's writing the preface to Vivienne de Watteville's *Speak to the Earth: Wanderings and Reflections Among Elephants and Mountains* (1935) and the fact that Hemingway had planned to use a passage from *Speak to the Earth* as epigraph for "The Snows of Kilimanjaro" in 1936 ("Edith Wharton, Ernest Hemingway, and Vivienne de Watteville, *Speak to the Earth*" in Tintner's *Edith Wharton in Context: Essays on Intertextuality* [Tuscaloosa: University of Alabama Press, 1999], pp. 134–138).

16. Jo Ann Middleton rehearses the story of Hemingway's Nov. 25, 1923, letter to Wilson (see Wilson's *The Shores of Light: A Literary Chronicle of the Twenties and Thirties* [New York: Farrar, Straus, and Young, 1952], p. 118) in her *Willa Cather's Modernism: A Study of Style and Technique* (Rutherford, NJ: Fairleigh Dickinson University Press, 1990). For the placement of Cather into modernist circles see also M. Catherine Downs, *Becoming Modern: Willa Cather's Journalism* (London: Associated University Presses, 1999).

17. See my "The Intertextual Hemingway" in *A Historical Guide to Ernest Hemingway* (New York: Oxford University Press, 2000), especially pp. 186–192.

18. Frederic Joseph Svoboda, *Hemingway and The Sun Also Rises: The Crafting of a Style* (Lawrence: University Press of Kansas, 1983), p. 85.

19. J. Gerald Kennedy, *Imagining Paris: Exile, Writing, and American Identity* (New Haven, CT: Yale University Press, 1993); see also Donald Pizer, *American Expatriate Writing and the Paris Moment: Modernism and Place* (Baton Rouge: Louisiana State University Press, 1996); Marc Dolan, *Modern Lives: A Cultural Re-reading of* The Lost Generation (West Lafayette, IN: Purdue University Press, 1996); and various essays in *French Connections: Hemingway and Fitzgerald Abroad*, ed. J. Gerald Kennedy and Jackson R. Bryer (New York: St. Martin's, 1998).

20. Pizer, *The Paris Moment*, p. 1; hereafter cited in text.

21. George Wickes, "The Right Place at the Right Time," *French Connections* (New York: St. Martin's, 1998), p. 4.

22. Gertrude Stein, "An American and France," *What Are Masterpieces* (Los Angeles, CA: Conference Press, 1940), p. 61.

23. Gertrude Stein, *Paris France* (New York: Scribner's, 1940), pp. 11, 12.

24. J. Gerald Kennedy, "Figuring the Damage," *French Connections* (New York: St. Martin's, 1998), p. 339.

25. Ibid., Kennedy quotes from Hemingway's *A Moveable Feast*, p. 119.

26. Michael S. Reynolds, "The Sun in Its Time: Recovering the Historical Context," *New Essays on* The Sun Also Rises, ed. Linda Wagner-Martin (Cambridge, UK: Cambridge University Press, 1987), p. 46.

27. Michael S. Reynolds, *Hemingway: The Paris Years* (Cambridge, MA: Blackwell, 1989), p. 327; he quotes here from Hemingway's manuscripts at the John F. Kennedy Library.

28. Marc Dolan, *Modern Lives* (W. Lafayette, IN: Purdue University Press, 1996), pp. 160. Dolan makes the point that in this myth of the Lost Generation, readers and critics "moved through a reiterated narrative that often bore a striking resemblance to the sequence of moods that so insistently dominated Fitzgerald's historical thinking in the early 1930s: from youthful exuberance (the 'younger generation' of the early 1920s) to self-absorbed decline ('a lost generation' in the late 1920s) to conspicuous decadence ('the lost generation' of the early 1930s). In time, this coincidence would mark a shared retrospective perception of the narrative flow and segmentation of recent American history."

29. Wickes, "The Right Place at the Right Time," *French Connections*, p. 12.

30. Paul Fussell, *The Great War and Modern Memory* (New York: Oxford University Press, 1975), p. 7; hereafter cited in text.

31. Robert Lewis, *A Farewell to Arms* (New York: Twayne, 1992), p. 5.

32. Manuscripts of Ch. 40, *A Farewell to Arms*, Hemingway Collection, John F. Kennedy Library.

33. Manuscripts of Introduction, *Men at War*, Item #19, Hemingway Collection, John F. Kennedy Library.

34. Michael S. Reynolds, *Hemingway: The Final Years* (New York: Norton, 1999), p. 210.

35. Michael S. Reynolds, *Hemingway's First War* (Princeton, NJ: Princeton University Press, 1976), p. 139. Keeping scrapbooks would have been natural for Ernest; his mother was a seemingly inexhaustible scrapbook maker; see her collections of photo albums and scrapbooks made for and about Enrest in the Hemingway Collection, John F. Kennedy Library.

36. Ibid., pp. 154–158. Reynolds notes more than casual similarities between Hemingway's novel and *Charterhouse*. He also points out that *Frederic* Stendhal, *nom de plume* for *Henri* Beyle, gave Hemingway the source for both parts of Frederic Henry's name.

37. Ibid., pp. 105–180.

38. Michael S. Reynolds, *Hemingway's Reading, 1910–1940* (Princeton, Princeton University Press, 1981), p. 99.

39. Ambrose Bierce, *Tales of Soldiers and Civilians and Other Stories* (New York: Penguin, 2000); "An Occurrence at Owl Creek Bridge," pp. 11–19. The selec-

tion from Bierce's first book of stories, *In the Midst of Life* (the British title, taken from *The Book of Common Prayer*, "In the midst of life, we are in death"; United States title, *Tales of Soldiers and Civilians*, both 1892) includes a range of Civil War stories including "A Horseman in the Sky," "Chickamauga," "A Son of the Gods," "One of the Missing," "Killed at Resaca," "The Affair at Coulter's Notch," "The Coup De Grace," "Parker Adderson, Philosopher," and "One Kind of Officer." Many of Bierce's stories deal with the fear of death, while others have a supernatural element that deflects attention from the bloody struggle that the Civil War was—though not always presented so truthfully in postwar fiction.

5　Ideas

Most of the thematic emphases of literature the world over are incorporated in Hemingway's mixture of romance and war novel. Within the American literary tradition of using as subject a man's inner quest for a meaningful self—whether that quest took the character to the frontier, as in James Fenimore Cooper's novels, or to the ocean, as in Herman Melville's, or to another country, as in Henry James's—Hemingway's *A Farewell to Arms* establishes Frederic Henry as a true, and somewhat conventional, American hero.

To be engaged in war may be the ultimate test of manhood. The outcomes of performance in either battle or as a noncombatant in the military are stark: death or life. Life after war might be a limited one, however, marred by either physical or psychological debility. Either way, the odds are indisputably high.

Frederic Henry, in the milieu of war, almost unconsciously becomes the prototype of the twentieth century existential figure. In a world of confusion, with military events hostile to any individual's well-being, the person alone has no philosophic star to guide by. His duty is to take orders. Privileging himself as a thoughtful, knowledgable person has no place in the soldier's arena: he must recognize that he is only a small bit of fodder for the machinery of war.

Soldiers cannot even think about any kind of personal health, much less the concept of self-actualization. Serving one's country becomes the single, and primary, goal.

Such a goal, however, is usually directionless. Mandated by the circumstances of "serving" in the military, a person's own choices are severely limited: the very point of military discipline is to replace one's personal choice. The notion of courage, then, is also dramatically changed. To follow a superior's order may wipe out any volition. It was this dilemma that so attracted Hemingway to Stephen Crane's Civil War novella, *The Red Badge of Courage*. To call a fearful boy's behavior "courage" is to insist on more realistic definitions—or, more appropriately, to insist that courage under someone else's command is very different from personal courage.

In *A Farewell to Arms*, Hemingway deals with this impossible situation through the use of metaphors and hesitant stream-of-conscious passages. Except for the paragraph about inflated language, he seldom gives his reader lessons in either social studies or psychology: he writes about the characters he fashions as human, and gives them words that seem germane to the situation. The only passages in which he treats the issue of courage and/or bravery comprehensively are in the scenes of Frederic's leaving Catherine, when he meditates during their night together, "we were never lonely and never afraid when we were together. . . . If people bring so much courage to this world the world has to kill them to break them, so of course it kills them. The world breaks every one and afterward many are strong at the broken places. But those that will not break it kills. It kills the very good and the very gentle and the very brave impartially. If you are none of these you can be sure it will kill you too but there will be no special hurry" (249). Earlier, in a dialogue between the two, Frederic had reassured Catherine that "they" wouldn't get her "Because you're too brave. Nothing ever happens to the brave." When she points out that the brave also die, he responds that they die only once—a tautology that might sound poetic but is only nonsense. Catherine also points that out to him, ending with the last word: "He knew a great deal about cowards but nothing about the brave. The brave dies perhaps two thousand deaths if he's intelligent. He simply doesn't mention them" (139–140).

It is noticeable that Hemingway uses these words about the brave to refer to Catherine. For a male speaker surrounded by men in battle, such a shift in reference comes as a surprise. Inherent in the concepts of courage and bravery is the gendered consideration of manliness. In days of earlier American literature, the military was the province of men; women were excluded entirely. The military was one of the safely male areas where men might choose to serve, in part as a way to escape the domestic—the home and family, church, and community that were increasingly in the twentieth century becoming areas of women's control. (In fact, in the late nineteenth century, the phrase "separate spheres" grew up to connote the kind of division of power in middle- and upper-class families, and in the cultures those families dominated.)

It is this gendered allocation of power that gave rise to some of the more recent questioning of the military (seen during our history with the Vietnam War). If to be a man is to make your own situation, then to voluntarily relinquish such decision making is to act—in effect—against oneself. Frederic Henry's attempt in A *Farewell to Arms* to adjudicate his own "separate peace" as he deserts and flees with Catherine (and as the wounded Nick Adams character in the In Our Time vignette had coined the phrase initially) is one means of bridging the seemingly wide division between obeying military orders and making decisions personally.

Hemingway's narrative strategy in A *Farewell to Arms* is to put the outright criticism of war into the mouths of the young Italian mechanics, rather than attributing the criticism to Frederic Henry. Even though he later deserts, Henry seems a bit incredulous at the harshness of Passini's judgments (it is Passini, who here shows no belief at all in the war effort, who is killed in the shell explosion that wounds Henry):

> "Tenente," Passini said. . . . "Listen. There is nothing as bad as war. We in the auto-ambulance cannot even realize at all how bad it is. When people realize how bad it is they cannot do anything to stop it because they go crazy. There are some people who never realize. There are people who are afraid of their officers." (50)

When Henry tries to get Passini to blame the wealthy ammunitions manufacturers, or other war profiteers, by responding "Also they make money out of it," Passini shatters his liberal beliefs by saying simply, "Most of them don't. . . . They are too stupid. They do it for nothing."

Immediately juxtaposed with this somewhat elevated discussion (though Passini avoids the ultra-patriotic words that Henry despises) is the scene of Henry's going to a headquarters building in search of food for his men. There is only cold macaroni and hard cheese, but there is also the atmosphere of relief inside the building that the attack is starting. As if to foreshadow that attack, the major notices, "Outside something was set down beside the entrance" (52). When the major says, "Bring *him* in," the reader has the same kind of disbelief that Henry experienced: a wounded man became a "something" in the day-to-day business of running the war. And immediately following this brief scene is the description of both Henry's wounding, and its accompanying out-of-body consciousness, and Passini's death.

Paul Fussell writes about what he calls "military memory":

> Everyone who remembers a war first-hand knows that its images remain in the memory with special vividness. The very enormity of the proceedings, their absurd remove from the usages of the normal world, will guarantee that a structure of irony sufficient for ready narrative recall will attach to them. And the irony need not be Gravesian and extravagant: sometimes a very gentle irony emerging from anomalous contrasts will cause ... "certain impressions [to] remain with one—a sunrise when the Huns are quiet, a sunset when they are raising a storm, a night made hideous by some distant cannonades. ... " One remembers with special vividness too because military training is very largely training in alertness and a special kind of noticing.[1]

Like the "something" deposited outside the door of the tent, Hemingway's *A Farewell to Arms* is filled with slight details that open out only later in the novel, making readers return to their first introduction as if to process these details anew.

One of these is the quick mention of "the new graves in the [hospital] garden" that Henry—now hospitalized in Milan—observes as he goes for his walks and for his physical therapy, generally conducting himself as a person in recovery (75). Just a few feet from his room, however, lie the buried bodies of fellow soldiers who have died on the other side of the curtain that shrouds his bed. Another is the equally brisk mention of his going to sleep in Milan, watching "the beams of the search-lights moving in the sky," and his subsequent waking—"sweating and scared and then went back to sleep trying to stay outside my dream" (88). Italy is clearly a country at war, vigilant in keeping watch for any impending bombing. And Frederic Henry is clearly a man traumatized by his near-death wounding, a horrifically surprising attack that came in the darkness. Another is the ambulance major's description of the war (on Henry's return to action), which he consistently calls "very bad. ... You couldn't believe how bad it's been" (167) and in the midst of the description, saying simply "we lost three cars."

Drawing on the author's careful planting of the assumptions people bring to war—and in his assumptions the character Frederic Henry was no less naïve than the other young soldiers or drivers—here Hemingway punctures another of those assumptions—that driving ambulances was not dangerous. Three of the less than a dozen ambulances under the major's jurisdiction were lost—the cars' men, presumably, dead. Just as Henry himself was blown up by a mortar shell, whoever was on the lines—regardless of which uniform he wore or what his responsibility was—was in danger of dying.

Hemingway uses this fallacy of assumption twice in the novel. One assumption is that ambulance personnel are, somehow, safe. Yet he gives us the deaths of Passini and Aymo, and Henry's wounding, to counter that public knowledge. Another is the fallacy that women no longer die in childbirth. Frederic thinks about these assumptions in almost the same language (the Catherine-dying-in-childbirth scene is another of the stream-of-consciousness passages): "And what if she should die? She won't die. People don't die in childbirth nowadays. That was what all husbands thought. Yes, but what if she should die? She won't die. . . . [W]hat if she should die? She can't die. Yes, but what if she should die? She can't, I tell you. . . . [B]ut what if she should die? She can't die. Why would she die? What reason is there for her to die?" (320). With the changing of insistent verbs, the quick repetition of short sentences, the blunted effect of the somber pattern of repetition as the reader begins to see how sure, even if implausible, Catherine's death is becoming, Hemingway builds toward the character's actual (quiet and gentle) death with all the bravado Frederic Henry can muster. But to the last question, "What reason is there for her to die?" the reader knows that such reasonlessness is precisely the point.

Catherine's death almost takes the fall for the fact that Hemingway writes very little unpleasant description of the battles of war per se. One of the problems with marketing war novels was that readers did not want to know what trench warfare or the scenes on the hillsides of the Marne were like. As Fussell notes,

One of the cruxes of the war, of course, is the collision between events and the language available—or thought appropriate—to describe them. To put it more accurately, the collision was one between events and the public language used for over a century to celebrate the idea of progress. Logically there is no reason why the English language could not perfectly well render the actuality of trench warfare: it is rich in terms like *blood, terror, agony, madness, shit, cruelty, murder, sell-out, pain* and *hoax,* as well as phrases like *legs blown off, intestines gushing out over his hands, screaming all night, bleeding to death from the rectum*, and the like. . . . The difficulty was in admitting that the war had been made by men and was being continued *ad infinitum* by them. The problem was less one of "language" than of gentility and optimism; it was less a problem of "linguistics" than of rhetoric. Louis Simpson speculates about the reason infantry soldiers so seldom render their experiences in language: "To a foot-soldier, war is almost entirely physical. That is why some men, when they think about war, fall silent. Language seems to falsify physical life and to betray those who have experienced it absolutely—the dead."[2]

In both Fussell's book and in *A Farewell to Arms*, the soldier's reliance on communicating with relatives and friends back home by sending the Field Service Post Card illustrates the failure of civilized language—and the soldier's reluctance to invade his family's private and safe space with the language that could do justice to his experiences. On the postcard, categories are harmless yet reassuring:

I am quite well.
I have been admitted into hospital
sick   and am going on well.
wounded   and hope to be discharged soon.[3]

At two points in Hemingway's novel, Henry sends these postcards to avoid being in touch with his family. Each time he checks only "I am quite well." The first time he relies on these "official language" messages is when he has begun to learn what war is really about. The second time, however, is used to provoke the reader into assessing Frederic's state of mind once he has deserted. He uses the Field Service card during the idyllic months that he and Catherine live as a couple complete in themselves, awaiting the birth of their child. That the second instance seems to be as inexpressible as the first gives the reader the same kind of concern as does the dialogue between Catherine and Frederic when they reassure each other that they will never need to meet the other's father. In the scene where they talk about Catherine's past craziness and look ahead to the birth of their child, Catherine comments that wine had given her father the gout.

"Have you a father?"
"Yes," said Catherine. "He has gout. You won't ever have to meet him. Haven't you a father?"

"No," I said. "A step-father."

"Will I like him?"

"You won't have to meet him."

"We have such a fine time," Catherine said. "I don't take any interest in anything else any more. I'm so very happy married to you" (154).

The enormity of the couple's pretense—why does Hemingway give Frederic a step-father rather than a father, since it was his father he loved and that father still lived—and, more startlingly, Catherine's valorizing of their withdrawal from all the world, even their own families, under the guise that they have married, which they have not, creates more than irony: it clearly signals the readers that the "craziness" thought to be long in the past may still be with them, only this time, that it may be infecting both of them. The wages of war, the distillation of what war means— complete and utter separation from the known world, the world that makes a person human—impacts the reader here with first puzzlement and then despair. The least reconcilable dialogue is yet to come, however. Frederic Henry asks Catherine:

"Where will you have the baby?"

She replies, "I don't know. The best place I can find."

Operating now, as Henry says, in his "clear and cold" factual mode, he continues, "How will you arrange it?" And Catherine replies, as much in a fantasy of denial as he,

"The best way I can." (153–154)

Serving in a wartime army, living in a foreign country, unmarried and illegitimately pregnant, Catherine has nothing but a fantasy power. She has no rights, no way of providing for her hospitalization, no reason to be abroad but to serve in the hospital staff—and once her pregnancy becomes advanced, she will lose that sinecure. Juxtaposing these scenes as Hemingway does, the reader sees the necessity for Henry's using the Army Zona de Guerra postcards, "strange and mysterious" though he finds them (36). As Hemingway makes clearer and clearer, nothing is stranger and more mysterious than this illusory romance that Catherine and he have created.

To return to Frederic Henry as he is nearer the start of A Farewell to Arms, however, is to show how illusory was his first conception of war. He admits, "It seemed no more dangerous to me myself than war in the movies"

(37). Henry's behavior strikes the reader accordingly: this is a young American who goes out with his friends, drinks too much, chases whores, and amasses statistics after a weeks-long leave that makes him one of the cocks of the walk. He is also something of a United States nativist: he has moments of wishing he were with the British forces rather than the Italian (after all, in Oak Park and other parts of the States, the men he serves with would be designated "wops"). He wonders about the Italian stereotypes and thinks about the difficulty of learning their language. He thinks of them as being marked by their Catholicism (the reason for the continued appearance in the novel of the young priest), by their wine drinking, by their lustiness (which the confessional in the Catholic church makes amends for), and by their hail-fellow-well-met characteristics. Even in the midst of learning to know Italians, he wishes for the English, "big and shy and embarrassed and very appreciative together of anything that happened. I wish that I was with the British. It would have been much simpler" (37). (Hemingway's nativism also prompts the dialogue about how comic the Japanese are, "a wonderful little people fond of dancing and light wines," [76], and much of the pidgen English kind of quality of his prejudicial statements might be ignored under the guise of translation problems.)

Wendy Steiner sees World War I as the most powerful of forces shaping American literature early in the twentieth century. She speaks particularly to the polite and patriotic phrasing of the fiction and essay intended to be polemic, to draw the United States into the war conflict, and to the way that expression jarred against the voicing of "the shattered despair of younger novelists," whose naturalistic mode gave the reader lines such as Henry Miller's "the boys from the north side and the boys from the south side—all rolled into a muck heap and their guts hanging on the barbed wire. . . . The whole past is wiped out." In Steiner's words, the younger writers' "bitter analysis polarized the generations, the sexes, and the aesthetic orientations of everyone concerned. The parents who had proudly sent their sons to die for their country, the women who rejoiced in the nobility of soldiers' blasted experience, and the traditionalists who eagerly embraced the war as a lesson in morality and propriety were equated with the cause of the war itself."[4]

In one of his earliest stories, "Soldier's Home," Hemingway had exploded the myth that a soldier—one who had seen any war at all—*could* return home. The story begins with the dilemma that Harold Krebs, who had seen action and was full of honest accounts of battle, faced when other men prided themselves on recounting inflated narratives. The language of his war had already been usurped—and dishonestly so. While he focused his enmity toward his mother and the complacent community, Harold Krebs knew at heart that the anger was within himself, was somehow his fault. Steiner notes that writers who dealt with the subject of World War I were implicitly drawn to the topic of such guilt. She says, "The dislocation brought on by World War I, the fact that even the winners came home to a world they could not live in, provoked a profound analysis of the phenomenon of victimization. Woodrow Wilson's argument for neutrality had been based on the need to avoid the dynamic of physical battle, on the grounds that the difference between winner and loser was too slight. The United States, he claimed, could not 'fight Germany and maintain the ideal of government that all thinking men share. . . . A ruthless brutality will enter into the very fibre of our national life'" (850).

Hemingway's handling of this problem within *A Farewell to Arms* was to create the character of Ettore, the American of Italian descent who is fighting in the Italian army. Even the glamour of Ettore's living in San Francisco—though a buddy calls him "just a wop from Frisco"—cannot keep his reprehensible qualities from Henry's and Catherine's criticism. Ettore Moretti is a man on the make, regardless of national characteristics. He wants all five of the medals he says he has been awarded ("But the papers on only one have come through") because they enhance his womanizing power. He comments to Frederic that with his silver medal, "[T]he girls at the Cova will think you're fine then. They'll all think you killed two hundred Austrians or captured a whole trench by yourself." Tactless and offensive, Ettore shows Frederic (whom he calls "Fred" twice in this scene, the only time anyone in the novel deviates from Frederic Henry's chosen name) the "deep smooth red scar" on his arm. He boasts about his other two wounds that will make the three "wound stripes" on his sleeve almost as eye-catching as his medals. Ettore is the soldier who fights only for booty, of whatever kind (119–123).

In this negative definition of war hero, Hemingway posits everything objectionable to those who understand the horrible process of battle. He also gives the reader a contrast to the braggart Ettore (and the much more passive, but perhaps not any more heroic, Frederic Henry). In the character of Gino, the ambulance driver who explains to Frederic that "it really had been hell at San Gabriele," Hemingway gives the reader an observer of war who presents facts truthfully, with no self-aggrandizement. Instead, Gino uses his narrative in order to admit to his fear.

He said the Austrians had a great amount of artillery in the woods along Texnova ridge beyond and above us, and shelled the roads badly at night. There was a battery of naval guns that had gotten on his nerves. I would recognize them because of their flat trajectory. You heard the report and then the shriek commenced almost instantly. They usually fired two guns at once, one right after the other, and the fragments from the burst were enormous. He showed me one, a smoothly jagged piece of metal over a foot long. It looked like babbitting metal.

"I don't suppose they are so effective," Gino said. "But they scare me. They all sound as though they came directly for you. There is the boom, then instantly the shriek and burst. What's the use of not being wounded if they scare you to death?" (182)

Gino's discourse echoes that of the major, who is not afraid to tell Frederic Henry upon his return from the Milan hospital how bad things have been over the summer and fall. The Italians had lost 150,000 men on the Bainsizza Plateau and on the San Gabriele, and another 40,000 on the Carso. He said bluntly, "If they killed men as they did this fall the Allies would be cooked in another year. He said we were all cooked but we were all right as long as we did not know it. We were all cooked. The thing was not to recognize it" (133–134).

In a kind of counterpoint, a weary and visibly "thinner" Rinaldi tells Frederic Henry matter-of-factly, "This war is killing me. I am very depressed by it. . . . All summer and all fall I've operated. I work all the time. I do everybody's work. All the hard ones they leave to me" (167). But eventually Henry goes back to the front and—despite the verbal warnings he has had—is stunned by what he sees: the destruction of the forests and the ground where the troops have been shelled, the "many iron shrapnel balls in the rubble of the houses and on the road beside the broken house where the post was" (185). The physical waste is bringing the bludgeoning character of war closer to Henry.

It is when Henry sleeps at post during the night that the full force of the possibility of enemy attack hits him; the fear that Gino had described takes over.

The wind rose in the night and at three o'clock in the morning with the rain coming in sheets there was a bombardment and the Croatians came over the mountain meadows. . . . They fought in the dark in the rain and a counter-attack of scared men from the second line drove them back. There was much shelling and many rockets in the rain and the machine-gun and rifle fire all along the line. They did not come again. . . .

The wounded were coming into the post, some were carried on stretchers, some walking and some were brought in on the backs of men that came across the field. They were wet to the skin and all were scared. We filled two cars with stretcher cases as they came up from the cellar of the post and as I shut the door of the second car and fastened it I felt the rain on my face turn to snow. The flakes were coming heavy and fast in the rain.

When daylight came the storm was still blowing but the snow had stopped. It had melted as it fell on the wet ground and now it was raining again. There was another attack just after daylight but it was unsuccessful. We expected an attack all day but it did not come until the sun was going down. . . . We expected a bombardment but it did not come. It was getting dark. (186)

Hemingway's emphasis here is not on the damage done by the shelling and the attacking, but rather on the state of mind of Frederic Henry and the others, whose job was to wait, to keep watch, to convey the wounded, to try to save lives.

After this scene, with its countless examples of brave men doing their jobs with no thought of medals or wound stripes, Hemingway juxtaposes the scene of Frederic Henry nervously preparing for the evacuation and asking his superior officer what the policy is for using the ambulances during a retreat. What he is told shocks him. The ambulances will be used to carry hospital supplies and equipment, not to save the wounded. The wounded are left behind. When a country has a chance to be a winner, human life is worth saving. But when the country is on the run, its armies in retreat, all human life can be extinguished—with no guilt or repercussions. The people in charge of humanitarian efforts are intent on saving only themselves and their equipment.

In some ways, this context makes the decision of Catherine Barkley, V.A.D. who was brought to Italy to aid the wounded, somewhat more understandable. Once a country was losing, even the medical personnel saved themselves first. Fergie would be transferred out, and no matter how badly the wounded needed aid, the hospital would provide no human comfort—perhaps shelter, but not personnel.

It seems fair to say that what Frederic Henry learns in the process of becoming a military man is that one acts primarily to save himself. In contrast to the rules and lessons of the service, Hemingway shows the less educated (in this novel, the ambulance drivers and mechanics) and people separate from the military forces as the only true observers of the horrors of warfare. Positioning Frederic Henry between those two camps, Hemingway allows his protagonist a range of legitimate behaviors. In James Phelan's reading of Henry, for example, the character illustrates what Phelan sees as *A Farewell to Arms*'s primary plot, "a coherent process of growth and change in Frederic Henry that culminates, tragically and ironically, in the moment of his greatest loss. Furthermore, I believe that Hemingway's representation of this process cannot be appreciated until we combine our attention to style, character, and structure with careful attention to voice."[5] In Phelan's discussion of the novel, he draws parallels between the way Hemingway makes the reader identify, first, with the naïve Henry—albeit with some criticism for his egotism and machismo—and the way that somewhat critical identification changes into understanding as the novel goes its carefully drawn way.

Phelan sees immense distance between Hemingway as author and Frederic Henry as character, particularly at the novel's start. "For all the authority of his voice at the beginning of the narrative, Frederic Henry is strikingly ignorant; the implied presence of Hemingway's voice, which gives the sentence its pointed irony, makes Frederic's voice naïve. This gap between Frederic and Hemingway is arguably the most important revelation of the first chapter. It establishes a tension between author and narrator that is one major source of our continued interest in the narrative, and it helps define the major initial instability of the narrative: Frederic's situation in a war whose effects and potential consequences he is ignorant of" (64).

By concentrating on the style of the way the character's voice interacts with the unnamed, third-person, authorial voice, Phelan is able to enrich the reading of Henry that summarizes his sorrowful learning experiences throughout the narrative as "maturing." Surely a man does not need to escape being killed (several times), become a killer himself, and lose both his child and his wife in order to mature. Hemingway may have thought of himself as a realist, but he was never aiming for martyrdom—for either Frederic Henry or himself.

One of the most-detailed presentations of the role of "retrospective narration" in Hemingway's characterization of Frederic Henry is James Nagel's essay, in which he argues that the Henry the reader knows is not conveyed through a realistic, chronological description of the man enduring World War I: "*A Farewell to Arms* is fundamentally not a realistic novel about World War I narrated by Ernest Hemingway; it is, rather, a retrospective narrative told by Frederic Henry a decade after the action has taken place for the purpose of coming to terms emotionally with the events."[6] Enriched with the 1990s critical interest in self-narration, Nagel's is the current view of reading Henry so that the obvious moral impasses of the novel can be assessed in fairly complex ways. Frederic Henry during the war was a young man, relatively inexperienced. The Frederic Henry who narrates the novel has learned from both the war and his great love: he is a different character.

Phelan's analysis gives us a more complex approach to voice and figuration, as he points out, to counter the ease with which this retrospective view can be assimilated:

> The rub in seeing Frederic as the victim rather than the source of irony is that if unselfconscious Frederic has learned about the war and the world at the time of the action, then his knowledge should always be a part of his perspective as he retells the story. In other words, Frederic writes as if he does not know what he in fact knows. (82)

Phelan's approach is also one of the few that focuses on the interaction between Henry and the young priest. While Hemingway's triangular design—Rinaldi, the priest, and Catherine as Henry's objects of value—is clearly set up from the start, little critical attention has been paid to his friendship with the priest. It is almost as though the critics have adopted the pose of the officers at the mess, and see the priest as an object of ridicule rather than a spokesperson for one whose life is directed toward a goal.

The character of the priest—young himself, and intentionally unnamed except by profession—in many ways establishes the innocence of Frederic Henry as young soldier: even as he is being corrupted by drink and sex, his higher motivation (his military service) is idealistic. Why else has he volunteered for any involvement in the war at all?

As Phelan points out, it is in Henry's conversations with the priest after he has returned from his convalescence in Milan that the reader sees how disillusioned the young American has become.

> [Priest] "I had hoped for something."
> "Defeat?"
> "No. Something more."
> "There isn't anything more. Except victory. It may be worse."
> (179)

Phelan notes that "Frederic's voice here now echoes Passini's; the conventional wisdom has been replaced by the values of the Italian peasant. Furthermore, as Frederic voices values more in line with Hemingway's, the authoritative quality of the voice is softened to some extent" (71).

It can be said that, throughout *A Farewell to Arms*, the presence of the priest has a reassuring, almost a tranquilizing, effect. But it is also from the priest that Frederic is given permission to value his love for Catherine. As the priest tries to understand how Henry, whom he likes and admires, can deny any love for the God who is his very life, he confirms Henry's potential for loving: "When you love you wish to do things for. You wish to sacrifice for. You wish to serve" (72). But Henry—even in the midst of his passion for Catherine—says flatly, "I don't love." The priest maintains his reassuring role by saying, "You will. I know you will. Then you will be happy." Henry, however, in one of the cruder moments of nonfeeling that Hemingway gives the character, replies complacently, "I'm happy. I've always been happy." The interchange is strange in what Henry might think is the expression of his brutal honesty, but in effect, he robs the priest of parts of his own belief system. Frederic Henry may be a person with no illusions, but he also shows himself incapable of appreciating the kindness of friendship. To ameliorate this cynical impression, Hemingway closes the scene by showing the wounded Henry going off to sleep, thinking of the priest's Abruzzi—"what was lovely was the fall to go hunting through the chestnut woods"—rather than fearing either attack or his own customary nightmares (73). This scene, coupled with the one referred to earlier, when the priest tells Henry how terrible the summer had been, is the end of Hemingway's use of the young priest. From then on, reliance on language gives way to the efficacy of action.

Robert Lewis points to Hemingway's belief that words are treacherous. Several scenes "link the motif of talking with that of thinking. The former language activity is open; the latter, closed within the head of the thinkers. Throughout Hemingway's other work (as well as throughout *A Farewell to Arms*), nonthinking is a valid, even valuable state. . . . [A] way of coping with irrational and absurd reality."[7]

It is the priest who cuts through the brash language Rinaldi has used to welcome Frederic back. . . . "How are you really?" Lewis calls their ensuing conversation a "minidrama in epistemology applied to their understanding of the war" (135). Incomprehensible though it may be to outsiders, the war demands Hemingway's cryptic and restrained choices of words, many of which are negatives. When the priest asks Frederic—who has just commented that any belief in victory is impossible—what he does have belief in, he answers, "In sleep" (179).

Effectively cutting the priest and his conversation off, Frederic yet reaffirms their friendship, promising "We'll have a walk and talk together" when he again returns (180). The language of war has ceased to bridge the distance between people caught in the travesty of fighting other human beings, but the human beings themselves remain valuable.

Whenever he appears in A Farewell to Arms, the nameless priest prompts the reader's reference to Frederic Henry's belief system. There are many scenes in the novel ostensibly "about" religion. As Lewis contends, "religion is significant throughout the novel, whether in the character of the priest or in the absence of religion in the lives of most of the other characters" (38). Even while these characters seem irreligious, however, the text is filled with both religious objects and religious vocabulary—the Saint Anthony medal and the prayers of the supposed Catholic Italian ambulance drivers; the references to souls, belief systems, and various threats of death. Count Greffi, for example, looks back from his near century of life to comment on the soul, and the priest, in his urging Frederic to go to the Abruzzi, creates a place that seems to serve as a spiritual refuge, "the homeland where nature and human beings cohere, where life is good"—and, by implication, pure. As Hemingway uses the mention of the land, in fact, it is seen to be (in Lewis's description) "an area isolated in both time and place, a pastoral haven remote from both the war and the cities of the plains that attract the profane" (110).

If A Farewell to Arms were intended to be only a war novel, or even only the combination of war novel and romance that most readers see it as being, Hemingway's emphasis on the spiritual would be less necessary. But to write the quest story, the narrative of Frederic Henry as pilgrim, Hemingway had to provide the clear, sweet moments of spiritual possibility as contrast to the urban, mechanized, blood-soaked landscape of war.

To break into the convention of the war novel frees Hemingway from a number of constraints. It allows him to draw a hero who in his conflicted state deserts his military duty rather than losing his life by upholding it. Individual life is thus privileged above any common, nationalistic good. The primary plot of a war novel is usually the account of battles that, all too inevitably, lead to either victory or death—sometimes both. In contrast, Hemingway's reader comes to the close of A Farewell to Arms relatively ignorant of World War I's outcomes. In fact, Hemingway's breaking out of the paradigm of war novel has allowed him to emphasize the domestic narrrative over that placed on the battlefield. As Margaret Higonnet and her coeditors write in the introduction to *Behind the Lines, Gender and the Two World Wars*,

> Even when women writers describe the wartime losses that they have suffered as women—as wives, mothers, and lovers—they are displaced, for the primary loss in war literature is inevitably death; mourning is secondary.[8]

What Hemingway does in *A Farewell to Arms* is make mourning primary: the structure of the book, and therefore its impact, depends on the well-being of Catherine and the child. That Hemingway also reverses the character of the bereaved—as well as the character lost—is another surprise. Lament as the reader does the known losses of life during the First World War, the only scenes of death in *A Farewell to Arms* give him or her the deaths of Passani and Aymo, modest figures dead through random and therefore meaningless acts. Hemingway does not tell the stories of men who perform valiantly in the fields of war. His characters either die accidental deaths, or else—like Bonello and Frederic Henry—desert.

Because of Hemingway's scenes of dialogue between Henry and the ambulance drivers, as well as between Henry and Rinaldi, the officers, and the priest, the reader remains conscious of war and all its philosophical justifications. But because none of these passages of discourse ever praises the war, the author succeeds in debunking the rhetoric of patriotism. As the introduction to *Behind the Lines* remarks, "Much of the strength of men's literature of war derives from the tension between patriotism and criticism" (15). *A Farewell to Arms* comes down hard on the side of criticism of war. Unrelieved in his censure of World War I, Hemingway crafts a book that never posits so much as a shimmer of glamour, romance, or honor in men's activities in the field.

Given the literary fact that the war novel is held to be a male-dominated genre, with men of war serving as protagonists and adversaries, what Hemingway achieves in *A Farewell to Arms* is a moving story of people caught in the unreasonableness of war who are yet intent on creating a world that is balanced, honorable, and even guided by rational principles.

Jane Marcus points to Hemingway's uncharacteristic choice of the humble ambulance drivers and mechanics—foreign and undistinguished military people, not officers leading a charge—as a signal of how different even the war segments of the novel are from the expected. In the growth to maturity of Aymo and the others, she sees a parallel with the changes in Frederic Henry. As she notes,

> The ambulance drivers are equally made into "men" by the require-
> ments of their jobs. They must overcome their fear of open spaces
> and the dark and drive long distances in the night with their cargo
> of maimed men.[9]

In their service to aid and transport the wounded, these figures can be identified as more feminine than masculine. They care for others; they—for the most part—are armed to protect themselves and their vehicles rather than to fight as aggressors in the lines. Indeed, it is unexpected that the male characters in A Farewell to Arms are *not* fighting men.

Yet, in what Marcus defines as an important sexual pattern, Heming-way's characters do fit an expected gender pattern. Marcus points out, "In wartime, the impotent male is a vampire. . . . [M]en must be potent. Women must be maternal" (131). There is no question that Catherine and Henry play out these established sexual roles: for all the inconve-nience of an unexpected pregnancy, in fact, Henry might be said to have proved his potency beyond question.

In Hemingway's skillful structuring, there are implied changes in Henry's virility. At several points in the book, his whole being is trauma-tized. The most important of these places is Book III, which serves as the novel's pivot. The massively disillusioning events of the war that seems in the process of being lost causes the same kind of shock to Henry's psycho-logical system that the mortar shell injuries did to his physical body. Once back in the lines, he assumes command of the ambulances and their driv-ers, but his judgment is shaken. He had volunteered for neither retreat nor defeat.

As simply as the language Hemingway chooses to describe it, the for-mer began:

> The next night the retreat started. We heard the Germans and Aus-
> trians had broken through in the north and were coming down the
> mountain valleys toward Cividale and Udine. The retreat was
> orderly, wet and sullen. In the night, going slowly along the crowded
> roads we passed troops marching under the rain, guns, horses pulling
> wagons, mules, motor trucks, all moving away from the front. There
> was no more disorder than in an advance (188).

With the incremental repetition he often used to achieve tone, Hemingway's next paragraph establishes the pervasive rain, mud, and hopelessness. About the crush of refugees, the hysteria, the bundles of life's treasures, he says nothing. Only the stifled push of evacuation, and finally, "The column stalled again in the night and did not start" (195). And of course, "It was still raining" (198).

Frederic Henry and his drivers—Bonello, Piani, and Aymo—maintain their stoic composure. They give rides to two pairs of people—two "sergeants of engineers" separated from their Italian unit and two adolescent sisters who fear for their lives, and their virginity. It is through Henry's interactions with both pairs that Hemingway charts his character's disintegration.

With the young sisters, who speak so little English that they are dependent on body language rather than words, the ambulance personnel need to make them understand they are in no danger. Hemingway's attention falls first on this pair, because their fearfulness adds a kind of dark comedy to the good-hearted efforts of the men to transport, feed, and comfort them. When Aymo mistakenly touches the thigh of the older sister, a gesture of assurance, she "drew her shawl tight around her and pushed his hand away. . . . The girl looked at me fiercely" (195). In a paragraph describing the fear of what Henry calls these "two wild birds," Hemingway plays on the shock value of coarse language—whatever its dialect.

> [Aymo] turned to the girl. "Don't worry," he said. No danger of——,"
> using the vulgar word. "No place for——." I could see she understood the word and that was all. Her eyes looked at him very scared.
> She pulled the shawl tight. "Car all full," Aymo said. "No danger
> of——. No place for——." Every time he said the word the girl stiffened a little. Then sitting stiffly and looking at him she began to cry.
> I saw her lips working and then tears came down her plump cheeks.
> Her sister, not looking up, took her hand and they sat there
> together. The older one, who had been so fierce, began to sob (196).

In a later interchange, the men ask the girls if they are virgins (which they are), and the girls seem cheered by receiving acknowledgment. Their predicament, and their virginity, sends Frederic Henry into a reverie about Catherine, their great love, and the stream-of-consciousness tapestry of lines from the lyric "Western wind." The condition of human love is itself drastically changed in the presence of war—and what war does to its practitioners.

The scenario of the two sergeants of engineers seems meant to illustrate how corruptible men at war can become. On the second day of the retreat, conditions worsen. The drivers make the young sisters leave them and join the populace at large, where they will be more anonymous and perhaps safer. The sergeants, however, will be useful once the ambulances leave the main roads and try to reach Udine by crossing the countryside. When the sergeants try to bolt, seeing that the ambulances will never make the trek, Frederic Henry shouts his orders:

"Get busy," I said, "and cut brush."

"We have to go," one said. The other said nothing. They were in a hurry to start. They would not look at me.

"I order you to come back to the car and cut brush," I said. The one sergeant turned. "We have to go on. In a little while you will be cut off. You can't order us. You're not our officer."

"I order you to cut brush," I said. They turned and started down the road.

"Halt," I said. They kept on down the muddy road, the hedge on either side. "I order you to halt," I called. They went a little faster. I opened up my holster, took the pistol, aimed at the one who had talked the most, and fired. I missed and they both started to run. I shot three times and dropped one. The other went through the hedge and was out of sight. I fired at him through the hedge as he ran across the field. The pistol clicked empty and I put in another clip. I saw it was too far to shoot at the second sergeant. He was far across the field, running, his head held low. I commenced to reload the empty clip. Bonello came up.

"Let me go finish him," he said. I handed him the pistol and he walked down to where the sergeant of engineers lay face down across the road. Bonello leaned over, put the pistol against the man's head and pulled the trigger. The pistol did not fire.

"You have to cock it," I said. He cocked it and fired twice. He took hold of the sergeant's legs and pulled him to the other side of the road so he lay beside the hedge. He came back and handed me the pistol.

"The son of a bitch," he said. He looked toward the sergeant. "You see me shoot him, Tenente?"

Hemingway's style intensifies the impersonality of this execution. Bonello's bragging, Henry's demand for authority (and the long-recognized penalty for disobeying an officer, even though—as the sergeant had said—Henry was not their officer), the sense that killing was what a person had to do in wartime all jar against the very humane treatment these same men had just given to the young Italian girls. But in each case, the military men are following the prescriptions of their "duty"—to protect women and children, to create military order. The double-bind of following orders, even if those orders are not one's own and serve no purpose (especially in the light of a retreat that cannot salvage much), traps Frederic Henry here, despite his sense of himself as a fair person.

Hemingway's description works to make the reader question Henry's act. The spareness of Henry's orders to the men—to cut brush, to halt—seems intended to shortcut the phrase the sergeants might have anticipated. At no time does Henry threaten to shoot them, and never has his gun been in evidence.

The word choice "dropped one" also places the killing into the realm of sport shooting, as does Piani's kidding that Bonello "killed him on the sit. . . . He wasn't flying very fast when you killed him" (207). The sense of the impersonal continues as the sergeant's body is undressed to provide material to put under the ambulance wheels, leaving him clothed only in his long underwear; whatever dignity remains is to death lost. And Bonello's sense of accomplishment—"all my life I've wanted to kill a sergeant"—also chills the reader.

Even though Hemingway may be trying to balance whatever scales of justice exist in war, the fact that the sergeants eat before the drivers, try to steal a clock from the abandoned farmhouse, and dislike the ambulance drivers hardly stacks up beside the death of one of the sergeants (unnamed, unmourned, distinguished only as the one who talks the most).[10]

After the killing of the sergeant, Frederic Henry is hit with guilt about what he has done to his own men. He seems never to think about the execution. But about the ambulance drivers, he says, "It was my fault. I had led them up here" (205) and he feels much worse when Aymo is shot by a sniper (who may be an Italian). Hemingway shows Henry's rational military thinking ("We could avoid the main line of the retreat by keeping to the secondary roads beyond Udine. I knew there were plenty of side-roads across the plain. I started down the embankment").

But as soon as Henry calls for his men to follow, a shot hits the embankment. His command "Come on" is immediately changed to "Go on back," but Aymo, "as he was crossing the tracks, lurched, tripped and fell face down. We pulled him down on the other side and turned him over. 'His head ought to be uphill,' I said. Piani moved him around. He lay in the mud on the side of the embankment, his feet pointing down-hill, breathing blood irregularly. The three of us squatted over him in the rain. He was hit low in the back of the neck and the bullet had ranged upward and come out under the right eye. He died while I was stopping up the two holes" (213).

That both Bonello and Piani question Frederic Henry's leadership comes out clearly as the three of them sit together, mourning their friend. Bonello asks, "Who's dead next, Tenente? Where do we go now?" (214) Later that rainy night, when they stop to rest, Bonello deserts and Piani covers for him, saying that he was afraid to die. He would rather be a pris-oner. (In the novel itself, having witnessed—and been a part of—the killing of the sergeant surely made Bonello tentative about his own deser-tion. Who could be sure that Frederic Henry would not draw on him?) The context of war that Hemingway has pictured makes Bonello's—and, as a foreshadowing, Frederic Henry's—choice understandable.

Hemingway returns the reader to the concept of bravery, by interrogat-ing the relationship between living and dying, and being brave, being a patriot. None of the dead was brave, but neither did the dead do any harm. One of the reasons the ambulance drivers are apt characters for this novel is that they have so little to gain by being courageous: they instead have jobs to do, and they try to do them. They do not give orders; they are on the humanitarian side of conflict. Yet of the three drivers Frederic Henry had started his journey with, only one remained. The novel also returns the reader to the echo of Henry's explaining to Catherine that he is not a brave man. Using the metaphor of a baseball hitter, Henry says, "I know where I stand. I've been out long enough to know. I'm like a ball-player that bats two hundred and thirty and knows he's no better" (140). Being a mediocre player is better, at that, than killing people—either intentionally as he did with the sergeant or accidentally as he did with Aymo.

To view Henry's aggressive act as evidence of the military right, if not of machismo, is to call into question Scott Donaldson's reading that Fred-eric is at heart passive, if not cowardly, able to get others to either suggest what should be done or to take action themselves (as Bonello finished off the sergeant).[11] Thomas Strychacz contributes a more complex assess-ment of Hemingway's early male characters, people Strychacz sees as driven by their need to perform in manly ways. As he says, "Performance itself does not guarantee manhood; but manhood does require successful performance. Fashioning manhood 'while the crowd hollers' and looks on is the crucial drama men undertake in Hemingway's early work: the moment when his characters undergo their most intense experiences of authority or humiliation."[12] (As an aside to the use of the word *manly* is novelist Jim Harrison's comment in the *New York Times Magazine* that the concept of being "manly" differs. For Harrison, who grew up in mid-Michigan, men who "fished and hunted strenuously" might not consider those activities particularly masculine. Rather, according to Harrison, "That idea seemed to derive from writers of city origin like the tortured Hemingway, who, though a very great writer, seemed to suffer from a prolonged struggle with his manhood."[13])

This kind of self-dramatization Strychacz names occurs regularly in Frederic Henry's relationship with Catherine, and is one of the reasons Fergie mistrusts him. There are the initial evenings when he drinks too much and arrives late, so that he cannot be with Catherine. There is his overweening confidence in the Milan hospital when he pulls her into his bed as soon as she arrives, and his disruptive insistence that she work the night shift so that they can make love. (Hemingway gives us the charming "Come back to bed, Catherine. Please" to endear Henry to the reader as well as to his lover, (102); he works hard to show how effective Henry's charm is, not only in Milan but throughout their Switzerland escape.) Ironically, it is in the midst of Henry's passion for Catherine that when the priest describes to him what love is, Henry denies ever having loved. Perhaps it should not be such a surprise when he responds as he does to Catherine's admission of her pregnancy. In a scene that serves as culmination of her self-effacement, her wanting to be him, for them to be the same person, she apologizes for having become pregnant from their frequent bouts of intercourse.

> "Nothing. Nothing's the matter."
> "Yes there is."
> "No nothing. Really nothing."
> "I know there is. Tell me, darling. You can tell me."

The outcome of their conversation proves that Catherine's assessment was right—Frederic is not happy about the pregnancy, despite his protestations, and she is made to be the apologizer after all. "I'm going to have a baby, darling. It's almost three months along. You're not worried, are you? Please please don't. You mustn't worry. . . . I did everything. I took everything but it didn't make any difference." Rather than empathize with what she has been through during the last months, however, Frederic replies inanely, "I'm not worried."

Later, when the conversation resumes, Frederic shows his true feelings as Catherine asks,

> "You aren't angry are you, darling?"
> "No."
> "And you don't feel trapped?"
> "Maybe a little. But not by you."
> "I didn't mean by me. You mustn't be stupid. I meant trapped at all."
> "You always feel trapped biologically."
> She went away a long way without stirring or removing her hand.
> "'Always' isn't a pretty word."
> "I'm sorry."
> "It's all right. But you see I've never had a baby and I've never even loved any one. And I've tried to be the way you wanted and then you talk about 'always.'"
> "I could cut off my tongue," I offered.
> "Oh, darling!" she came back from wherever she had been. "You mustn't mind me.
> We were both together again and the self-consciousness was gone. "We really are the same one and we mustn't misunderstand on purpose" (137–139).

The assault readers feel in this scene stems from Frederic Henry's utter lack of sympathy for Catherine, a lack of sympathy that is clear from his stiffly withheld emotions. His response is not only monosyllabic ("No") or terse ("I'm not worried," "I'm sorry") or glib ("I could cut off my tongue") but some lines are insulting: "You always feel trapped biologically. . . . Maybe a little. But not by you." What Hemingway carefully omits is any evidence that Frederic is happy about the baby—or even accepting of it. This collective response erases earlier evidence of his charm, or of his genuine caring for this woman. On her own in foreign countries, and those countries at war, Catherine knows better than to involve him into her necessary planning. His quip about cutting off his tongue hardly serves as any serious apology, just as *his* feeling of "being trapped" hardly compares with *her* situation.

It is this scene that has angered women readers (and some men) throughout the last thirty years. Yet Sandra Whipple Spanier reads Catherine as the code hero in this novel, and pays tribute to her ability to lose herself within the relationship. Spanier acknowledges that the character of Catherine offends some readers; she notes that "it is hard for them to see the subordination of the individual ego to a personal relationship as a mark of maturity. Rather than being respected for her self-knowledge and clear-eyed pragmatism as she attempts to construct a sane context for her existence in an insane world, Catherine has been perceived as lacking in character because she has chosen to define herself in terms of a relationship."[14] While Spanier builds an impressive case for Catherine as a wise and surviving lover, as does Ernest Lockridge, *A Farewell to Arms* provides too many instances of Frederic Henry's immaturity, his habit of using Catherine, even to creating the grieving facade as he does at the end of the novel's narrative. If Catherine Barkley were alone in the novel, Spanier's case might be stronger.

In a recent essay about language in *A Farewell to Arms*, Gary Harrington notes that seldom in the novel does the reader find any warmth in Frederic's "love" for Catherine. He uses as examples the frequent references to prostitutes, the notion that neither of the lovers will ever meet each other's families, and the naming of Catherine as "your English" and the "English you go to see every night at the hospital." Harrington's point is that this novel, too, like *The Sun Also Rises*, is filled with puns, puns that when read correctly add to the unpleasantness of the tone of the great love relationship:

> However, whether Frederic likes it or not—and he does not—Catherine carries the child to term. After the delivery, Frederic goes to the restaurant where he "read[s] the paper of the man opposite" (329). The news provides details of "the break through on the British front," a somewhat graphic pun relating both to the Caesarean operation and to the resultant hemorrhaging which at that moment afflicts Catherine. Not coincidentally, early in the novel both Frederic and Rinaldi refer to Catherine as "the British" (32). . . . A closely related play on words occurs in Frederic's description of the weather after his lunch on the day of the delivery. Frederic reports that "The day was cloudy but the sun was trying to come through" (318), just as the couple's son is at that moment trying unsuccessfully on his own to "come through."[15]

Harrington's note to this commentary is itself pertinent, as he refers to another of those pieces of information about pregnancy that Frederic simply blotted out—Catherine's narrow hips. He refers to another play on words during the retreat, when Frederic tells Aymo to let the sisters leave because "they won't be very useful. . . . You ought to have some one that could push. . . . Pick up somebody with a wide back" (199).

Another of Harrington's points is that even as Catherine is struggling for her life, Frederic asks the doctor only "Will that scar flatten out?" as if only her appearance matters to him. Harrington continues, "the remark anticipates Frederic's own emotional wound being reduced in the future to an affectless reminiscence; considering his atonal narration throughout *A Farewell to Arms*, he seems to have arrived at some approximation of this condition by the time that he begins to tell their story. This emotional leveling finds an analogy in Frederic's recounting late in the novel his memory of the ants on the log in the fire" (71).

To view Frederic Henry as emotionally stymied goes against the grain of most extant criticism, which wants to find him changed—for the better—because of his involvement with Catherine. The very fact that he can narrate his mournful story (his narration becoming *A Farewell to Arms*) bespeaks his comparative health. For Jamie Barlowe-Kayes, however, the whole matrix of narration—Hemingway's craft and intention, Frederic Henry's ostensible meanings, Catherine's words as a part of that composite—is suspect. Barlowe-Kayes suggests a more comprehensive way of reading the character of Catherine in relation to that of Frederic Henry when she insists that both figures exist in an unstabilized space. The crux is, according to this critic, that Catherine must be read as "a subject, not an object."[16] The reader must see that Catherine Barkley's supposedly superior knowledge as it relates to war—and which she uses to educate Henry—is of little value in saving her own life. Readers may accept the idea that Catherine has superior knowledge as a way of giving her character a superior position. But it remains Hemingway's role to decide what kind of knowledge is valued:

> [H]er "knowledge" about war is not finally attachable to her experience, other than vicariously. She knows no more about dying in war (even as a nurse) than Frederic knows later about dying in childbirth. Thus, whatever subjectivity might seem to be implied in her articulation of the text's privileged information is instead undermined when she is re-read as Hemingway's version of an attractive puppet who speaks knowingly about what he does not allow her to know (179).

Barlowe-Kayes also points out that Catherine's willingness to both "'educate' Frederic Henry and to subordinate herself to his desires—

almost to the point of abandoning her responsibilites—[provides] yet another screen behind which Barkley's objectification is hidden to Hemingway himself and to many Hemingway critics." Catherine therefore cannot be read, or judged, outside of the cultural context that has itself shaped the kinds of responses a good, and particularly a loving, woman would be allowed to make.

Barlowe-Kayes concludes that "Hemingway's text, as a representation of the traditions of gender relations, repeats that tradition's inherent, unacknowledged objectification of women. As a metaphor, Barkley also iterates Hemingway's praise for acquiescent, self-sacrificing, fully supportive women" (180).

For the general reader, however, it is hard to deny the supposed reality of Catherine and Frederic: characters exist in fiction not to provide practice in applying reading theory, but to capture the imaginations of readers. One of the main problems with Catherine Barkley as heroine, or as hero, is that she wants so desperately to lose herself in Frederic Henry's identity. Where is the incipient feminist, the courageous woman who cares for the wounded in war? Where is the twentieth century's "new woman"?

Some of these issues are hard to decipher because a great many segments of *A Farewell to Arms* borrow from the patterns of classic romance. Once the reader meets Catherine, all elements of conventional romance are introduced. The meeting occurs in a garden. Catherine—dressed in white, aristocratic, educated, later described as a "goddess"—is protected by a nurse, her friend Fergie; and Rinaldi as the magical introducer suggests the French epic, *The Song of Roland*'s second of the same name. Catherine herself calls attention to the "game" of romance, with its rituals; and we are given the phallic object of the stick and the beauty of her long, uncut hair as well as her tall blondness to complete the romantic trope.

Lisa Tyler's important essay comparing Emily Brontë's *Wuthering Heights* and *A Farewell to Arms* describes borrowings—women named Catherine, each carrying a fetus named Catherine; both Englishwomen with the same physical characteristics; both trying to reclaim a lost adolescent love. Rain shrouds both books; dialogues are symbolic (and redolent, in the Hemingway novel, of lines from *Heights*); the love relationships are exclusive. The passion of the lovers is also unholy: neither woman is religious, neither recognizes life after death.[17]

John Cawelti's definition of romance underscores the use of one or the other (or both) of the lovers' deaths to reveal the level of their passion. He cites the stories of Tristan and Isolde, and Romeo and Juliet, to show that readers believe that "the intensity of the lovers' passion is directly related to the extent to which their love Is doomed."[18] Hemingway plants a number of signals throughout A Farewell to Arms that doom, not joy, is the tone of the love affair. And while many readers might attribute the somberness of the book to its being set during a brutal war, others would recognize the dark risks that the experience of great passion carries.

Many of these signals can also be read as indicating that A Farewell to Arms is meant to be a courtly love story. (Even as Hemingway is writing the sexual descriptions for everything except Frederic's and Catherine's love making, he reminds his readers of the chastity, of the abstinence typical of the court romance.) Hemingway had grown up reading the Arthurian legends, and his use of the wounded Jake Barnes in The Sun Also Rises draws partly from the wounded Arthur, king whose land will be barren unless he is rescued by a virgin knight bearing a bloodstained lance—the young matador Pedro Romero.

Then, too, as early as 1924, Hemingway's friend Eric Dorman-Smith remembers discussing the French "Arthur" story, Chanson de Roland, with an excited Hemingway.[19] The story of Roland (sometimes called "Orlando") threads under A Farewell to Arms, as it does Hemingway's later novel For Whom the Bell Tolls and Virginia Woolf's 1928 Orlando.

Roland's tale has become legend. In it the man of integrity must survive and prosper even though his family betrays him. Orphaned or abandoned, the hero finds his role of service with the Emperor Charlemagne. With his cousin Rinaldo, Roland/Orlando does numerous great deeds as the emperor's paladin, but his most memorable is sacrificing himself and his troops to save Charlemagne. That battle occurs at the monastery of Roncesvalles, where sacrifice and purity are the marks of nobility.[20]

To transfer this skeletal outline to the themes of A Farewell to Arms is not difficult. Rinaldi, the other officers, and Frederic Henry are the paladins of the Allies: they are men given to compassionate service (Rinaldi as physician, Henry as ambulance driver). They are not in the business of conquering people and land for their own benefit. Both see the value in Catherine, though Rinaldi (usually the more successful lover) loses out in this instance.[21]

Hemingway adds a dimension of sexual tension to his novel by making Rinaldi less chaste, more avaricious. His sexual appetite for women is clear, and he consistently flirts with Henry as well. As roommates, Rinaldi and Henry share an intimacy that the protected Oak Park Hemingway had never known. "You're dirty," Rinaldi tells Frederic as he returns from his leave. "You ought to wash" (11). In the midst of asking for sexual details of his various exploits, Rinaldi makes Henry aware of his body. Notice this contradictory descriptive entrance: "We shook hands and he put his arm around my neck and kissed me. 'Oughf,' I said" (11).

The pattern is repeated nearly every time Henry returns to their room: the American relates nonphysically to the Italian man's advances-which-might-not-really-be-advances: "You have that pleasant air of a dog in heat. . . . Good night, little puppy" (27); Rinaldi calls Henry "baby" (41), "Poor dear baby" (64), "We won't quarrel, baby. I love you too much. . . . We are war brothers. Kiss me good-by" (67). After Henry is wounded, Rinaldi "came in fast and bent down over the bed and kissed me" (64); "Rinaldi kissed me. You smell of lysol. Good-by, baby. Good-by" (77). As Rinaldi admits during the first visit to the hospital:

> I wish you were back. No one to come in at night from adventures. No one to make fun of. No one to lend me money. No blood brother and roommate. Why do you get yourself wounded? (65)

He uses a sexual image to tell Henry he is jealous of his friendship with the priest:

> "Sometimes I think you and he are a little that way. You know." And when Henry is angry, Rinaldi continues, "you are just like me underneath. . . . You are really an Italian. All fire and smoke and nothing inside. . . . We are brothers and we love each other." (65–66)

Like the novel published twenty-five years after Hemingway's death, *The Garden of Eden*, *A Farewell to Arms* has a texture that allows more sexual readings than the primary heterosexual pairing of Catherine Barkley and Frederic Henry. But it is the romance plot, with that couple's great love, that has received the most critical attention. Judith Fetterley's now-famous criticism of the book, "Hemingway's 'Resentful Cryptogram,'" ascribes what she calls the structural "deviousness and indirection" of the narrative to Hemingway's hostility toward strong women. She challenges his verbiage about "idyllic union," "their Swiss idyll," and "genuine commitment" when such language is set against the fact that Catherine dies, and dies because she is female.[22]

Fetterley places the pair within the context of war, noting that for men to die in battle is noble, but for Catherine to die in childbirth is willfulness that she somehow might have controlled.

The difference between what men deserve in the world which produces these doctors and soldiers and priests and what women deserve can be seen in the disparity between the treatment of Catherine's death and the treatment of the deaths of men at war. "'You will not do any such foolishness,' the doctor said. 'You would not die and leave your husband'"; "'You are not going to die. You must not be silly.'" The tone here is appropriate to a parent addressing a recalcitrant child and the remarks are at once a reprimand and an implicit command which at some level assumes that Catherine is in control of whether she lives or dies. Indeed, Catherine herself has internalized the attitude of her doctor. She presents that *reductio ad absurdum* of the female experience: she feels guilty for dying and apologizes to the doctor for taking up his valuable time with her death—"I'm sorry I go on so long." (63)

Fetterley's point is that the soldier who has hemorrhaged to death in the ambulance above Henry was not apologizing; Catherine's death is, however, accompanied by guilt because "As long as there is a man around who needs her, she ought not to die" (64).

So far as the argument that Catherine instructs Frederic, making him into a better man, Fetterley sees that role of providing wisdom to be another kind of trap. "On the simplest level, Catherine allows Frederic to avoid responsibility and commitment. But in so far as this allows him to avoid growing up, she has failed him and is thus subject to hostility on this account. She is equally subject to hostility for having complicated his life and come so close to thrusting responsibility on him. . . . Catherine has betrayed Frederic. . . . The point is that whatever way you look at it, Catherine is bad news. Thus we might finally see her death as the unconscious expression of the cumulative hostilities which Frederic feels toward her. Essentially, she gets what is coming to her" (72).

Frederic Svoboda draws this consideration of the self-sufficiency of romance into a larger context when he meditates that "the Hemingway protagonist often seems to exist like Hemingway in a moment after: after the nineteenth century, after wilderness, after innocence, after loss."[23] Of all the themes that can be defined, particularly in connection with the male protagonist, perhaps the most pervasive is that of loss, loss that often produces a great effect upon the reader. A *Farewell to Arms* becomes one of Hemingway's great works because in it, according to Svoboda, "That essential sense of the seriousness of life—and sometimes of its joy—is underscored by its occurring against a backdrop of love and war, certainly two of the world's most serious undertakings" (171).

If many of the themes of the novel can be drawn from the military and war-linked parts of the novel, it is partly because such conflict is so clearly gendered. Men's roles in war are predictable, just as they are predictive of the characters of the person involved with the conflict. Accordingly, to comment on the themes of such a narrative from the perspective of its women characters means realizing that the women in the novel will of necessity play the responsible roles assigned to women during wartime. Catherine Barkley is as surely trapped by her role as Frederic Henry is by his.

Catherine's role in her life with Frederic Henry is to love and support him. As Hemingway had written to F. Scott Fitzgerald about the ways he tried to work romance into much of his writing, "Love is also a good subject as you might be said to have discovered."[24] As numerous critics have also understood, the traditional place of the woman in love is a subordinate one.

NOTES

1. Paul Fussell, *The Great War and Modern Memory* (New York: Oxford University Press, 1975), pp. 326–327; the quote uses words from Stephen Hewett's *A Scholar's Letters from the Front*, p. 46.

2. Ibid., pp. 169–170; Louis Simpson's comment from *The Poetry of War*, p. 172.

3. Quoted in Fussell, *The Great War*, p. 184. And see Eric Leed, *No Man's Land: Combat and Identity in World War I* (Cambridge, UK: Cambridge University Press, 1979) and Angela Smith, *The Second Battlefield* (New York: Palgrave, 2000).

4. Wendy Steiner, "The Diversity of American Fiction," *Columbia Literary History of the United States* (New York: Columbia University Press, 1988), pp. 848–849. See Steven Trout, "'Where Do We Go From Here?': Ernest Hemingway's 'Soldier's Home' and American Veterans of World War I," *Hemingway Review* 20, no. 1 (Fall 2000), pp. 5–22 and John J. McKenna and David M. Raabe, "Using Temperament Theory to Understand Conflict in Hemingway's 'Soldier's Home,'" *Studies in Short Fiction* 34, no. 2 (1997), pp. 203–213.

5. James Phelan, *Narrative as Rhetoric, Technique, Audiences, Ethics, Ideology* (Columbus: Ohio State University Press, 1996), p. 60; hereafter cited in text.

6. James Nagel, "Catherine Barkley and Retrospective Narration in *A Farewell to Arms*," in *Ernest Hemingway: Six Decades of Criticism* (E. Lansing: Michigan State University Press, 1987), pp. 171–185; see also Peter Balbert, "From Hemingway to Lawrence to Mailer: Survival and Sexual Identity in *A*

Farewell to Arms," *Hemingway Review* 3, no. 1 (Fall 1983), pp. 30–43, who comments on the way Frederic's "practical, soldierly, but delimiting brand of merely 'survivalist' ideology" becomes broader and richer once he loves Catherine.

7. Robert W. Lewis, *A Farewell to Arms: The War of the Words* (New York: Twayne, 1992), p. 134; hereafter cited in text.

8. Margaret Randolph Higonnet, Jane Jenson, Sonya Michel, and Margaret Collins, "Introduction," *Behind the Lines: Gender and the Two World Wars* (New Haven, CT: Yale University Press, 1987), pp. 1–17; this excerpt p. 14; hereafter cited in text.

9. Jane Marcus, "Corpus/Corps/Corpse: Writing the Body in/at War," *Arms and the Woman: War, Gender, and Literary Representation*, ed. Helen M. Cooper, Adrienne Auslander Munich, and Susan Merrill Squier (Chapel Hill: University of North Carolina Press, 1989), pp. 124–167; this excerpt p. 142; hereafter cited in text.

10. Among critics who discuss Henry's killing the sergeant are Millicent Bell, "Pseudoautobiography and Personal Metaphor" in *Modern Critical Views of Ernest Hemingway's* A Farewell to Arms (New York: Chelsea House, 1987), pp. 113–129; Lewis, *A Farewell to Arms*; Paul Smith, "The Trying-Out of *A Farewell to Arms*," *New Essays on* A Farewell to Arms, ed. Scott Donaldson (Cambridge, UK: Cambridge University Press, 1990), pp. 27–52; and several essays in Gary Wiener's *Readings on* A Farewell to Arms (San Diego, CA: Greenhaven Press, 2000).

11. Scott Donaldson, "Frederic Henry's Escape and the Pose of Passivity" in *Modern Critical Interpretations of Ernest Hemingway's* A Farewell to Arms (New York: Chelsea House, 1987), pp. 97–112; this excerpt p. 112.

12. Thomas Strychacz, "Dramatizations of Manhood in Hemingway's *In Our Time* and *The Sun Also Rises*," *Hemingway: Seven Decades of Criticism* (E. Lansing: Michigan State University Press, 1998), pp. 45–57; this excerpt p. 57. Strychacz treats only *Sun* and the early stories in his discussion, but the relevance of his paradigm to Frederic Henry is clear.

13. Jim Harrison, "First Person Female," *New York Times Magazine* (May 16, 1999), pp. 100–101.

14. Sandra Whipple Spanier, "Catherine Barkley and the Hemingway Code: Ritual and Survival in *A Farewell to Arms*," *Modern Critical Interpretations of Ernest Hemingway's* A Farewell to Arms (New York: Chelsea House, 1987), pp. 131–148; hereafter cited in text. See also Ernest Lockridge, "Faithful in Her Fashion: Catherine Barkley, the Invisible Hemingway Heroine," *Journal of Narrative Technique* 18, no. 2 (Spring 1988), pp. 170–178.

15. Gary Harrington, "Partial Articulation: Word Play in *A Farewell to Arms*," *Hemingway Review* 20, no. 2 (Spring 2001), pp. 59–75; this excerpt, p. 70.

16. Jamie Barlowe-Kayes, "Re-reading Women: The Example of Catherine Barkley," in *Hemingway: Seven Decades of Criticism* (E. Lansing: Michigan State University Press, 1998), pp. 171–184; hereafter cited in text.

17. Lisa Tyler, "Passion and Grief in A Farewell to Arms: Ernest Hemingway's Retelling of Wuthering Heights," The Hemingway Review (Spring 1995), pp. 79–96, reprinted in Hemingway: Seven Decades of Criticism (E. Lansing: Michigan State University Press, 1999), pp. 151–169. See also Ernest Lockridge, "Faithful in Her Fashion: Catherine Barkley, the Invisible Hemingway Heroine," Journal of Narrative Technique 18 (1988), pp. 170–178.

18. John G. Cawelti, Adventure, Mystery, and Romance (Chicago: University of Chicago Press, 1976), pp. 39–42.

19. As noted in Michael S. Reynolds' Hemingway's Reading, 1910–1940 (Princeton, NJ: Princeton University Press, 1981), p. 93; see also Daniel Fuchs' "Ernest Hemingway, Literary Critic" in Ernest Hemingway: Five Decades of Criticism (E. Lansing: Michigan State University Press, 1974), pp. 39–56.

20. The best description of Hemingway's interest in this theme is Kim Moreland's The Medievalist Impulse in American Literature: Twain, Adams, Fitzgerald and Hemingway (Charlottesville: University Press of Virginia, 1996).

21. Early Hemingway writings suggest that he was more intrigued with Rinaldi than his role in A Farewell to Arms shows. The character appears in the vignettes of In Our Time, as well as in a manuscript titled "The Mercenaries" at the John F. Kennedy Library. Set in Petoskey, Michigan, and in Chicago, the story has as the "I" protagonist a man named "Rinaldi Rinaldo" (see Item #572–573, the Hemingway Collection).

22. Judith Fetterley, "Hemingway's 'Resentful Cryptogram,'" in Modern Critical Views of Ernest Hemingway's A Farewell to Arms (New York: Chelsea House, 1987), pp. 61–75; this excerpt, p. 61; hereafter cited in text.

23. Frederic J. Svoboda, "Great Themes in Hemingway," A Historical Guide to Ernest Hemingway (New York: Oxford University Press, 2000), pp. 155–172, this excerpt p. 169; hereafter cited in text.

24. Ernest Hemingway to F. Scott Fitzgerald, Letters, p. 177.

6 Narrative Art

A large part of the power of Hemingway's novel accrues from the way the author marshaled his newly earned understanding of structure and word choice and use. In retrospect, Hemingway made references to his having written an "accidental" novel in *The Sun Also Rises*: even though he had been working with such consummate craftsmen as Ford Madox Ford, Ezra Pound, John Dos Passos, and F. Scott Fitzgerald (not to mention the women writers whose works he knew well: Gertrude Stein, with whom he was a personal friend, as well as Virginia Woolf, Natalie Barney, and Edith Wharton), putting into practice the maxims that were the watchwords of modernism was difficult. As he wrote to Stein about his study of the paintings of Cézanne, which she had recommended,

> I'm trying to do the country like Cézanne and having a hell of a time and sometimes getting it a little bit. It is about 100 pages long and nothing happens and the country is well; I made it all up, so I see it all and part of it comes out the way it ought to. . . . [B] but isn't writing a hard job though?. . . . It used to be easy before I met you. I certainly was bad, gosh. I'm awfully bad now but it's a different kind of bad.[1]

Aside from the disingenuous close to that paragraph, Hemingway was truthful: he had written one of his most fully realized short stories, "Big Two-Hearted River."

Confident enough of his own ability to choose among the pieces of advice his friends provided, Hemingway was not trying to become a car-bon copy of any writer. His eventual animosity toward both Sherwood Anderson and Gertrude Stein is evidence of his trying to unhook himself from their "school."[2] The process of Hemingway's becoming the writer who was capable of composing *A Farewell to Arms* was itself torturous, and did not proceed in a linear fashion. One of the most interesting studies of this novel remains Bernard Oldsey's analysis of Hemingway's choices as he crafted both the beginning and the all-important ending—not to mention interior sections—of *A Farewell to Arms*. Possible only after the manuscripts of this book and much of Hemingway's other writing were available in the Hemingway Collection of the John F. Kennedy Library (first at the Trapelo Road location, before the Kennedy Library was built) in the later 1970s, such analyses provide the reader with a kind of roadmap of Hemingway's thinking about his work.

Oldsey's major contribution to the study of Hemingway as a writer draws from the actual pages of draft, or from handwritten emendations to or deletions from typed copy as well as proof sheets. His work makes pos-sible envisioning Hemingway's creative process, even though the writing of *A Farewell to Arms* was done in the midst of extensive geographical movement, as well as emotional changes: for one, the life-threatening birth of his and Pauline's first child (with the frightening possibility that either the child or Pauline—or both—might die); for another, the com-paratively unexpected death by suicide of his depressed father, a death that not only saddened Hemingway but left him—as the oldest son—feeling responsible for the financial well-being of his mother and his younger siblings. This mixture of grief and anger prompted some unpre-dictable elements in the characterizations of his protagonists.

In what had to have been a highly volatile period of his life, Heming-way as author relied on the kinds of writing he already knew how to do well. Once he had decided to write about World War I, not a trivial sub-ject, he drew from a number of personal resources. Hemingway knew he could write poetry: his reliance on repetition and the use of charged metaphors stemmed from his work with the poem. He knew he was adept at disguising the visibly "poetic" under a terse and sometimes monosyl-labic diction; his friend Ezra Pound had admired his prose poems from the first collections. Under the direction of Gertrude Stein, who helped him free his subconscious in order to focus on themes that were emotionally significant to him, he had learned to bring the rhythmic choices of poetry into his short stories. In the perfection of "The End of Something," "The

Doctor and the Doctor's Wife," and other stories, Hemingway had showed readers how integral to the work's effect were structure, diction, and metaphor.[3]

He had also proved, in nearly all his stories as well as his novel-length fiction, that he saw the keen importance of dialogue. The voices of Hemingway's characters as they interacted were perhaps the most significant means of describing those personae. Their language and the way their words were spoken—creating the métier of the scene itself—provided the heart of not only the scene but the relationship between the speakers.[4] Hemingway also knew that the façade of words spoken might be misleading or ironic—intentionally so; in this knowledge he went beyond the aesthetics of the realists, writers such as William Dean Howells or Theodore Dreiser, who prided themselves on using common words and sentence patterns as a means of portraying common persons. While much of Hemingway's dialogue might be couched in relatively simple language, it seems fair to say that very few of his characters were simple. Masking their psychological complexity under a vocabulary that seldom called for the use of a dictionary was one of Hemingway's contributions to American letters.

This obsession with all elements of craft, with making each word fulfill several aims, marked Hemingway as the essential modernist. Whereas the realists focused on bringing the whole relatively new spectrum of everyday America into literature, and the naturalists repeated the realists' insistence that detail was the means of convincing readers that portrayals were authentic—only adding the overlay of a god grown distant and even uncaring in the mechanistic modern world, the modernist writer fused the philosophic nihilism with a cryptic scene or image that, poemlike, spoke volumes about characters, their interactions, and their lives. Meticulous in what might appear to be casual word choice, the modern writer assessed every paragraph, every line, of writing: Was it clearly said? Did it have an appropriate effect? Was it enhancing what the modernist poets referred to as a work's *organic form?*[5] In the words of Ezra Pound,

> Good writing is writing that is perfectly controlled, the writer says just what he means. He says it with complete clarity and simplicity. He uses the smallest number of words. . . . Also there are various kinds of clarity. There is the clarity of the request: Send me four pounds of ten-penny nails. And there is the syntactical simplicity of the request: Buy me the kind of Rembrandt I like. This last is an utter cryptogram. It presupposes a more complex and intimate

understanding of the speaker than most of us ever acquire of anyone. It has as many meanings, almost, as there are persons who
might speak it. . . .

It is the almost constant labour of the prose artist to translate this
latter kind of clarity into the former; to say "Send me the kind of
Rembrandt I like" in the terms of "Send me four pounds of ten-
penny nails."[6]

Within *A Farewell to Arms*, Hemingway's craft as poet, prose poet,
short-story writer, novelist, and creator of dialogue came to fruition.

One of the best essays on the style of *A Farewell to Arms* was written by
Daniel J. Schneider in 1968. Emphasizing that the effect of the novel was
poemlike, in "Hemingway's *A Farewell to Arms*: The Novel as Pure
Poetry" Schneider read the novel as a single, well-constructed evocation
of emotion. Whether he studied word choice, sentence length, or the
choices and applications of such metaphors as that of rain, Schneider
emphasized that "cerebration tends to destroy passion."[7] Hemingway's
thrust to create a single emotional state was derived from what he knew
about writing poetry; in this novel he was after "the dominant state of
mind—the sense of death, defeat, failure, nothingness, emptiness" (255).
His intensity of aim shapes all his choices about his writing. Characters
are less important, since they too become pieces of the single effect; plot
lines are subordinated to the overall rhythms of the prose, rather than a
chronological logic of narrative.

Schneider sees the craft and its artistic evidence as paramount to what
Hemingway achieves in the novel: this is no plot-driven work, nor is it
primarily about either the war or the romance. It is about how a writer
makes hundreds of pages of story cohere with the dramatic intensity of a
lyric poem. For instance, as Schneider wrote, "The sense of failure and
impotence is . . . reinforced by the studious avoidance of action verbs.
Almost invariably Hemingway employs the copulative *to be*, and the
expletives *there were* and *there was* occur ten times in the twenty-one sentences of the chapter. . . . The repetitions give a sense of endless sameness
and weariness" (256–257). Like a lyric poem, Hemingway's novel
achieves that intensity of impression that is rare in prose fiction.

Michael Reynolds comments about his close study of the *Farewell to
Arms* manuscripts, that what impressed him most was the fact that many
of the pages were handwritten and then typed (and published) with no
changes. Referring to what he calls the manuscript's "remarkable smooth-
ness," Reynolds speculates that perhaps 45 percent of the pages appear

unrevised, with another 30 percent having very minor changes—one or two words.[8] What Reynolds describes here is the poet at work: following his subjective, almost visceral sense of how the language should fall, the poet in Hemingway created line after line of words that spoke to the emotion he was holding, and distilling, in his imagination. (This is a normative pattern throughout the earliest of Hemingway's short stories, particularly the short fiction that appeared in the collection *In Our Time*. I think it is during these years of Gertrude Stein's tutelage, her emphasis on the interior form available to any artist if he or she could just unearth the appropriate form, that Hemingway made his first strides toward becoming the accomplished writer he was. In fact, there is a high correlation between his early years as a writer—whether as poet or prose writer—and the polished effects of his prose during the 1920s. At intervals during his later career, most notably when he wrote *The Old Man and the Sea* and also during the years of "The Snows of Kilimanjaro" and the work culminating in *For Whom the Bell Tolls*, he was able once more to attain that fusion of what he wanted to write and what he found as the rhythm of the prose that could best create the work. In each case, an incredible balance between the internal demands of the writing and the author's never-simple personal life had to be achieved.[9]

Daniel Schneider sees the somewhat formulaic structure of Hemingway's plotlines as a natural outgrowth of his more poetic writing process. This is not a writer given to scrupulous timelines or cause-and-effect relationships between event and fact. In fact, in Schneider's words, "Hemingway is always reluctant to introduce actions that do not feed the dominant emotion. . . . The action, too, must obviously become, as nearly as possible, simple, intellectually uncomplicated, and . . . akin to lyric soliloquy."[10]

Hemingway early learned how to use silence. As John Reardon points out in his essay on ethics in writing, "There are places in Hemingway's stories as there are in *The Ambassadors* or in *Huckleberry Finn* when action suddenly ceases and one concentrates on the fulfilling moment. . . . The artist must work not only unhurriedly and with absolute attention, but like the sportsman and the hero, with the coverage of loneliness. In *Green Hills of Africa* Hemingway insisted. . . . 'Writers should work alone. They should see each other only after their work is done, and not too often then.'"[11] Reminiscent of the dedication typical of the imagists and modernists, Hemingway's focus too recalls Pound's maxim, "The mastery of any art is the work of a lifetime."[12] In the words of Ford Madox Ford, writing is "a priest's vocation. . . . To write honestly and well was the most important thing in the world."[13]

A Farewell to Arms has its share of well-placed silences. Congruent with the pace of the descriptive sections throughout the novel, these pauses serve as movie stills to sharpen the viewer's vision (or the reader's understanding), and to give the viewer/reader time to gather attention for the next movement of the text. Many of the still points occur toward the end of each of the five books of the novel; others impact somewhat more strongly because they are less expected. As Frederic and Catherine approach the Swiss shore, for example, Hemingway stops the action: "It was clear daylight now and a fine rain was falling. The wind was still blowing outside up the lake and we could see the tops of the white-caps going away from us and up the lake. I was sure we were in Switzerland now. There were many houses back in the trees from the shore and up the shore a way was a village with stone houses, some villas on the hills and a church" (276). The reader's mind is given to the likely pursuit of the boat with its deserting occupants; this quiet paragraph settles the sense of chase into a more tranquil mood.

Julian Smith's important essay, "Hemingway and the Thing Left Out," treats this concept by working with this novel and a short story, "In Another Country," which was written several years before *A Farewell to Arms*. Smith thinks the story—about the bereaved major whose young wife had so suddenly died—could easily be inserted into Hemingway's novel. His point is that structure in Hemingway's prose is not inevitable: thematic coherence is more important than linear progression. As Smith suggests, "[I]t would be an easy matter to insert 'In Another Country' either after the marriage conversation at the end of Chapter XVIII or between Chapter XXI, in which Catherine announces her pregnancy, and Chapter XXII, in which Henry loses his chance to go on leave with Catherine and is sent back to the front. The story fits so well into the novel that it seems The Thing Left Out. But though the novel does not need the story, the story needs the novel if it is to be read with any understanding of the narrator's reason for telling it."[14]

Smith's hypothesis is that the young American observes the Italian's deep grief, and sympathizes with the major, but has no premonition that his own beloved will also die. Smith sees as one visible link the fact that both the story and the novel were at one time connected (if not by title, by epigraph) with Marlowe's *The Jew of Malta* "by way of T. S. Eliot's 'Portrait of a Lady'":

Thou hast committed—
Fornication: but that was in another country,
And besides, the wench is dead. (190)

His readings build on Hemingway's posthumous comment (in *A Move-able Feast*) that the writer "could omit anything if you knew that you omitted and the omitted part would strengthen the story and make people feel something more than they understood" (188). That one of the provinces of the poet is the selection of detail—since the shorter form of expression demands that things are left out—fits well with Smith's notion here, whether or not "In Another Country" needs to become a part of the reader's thinking about *A Farewell to Arms*.

Michael Reynolds' assessment of the structure of Hemingway's 1929 novel is that it is composed of "five tightly interrelated short stories." He reads several of these prose books from this perspective; for example, "In the sequence [of escape] . . . the action began at Stressa and ended at Montreux, following the classic short-story formula: conflict (the threat of arrest), rising action (the flight up the lake), climax (safe arrival in Switzerland), falling action (problems with customs), denouement (set-tling for the winter at Montreux)."[15] The other climaxes in the other sections, according to Reynolds, are "Frederic's wounding, Catherine's pregnancy, Frederic's threat of execution, the lovers eluding the lake patrol, and the onset of Catherine's labor pains. . . . Each time Heming-way builds the tension a little higher" (42). Reynolds, too, sees the real cohesion within the novel as its metaphors and tone: "*A Farewell to Arms* is a massive defeat" (46).

At least partly because of the incremental shape of the novel, with one section building into the next, as the level of intensity builds as well, much critical attention has focused on the ending of *A Farewell to Arms*. The reason Robert Merrill calls the novel a tragedy is that the impact of Catherine's death is irreversible: not only do she and the child die, but it feels to the reader as if Frederic Henry's life is also at an end. Merrill qual-ifies his use of the term "tragedy," explaining that the form is newly con-ceived here because "the hero acts not mistakenly but supremely well, and suffers a doom which is not directly caused by his actions at all. The belief that life is a tragedy, *life* itself, has become the backbone for a new literary structure."[16]

Much has been made of the biographical fact that Hemingway was unsure about the way *A Farewell to Arms* was going to end. No reader can escape the fact that the text is relentlessly somber and that Hemingway consistently appropriates classic images of mourning—the rain, the shrouded forms, the darkness, the miasma of illness and war-related wounding and death—to suggest to the reader that, in Merrill's words, "the hero's doom is inevitable" (26). How Frederic Henry's "doom" would be figured was what remained for the author to explain. In that regard, the way the novel ends shapes the reader's only significant response—as Reynolds notes, sections keep building, keep intensifying, and one has only to find the lovers safe after rowing across the lake to feel a momentary relief. That relief does not last long, however: the world remains at war, and both Henry and Catherine have been a part of that conflict.

Bernard Oldsey's conclusive reading of the manuscripts of *A Farewell to Arms* clarifies the controversy about unresolved endings to the book. He states, "All of the conclusions in the Hemingway Collection presuppose Catherine's death."[17] In Oldsey's opinion, Hemingway was aware from the start that Henry would live to mourn; as he notes about the fact of Catherine's death, "This is, after all, Frederic Henry's story, and it is his reaction to Catherine's death that had to be depicted with revelatory force. All of the variant conclusions that Hemingway wrote for the novel are attempts to epitomize Henry's traumatized perception—from which, years later, the story unfolds" (79).

Oldsey points to the restrained description of her dying (very much different from the accounts of either Frederic's wounding or of the various military deaths), a description intended to almost repress the reader's attention. Catherine's death is one of the facts of the narrative, like the Italian losses during the summer. The reader must instead focus on how Henry takes that death, what he does to respond to it, to ameliorate it, to—at first—simply recognize and understand it. To accommodate the possibilities of Henry's reaction called for the numerous endings—some critics say thirty, some say fifty. Oldsey counts them at thirty-nine, remarking that Hemingway had come close to remembering correctly during the 1958 George Plimpton interview that was published in *The Paris Review*.

Oldsey further divides the drafts of possible conclusions into separate categories. Labeling these somewhat flippantly, he makes this grouping: "(1) The *Nada* Ending, (2) The Fitzgerald Ending, (3) The Religious Ending, (4) The Live-Baby Ending, (5) The Morning-After Ending, (6) The Funeral Ending, (&) The Original *Scribner's Magazine* Ending, (8) *The* Ending . . . (9) Miscellaneous Endings" (79). He contends that study of these endings serves to bring out the sometimes cryptic themes of the novel, themes that for one reason or another may not have been emphasized enough. With Hemingway as with all novelists, the ending of a book is the time to give the reader both a summary of and a resonance from even the most complex meanings. (With the luck of a beginner, Hemingway had found an effective ending for his first successful novel, *The Sun*

Also Rises, as Jake Barnes' behavior, and language, carried out the original sense of that character as bitterly aware but still vulnerable. Above all, enmeshed in the tenets of both modernism and imagism, Hemingway knew he wanted an ending for *A Farewell to Arms*—although at the time he wrote the endings, the novel remained untitled—that was both suggestive and definite.)

As Oldsey describes the "Nada" endings, they attempt to express Henry's recognition of "being-and-nothingness . . . everything is gone—all their love—and will never be again" (80). While the tone remains in the novel's conclusion, the nihilism is subdued: Henry's "nothing" has given him the book. The "Fitzgerald" endings relate to that writer's suggestion that Hemingway move the passage in Chapter 34 to the end—the "kills the very good and the very gentle and the very brave" passage. As the most "eloquent" section of the book, the passage deserved to be placed more prominently, Fitzgerald wrote.[18] From his long letter about the novel's manuscript, Oldsey quotes his prolegomenon about endings:

> The theory back of it I got from Conrad's preface to *The Nigger* [*of the Narcissus*] that the purpose of a work of fiction is to appeal to the lingering after-effects in the reader's mind.

Fitzgerald continued about having seen (at some time) "a sort of old-fashioned Alger book summary," which he did not like. He mentions his prior suggestion that the "kill the very good" passage be moved to the end, and restates Hemingway's reaction: "you were against this idea because you felt that the true line of a work of fiction was to take a reader up to a high emotional pitch but then let him down or ease him off. You gave no aesthetic reason for this—nevertheless, you convinced me" (81).

What Oldsey calls "the religious ending" pattern brings an almost "incongruous" emphasis on the spiritual into the novel's conclusion, incongruous because it needs to return to early chapters for any grounding at all in religious motifs. Oldsey notes, "With such a conclusion the priest would have emerged as the supreme mentor of this bildungsroman, not Rinaldi, Count Greffi, or even Catherine. However, a question imbedded in two of these religious attempts helps to explain why this kind of conclusion was rejected. Henry wonders how much of what the priest has is simply luck, how much is wisdom—and how do you achieve what the priest has if you are not 'born that way?'" (81)

This set of endings is in some respects related to what Oldsey calls "the live-baby" endings, in which the child lives—and the knowledge of his being alive comes before Catherine's death. Almost as if Hemingway realizes the bleak despair of the novel's effect on readers and is trying to lessen his nihilism, his attempts to save their son "would have meant another story; and with a touch of editorial wisdom reflecting that of the author, Henry realizes 'It is not fair to start a new story at the end of an old one'" (82). While Oldsey and others who have worked on Hemingway's manuscripts acknowledge his superb editorial decisions (unlike those of, say, John Dos Passos, who seldom made changes for the better of a work's total effect), the fact remains that Hemingway's careful word-by-word vetting of his drafts led to a product so polished that Scribner's personnel, including Max Perkins, seldom touched his writing.

The drafts of the conclusion most important to Hemingway, and most numerous in the Hemingway papers, are those dealing with Frederic Henry's realization of Catherine's death—and what her loss will mean to his life. What Oldsey names the "Morning-After" group tries to both summarize events after Catherine's death and evoke emotion, a pairing that is almost impossible. The reasonable marshaling of information that a summary requires—who wins the war? does Henry escape court-martial? where is Catherine buried? what happens to Rinaldi? the priest? Simmons? Ettore?—would scuttle the tone, the resonance, of loss. But as biographers point out, one of these summary endings *had* been set in galleys for the serial publication of the novel. Hemingway himself would have realized how "old-fashioned" such a conclusion was—he did not need Fitzgerald to introduce that term. The impetus for modernist fiction, the mode in which Hemingway had heretofore made his reputation, was its understated impact, its open endings. One of the strategies of the modern writer was to involve the reader in the process of interpreting: to make reading an active process. If the conclusion of any novel laid out everything that subsequently happened, the reader would be sent away without that necessary involvement.

Oldsey concludes that the *Scribner's Magazine* serial ending was a combination of many things—the "morrning-after" idea and "the funeral, suicide, lonely nights, the Fitzgerald suggestion, and the obverse-iteration method of stating-but-not-stating what happened after that particular night in 'March nineteen hundred and eighteen'" (83). But Hemingway held up the presses, and replaced that more conventional ending with one more like the present ending. He did not arrive at the polished version of the present conclusion, however, for nearly ten months: "Even in the very last phase of this process, Hemingway continued to write and rewrite to discover what should be said on the final page of the novel as a result of what had been said in the preceding three hundred and forty pages" (84).

Of the five typewritten versions of the present ending, Oldsey points out that each includes the stark metaphor that returns the novel to its poemlike impact: "It was like saying good bye to a statue."[19] Completely robbed of any dimension of her beauty, her physical body, or her person-hood, Catherine Barkley, dead, is only a lifeless *something*. Like Heming-way's early image of the *something* laid outside the hospital door, Barkley too is only an indiscriminate shape, perhaps not even a body. What gives this "statue" image its force is the rare burst of emotion Frederic Henry reveals as he throws the nurses out of Catherine's room:

> "You can't come in now," one of the nurses said.
> "Yes I can," I said.
> "You can't come in yet."
> "You get out," I said. "The other one too."

Frederic's brusque order reveals what his more mannerly conversation with the apologetic doctor had hidden—his gut-wrenching understand-ing that Catherine was dead. The novel concludes with the four-line paragraph that includes the "statue" image: "But after I had gotten them out and shut the door and turned off the light it wasn't any good. It was like saying good-by to a statue. After a while I went out and left the hos-pital and walked back to the hotel in the rain" (332).

To read the "statue" image somewhat more deeply is to understand the emotional reciprocity that existed in the love between Catherine and Frederic. Noncommittal as Frederic as lover tends to be (to the perceived animosity of more than a few critics), this conclusion reaffirms that it was less his love for Catherine that was in question than it was his ability to express that love. When does Frederic ever say how he feels about his beloved? Laconic and nostalgic, he tells the story of World War I and his escape from that horror through his love for Catherine in suitably terse language. Frederic Henry as narrator is given one set of patterns—in dic-tion, sentence rhythm, and focus—and his effective telling of the story depends on his consistency of voice. (The relief from that voice comes only in the actual descriptive passages—for instance, the passage of his wounding—when Hemingway moves to an omniscient third with touches of first person sometimes embedded.) Similarly, the reader is never privy to Catherine Barkley's interior consciousness. What one knows about Catherine's passion is also screened through Henry's recollections, and then reproduced in that terse male idiom that is characteristic of him. It is interesting that the only real conversations between the two characters occur early in the novel when Hemingway signals the reader that they are playing language games with each other—and with the sophisticated modernist reader as well.

Part of the hostility relative to gender issues in *A Farewell to Arms*, hostility that has grown during the past several decades, accrues from this narrative dilemma. And it is intensified because of the shortness of the last two books of the novel, when the opportunity for conversation of any kind between the two lovers is abruptly diminished because of the sheer brevity of the scenes required to move the action toward childbirth. By glossing over so much of the "separate peace" and the "other country"[20] Catherine and Frederic have created after their desertions, by summarizing what life was like, with its long walks and quiet evenings, Hemingway allows the reader to forget that Catherine is a genuine person. Unsuitable as it would have been to have her complain about her physical discomfort—and size—during those last months and weeks of her pregnancy, the reader needs some kind of reassurance that Catherine is still Catherine, rather than some idealized dream woman. In short, Hemingway writes no scenes that reveal what we must only suppose to have been Catherine and Frederic's real intimacy. Without language, without the expression of that closeness, their intimacy is only told about rather than imagistically given to the reader.

If a reader wants to find reasons to reject the patness of a great love story, Hemingway's choice of narrative method has set him up. Frederic Henry's laconic toughness plants the seed of doubt: how much does he care about Catherine and what happens to her? After all, his initial attraction to her was that he would have a steady lover and would not have to use the various women in the officers' whorehouse. Later, he was comforted and entertained by Catherine's presence in the Milan hospital. Still later, he knew she would escape the war with him—and deserting with Catherine was much more pleasant, and less lonely, than deserting by himself. (Her acceptance of his decision also justified that desertion to some extent.) Even his rowing across the lake to get them to Switzerland could be said to have been motivated by saving his own life; such a trip for a pregnant woman was not without risk. In short, within *A Farewell to Arms*, the reader has never seen Henry act to create a world for himself and Catherine that did not appear to be self-serving.

From the manuscripts of this novel comes one unpublished sentence that seems to figure in the author's judgment about what should be writ-

ten in the latter sections of A *Farewell to Arms*: "The position of the sur-
vivor of a great calamity is seldom admirable."[21]

In contrast to the character exposition early in the novel, when the
reader learns a comparatively large amount about Rinaldi (and about his
relationship with Henry) and even a fair amount about the unnamed
young priest, by the last two books of A *Farewell to Arms* character exposition has dropped out of the text. Supposedly, the reader knows the characters; attention must rather be given to event and action. But for the
new world of the physically intimate, the spiritually joined, lovers, Hemingway fails to provide details, information, conversation, any kind of
believable scene that convinces us of these emotional bonds. After a hundred pages about the male camaraderie at the Italian front, we get one-
sentence abstractions about Henry's love for Catherine.

Again in contrast, in the earlier parts of A *Farewell to Arms* when Hemingway had time to create scenes, we have seen Catherine nagging Frederic to leave the loud horse-racing crowd in order to be alone with
her—but the impact of that scene is ambiguous. The reader feels that
Henry goes with her unwillingly. Similarly, the hotel room scene, in
which Catherine says she feels like a whore, conveys more than a little
ambiguity, especially since Henry does not contradict her feelings and
since the novel spends almost as much space on the scene that follows,
his trying to cheat in order to secure a seat on the troop train. One implication of that juxtaposition is that Catherine may feel like a whore, but
poor Frederic has to travel in discomfort.

My point is that Hemingway's choices in selection of scenes and character interaction were not always apt. He does not give us—ever—any
interior way of understanding Catherine. By using Helen Ferguson to
convey Catherine's bravery, her willingness to relinquish her profession
and her self, he errs: readers don't care what Fergie thinks (she has not
been given any kind of authority within the text) and her interference
into the Catherine-Henry romance is more disruptive than it is helpful.
At no point in the novel does any of the stream-of-consciousness third-
person writing refer to Catherine; that more interior focus is always
applied to Frederic Henry or to matters that concern him and his masculinist life. In effect, narratively, Hemingway turned Catherine into a
statue long before her death. Perhaps the early scene of Henry's meeting
her in the hospital office, the pavilion of marble busts, indistinguishable
one from the other, does more than foreshadow her image in death: "marble busts all looked like a cemetery" (28). It may essentially explain that
for the author, Catherine was given just enough shape to serve as the lady

of the traditional romance, without usurping any real force of character from Frederic Henry.

Hemingway seems to try to rescue Catherine from narrative oblivion in the last scenes of her labor, complete with its pain, lack of coherence, and forceful language. But again, for the reader, Catherine's ordeal may exist to show once more how Frederic Henry is taking the process (one of the poorly chosen foci of these delivery scenes is how often Henry leaves the hospital and finds food, sustaining himself the last time as Catherine is bleeding her life away). During her labor, with an inappropriately sensual text, Catherine carries on several conversations that underscore some of the themes of *A Farewell to Arms*. (That some of her remarks here seem calculated to play on the sexualized relationship in the same ways earlier descriptions in *A Farewell to Arms* seems unfortunate.)[22]

Few critics would take the position of Leslie Fiedler, in his now-classic *Love and Death in the American Novel*, when he contends that Catherine has to die so that Frederic Henry escapes her becoming either "a bore" or "a mother," the fate of all his women characters. (Fiedler's real criticism is for the innocent boy-heroes of Hemingway's creation: "Poor things, all they wanted was innocent orgasm after orgasm on an island of peace in a world at war, love-making without end in a scarcely real country to which neither owed life or allegiance."[23]) There is, however, sentiment besides Fiedler's for seeing Catherine as an example of the fact that female characters in Hemingway's fiction exist largely in relation to the male. If the women are or become superior, they are that because the man will eventually learn from them: the process is symbiotic. In Hemingway's fiction, women are rarely central on their own terms.

Much of Fitzgerald's criticism of the novel, which he had read parts of in the *Scribner's* serialization and, eventually, in typescript, concerns the unreality of Catherine Barkley. His commentary makes clear that he thinks *A Farewell to Arms* is autobiographical; for instance, he tells Hemingway, "You are seeing him Frederic in a sophisticated way as now you see yourself then but you're still seeing her as you did in 1917 through a 19-year-old's eyes—in consequence unless you make her a bit fatuous occasionally the contrast jars—either the writer is a simple fellow or she is Eleanora Duse disguised as a Red Cross nurse. In one moment you expect her to prophesy the second battle of the Marne—as you probably did then."[24]

He also objected to the way Catherine sounded, reminding Hemingway that he might not now be listening to the way women talk, as he had when he was writing "Cat in the Rain" and several other of the *In Our*

Time stories. About Chapter 21, Fitzgerald noted, "This could stand a good cutting. . . . Sometimes these conversations with her take on a naïve quality that wouldn't please you in anyone else's work. Have you read Noel Coward?" (He continued, "Remember the brave illegitimate mother is an OLD SITUATION & has been exploited by all sorts of people you won't lower yourself to read," a comment about as negative as the reference to Noel Coward.) His chief problem with Catherine, however, remained her voice, and he suggested, "Catherine is too glib. . . . In cutting their conversations cut some of her speeches rather than his."

Criticizing Hemingway for the "dull" sections—at the race track, with the Italian singers, and the scene with Ettore Moretti—Fitzgerald really became intent on getting the war back into the novel: "the war goes further & further out of sight every minute." According to Scott Donaldson, "The ending troubled him [Fitzgerald] for the same reason. 'Seems to me a last echo of the war very faint when Catherine is dying and he's drinking beer in the Cafe.'" It is the war Fitzgerald terms "marvellous." And at the close of his letter, when he had written, "A beautiful book it is!," Hemingway wrote his own reply in the margin: "Kiss my ass."

While Fitzgerald's comments may have been less on-target than his remarks about Hemingway's earlier *The Sun Also Rises*, they were still insightful—and to a certain extent Hemingway paid attention to them. But the reason Fitzgerald found less to criticize was that Hemingway, always an apt pupil, had already become a proficient writer of fiction—as well as an able editor. It seems clear that, when he wrote the introduction to his anthology of war writing, and included all of Stephen Crane's *Red Badge of Courage*, he had planned the kind of stylistic and structural integrity that marked *A Farewell to Arms*. The reason he had to include Crane's work entire, Hemingway said, rather than excerpt it, was that "the Crane book could not be cut, at all. I am sure he cut it all himself as he wrote it to the exact measure of the poem it is: one of the finest books of our literature, it is as much of one piece as a great poem is."[25]

Various critics have commented on passages in *A Farewell to Arms* that seem precise, poetic, polished; and various others have seen the structure of the whole as being admirable (and very unlike most fictions about war). Again, in his introduction to *Men at War*, Hemingway commented on much writing that was based on World War I:

[T]here was no really good true war book during the entire four years of the war. The only true writing that came through during the war was in poetry. One reason for this is that poets are not arrested as quickly as prose writers would be if they wrote critically since the latter's meaning, if they are good writers, is too uncomfortably clear. The last war, during the years 1915, 1916, 1917, was the most colossal, murderous, mismanaged butchery that has ever taken place on earth. Any writer who said otherwise lied. . . .

But after the war the good and true books finally started to come out. They were mostly all by writers who had never written or published anything before the war.

The writers who were established before the war had nearly all sold out to write propaganda during it and most of them never recovered their honesty afterwards.[26]

In this passage, Hemingway meditates on the fact that, even while he had liked Barbusse's *Under Fire* and Dos Passos' *Three Soldiers*, he sees now that both are dated—the former, too filled with "screaming," the latter, with outmoded slang. His objections seem trivial. Perhaps more to the point is his insistence on truth, voiced earlier in the introduction. This is Hemingway's assessment of why he was able to write truly about war, as well as serve as editor for this collection:

When you go to war as a boy you have a great illusion of immortality. Other people get killed; not you. It can happen to other people; but not to you. Then when you are badly wounded the first time you lose that illusion and you know it can happen to you. After being severely wounded two weeks before my nineteenth birthday I had a bad time until I figured it out that nothing could happen to me that had not happened to all men before me. Whatever I had to do men had always done. If they had done it then I could do it too and the best thing was not to worry about it.

I was very ignorant at nineteen and had read little.[27]

When Hemingway achieves the kind of authenticity in *A Farewell to Arms* that he manages here, no reader questions his narrative. In fact, along with the published novel, there are random cut passages from the manuscripts that share that fluid force. For example, Michael Reynolds quotes an evocative passage from the manuscript about the effects of fear:

[T]he spells of fear were always physical, always caused by an imminent danger, and always transitory. I was in the second healthy stage, that of not being afraid when I was not in danger. I suppose the third stage, of being afraid at night, started about this point. I did not notice it start because I was rarely alone at night. Fear grows through recognition.[28]

Hemingway's center of interest in this novel, and in much of his writing about war, is the young and somewhat naïve soldier (or ambulance driver) for whom the experience of battle serves as the experience of nihilistic life. The character who lives at all must come to terms with his fears; denying them only forestalls eventual realizations. The powerful ending of A Farewell to Arms shows Frederic Henry in the midst of that bleak, and relentless, realization: "I went out and left the hospital and walked back to the hotel in the rain" (332). Isolated from the other men and women who had known the Italian front, bereft of his beloved and best friend, robbed of the child that might have been his, Henry could hardly be more alone. It is this resonance that bursts through A Farewell to Arms, however that second noun is defined.

So far as the writing of the novel is concerned, Bernard Oldsey places A Farewell to Arms within the context of all Hemingway's writing (having studied the manuscripts of much of that writing) and concludes: "The manuscripts show that Hemingway was not only a great natural writer, possessed of verve and linguistic flow, but also a fine editor of his own fiction. His sense of what was right, what would work, was uncanny. The papers reveal that he made very few, if any, incorrect decisions about how to begin or end a narrative."[29] His writing of this novel, then, was not atypical.

The process of his creating A Farewell to Arms is of interest, however, because the work is so complex, lengthy, and powerful. Michael Reynolds adds to the discussion of the novel's effective structure by describing other means of achieving its remarkable cohesiveness; he defined three structural principles at work throughout the novel. "First, there is the simple technique of foreshadowing; there is no major piece of action in the novel that has not been properly foreshadowed. Second, there is the device of the echo scene. Finally, there is the technique of reversing roles between characters."[30] To illustrate Hemingway's use of foreshadowing, Reynolds mentions Catherine's pregnancy, and the events leading to its possibility; Frederic Henry's attempts to pray, and the suggestions before his need to pray that he may need to do so; and the almost surreal parallels in Henry's condition both before he leaves Milan and before the retreat. For example, about the latter Reynolds notes, "During the night in Milan when Frederic is leaving Catherine to return to the front, he experiences in miniature what will happen on a larger scale during the retreat. In Milan Frederic leaves the Red Cross hospital to return to the front under less than ideal conditions: limping, jaundiced, and with a pregnant mistress. . . . In Milan, Frederic begins his journey to the train station with Catherine by his side. Moving down side streets in the rain, they make their way to a hotel where they have a last supper. . . . On the train Frederic is separated from Catherine, and he is surrounded by unknown and somewhat hostile soldiers. In the military retreat from Caporetto, Frederic begins with companions going down side roads in the rain. At night he stops at a farmhouse with Piani where they eat their last supper together. At the bridge he is separated from Piani by the hostile battle police" (242–243).

Perhaps of more import is what Reynolds calls Hemingway's "echo scenes," structures by which a primary scene seems to be repeated but changed, tilted, sometimes even reversed—with the effect of irony. To illustrate this technique, he mentions the several scenes between Henry and, first, Rinaldi and then the priest, as if in dialogue between opposing philosophical positions. More concretely, the image of going to Lake Maggiore—first for holiday and then to escape death for desertion. Scenes of executions—the Italian troops, with every tenth man shot; Henry's shooting the sergeant; the battle police executing officers during the retreat—build a similar echoing structure. Reynold's clearest example of this technique comes in his visibly ironic hotel scenes. In that comparison Henry first fantasizes about going to a hotel room with Catherine; then later, when they are in the room, fantasy is gone and there remains nothing but the sordid implication of their unblessed sexual union.

Reynolds also mentions the ironic use of seasons—Catherine's death occurs in the season of rebirth—and the pervasive seasonal cycles of battle and love that shape the time frame of the novel. He finds what he calls role reversal in the characters of Catherine and Frederic, first one strong and aware, then the other—then neither. He concludes that the general structure of A Farewell to Arms is based on nothing other than "the experience of defeat," no matter what battlefield one considers: the personal is as tragic as the military (282).

NOTES

1. Hemingway to Gertrude Stein, August 15, 1924 in Letters, p. 122.

2. See my "Favored Strangers": Gertrude Stein and Her Family (New Brunswick, NJ: Rutgers University Press, 1995), pp. 166–178.

3. See Michael S. Reynolds, ed. *Critical Essays on Ernest Hemingway's* In Our Time (Boston: Hall, 1983) and Richard Hasbany, "The Shock of Vision: An Imagist Reading of *In Our Time*" in my *Ernest Hemingway: Five Decades of Criticism* (E. Lansing: Michigan State University Press, 1974), pp. 224–240. In the latter, Hasbany notes, "The right word obsession led to precision. But the right word meant even more than this. For Pound using the right word was the means of keeping a language alive" (225). He quotes Pound saying "'The *mot juste* is of public utility. . . . We are governed by words, the laws are graven in words, and literature is the sole means of keeping these words living and accurate'" (in Pound's "Paris Letter," *The Dial* 62 [June 1922], p. 629).

4. Hemingway credited his prowess with dialogue to the fact that both Gertrude Stein and her older brother Leo, a cafe friend of Hemingway, had urged him to read Jane Austen (*"Favored Strangers,"* p. 171).

5. The Imagist poets, and particularly Pound, used this term as well as the concept of "absolute rhythm," the notion that every piece of writing must have "a rhythm which corresponds exactly to the emotion or shade of emotion to be expressed" (Pound, "Vorticism," *Fortnightly Review* 96 [September 1, 1914], p. 469). He says in his Imagist manifesto that an "organ base [is] a sort of residue of sound which remains in the ear" for the purpose of establishing mood ("Imagism," *Poetry* 1, no. 6 [March 1913], p. 205) and see Eric Homberger, "Pound, Ford and 'Prose': The Making of a Modern Poet," *Journal of American Studies* 5, no. 3 (December 1971), pp. 281–293.

6. Ezra Pound, *Literary Essays of Ezra Pound* (Norfolk, CT: New Directions, 1935), p. 50.

7. Daniel J. Schneider, "Hemingway's *A Farewell to Arms*: The Novel as Pure Poetry" in my *Ernest Hemingway: Five Decades of Criticism* (E. Lansing: Michigan State University Press, 1974), pp. 252–266, this excerpt p. 254; hereafter cited in text. William Adair, too, calls Hemingway "essentially a lyric writer; thus his basic impulse is to express, to find correlatives for, his vision rather than to re-create the 'real world' . . . [the novel] is constructed out of emotional 'counters,' the selection and arrangement of which is presided over by a dominant emotion" ("*A Farewell to Arms*: A Dream Book," *Modern Critical Interpretations of Ernest Hemingway's A Farewell to Arms* [New York: Chelsea House, 1987], p. 43).

8. Michael S. Reynolds, *Hemingway's First War* (Princeton, NJ: Princeton University Press, 1976), p. 27.

9. See my "Hemingway and the Limits of Biography" in *Hemingway: From Michigan to the World*, ed. Frederic J. Svoboda and Joseph J. Waldmeir (E. Lansing: Michigan State University Press, 1995), pp. 105–126.

10. Schneider, "Hemingway's *A Farewell to Arms*," p. 254. In his seminal 1966 book, *The Colloquial Style in America*, Richard Bridgman attributes much of Hemingway's lyricism to the influence of Gertrude Stein, particularly to her collection of interrelated poems, *Tender Buttons*. He sees much of Hemingway's early writing as "deliberately composed," with an eye to stylistic innovation: the young

author "had to learn how to construct a prose with sufficient internal coherence to resist the corrosion of time and how to develop sufficient internal complexity to redeem that prose from the curse of over-simplification" ("Ernest Hemingway," *Ernest Hemingway: Five Decades of Criticism*, pp. 160–188, this excerpt, p. 171).

11. John Reardon, "Hemingway's Esthetic and Ethical Sportsmen," in *Ernest Hemingway: Five Decades of Criticism* (E. Lansing: Michigan State University Press, 1976), pp. 131–144, this excerpt p. 138; Reardon quotes from Hemingway's *Green Hills of Africa*, p. 21.

12. Ezra Pound, *The Literary Essays of Ezra Pound* (Norfolk, CT: New Directions, 1935), p. 10.

13. As quoted by Arthur Mizener in *The Saddest Story: A Biography of Ford Madox Ford* (New York: World, 1971), p. xix.

14. Julian Smith, "Hemingway and the Thing Left Out" in *Ernest Hemingway: Five Decades of Criticism* (E. Lansing: Michigan State University Press, 1974), pp. 188–200.

15. Michael S. Reynolds, *Hemingway's First War* (Princeton, NJ: Princeton University Press, 1976), p. 42; hereafter cited in text.

16. Robert Merrill, "Tragic Form in *A Farewell to Arms*," *Modern Critical Interpretations of Ernest Hemingway's* A Farewell to Arms (New York: Chelsea House, 1987), pp. 25–32, this excerpt p. 26; hereafter cited in text.

17. Bernard Oldsey, *Hemingway's Hidden Craft* (University Park: Pennsylvania State University Press, 1979), p. 78. On p. 15, Oldsey reproduces the manuscript page on which Hemingway had written possible titles.

18. F. Scott Fitzgerald's letter; see Scott Donaldson, *Hemingway vs. Fitzgerald* (Woodstock, NY: Overland, 1999), pp. 125–135.

19. On p. 7 of manuscript #292 in the Hemingway Collection, the author tries this description of a woman dead, "She was like nothing. It was like holding a changed season or the autumnal equinox in his arms." John F. Kennedy Library.

20. Among Hemingway's list of titles for the novel are "A Separate Peace" and "A World's Room." Another that repeats this emphasis is "The Enchantment." In the section of titles that includes the latter, as well as "A Farewell to Arms," Hemingway has written "shitty titles" (Hemingway Collection, John F. Kennedy Library).

21. Unpaged manuscript page, *A Farewell to Arms* (Hemingway Collection, John F. Kennedy Library).

22. The kind of sexualization I'm referring to is anchored by Catherine's response to the gas used to anaesthetize her during severe labor pains. Her legitimately out-of-control request—"I want it now," "I want it again," "*I want it now*," "*Give it to me*," "*Give it to me. Give it to me*"—embedded with her praise for her "most wonderful doctor" makes the labor scene all too reminiscent of bad sex throughout modernist writing. What could not be put into polite language because nice women don't express their sexual needs, nor does published writing acknowledge either those needs or the language that conveys them, here appears

exclusively in the scenes of her painful labor. In that process, Catherine says nothing except these kinds of commands—unless she is urging both her men, her "wonderful" doctor as well as Frederic Henry, to go find food. What Hemingway seems to want to convey by this juxtaposition is the woman as both maternal and sexual; the scenes of her labor, however, end up giving the reader a great deal more of Frederic's menus than any sense of a great love between woman and man.

Hemingway's tendency to use descriptions that evoke the sexual in places that are not themselves about sex has been noted earlier. For instance, after his early leave-taking from Catherine, he idealizes their possible relationship in a scene heavily coded as sexual:

> I would like to eat at the Cova and then walk down the Via Manzoni in the hot evening and cross over and turn off along the canal and go to the hotel with Catherine Barkley. Maybe she would. Maybe she would pretend that I was her boy that was killed and we would go in the front door and the porter would take off his cap and I would stop at the concierge's desk and ask for the key and she would stand by the elevator and then we would get in the elevator and it would go up very slowly clicking at all the floors and then our floor and the boy would open the door and stand there and she would step out and I would step out and we would walk down the hall and I would put the key in the door and open it and go in and then take down the telephone and ask them to send a bottle of capri bianca in a silver bucket full of ice and you would hear the ice against the pail coming down the corridor and the boy would knock and I would say leave it outside the door please. Because we would not wear any clothes because it was so hot and the window open (38).

The passage continues with the two resting—"only a sheet" and the abstract language, "and the whole night we would both love each other all night in the hot night in Milan." The crudely emphasized but always indirect verbs—"get in," "put the__in the__and open it and go in," "take down"—are set within the slow moving, rhythmic tapestry of interaction (not to mention the fact that the primary sentence is composed of 164 words but, more importantly, of a dozen separate verbal constructions; and that that sentence follows the three-word introductory "Maybe she would"). The closing lines repeat the heat, the night, and the openness that accrues to the lovers. Frederic Henry's fantasy of forbidden sex with Catherine is made clear at least in part through Hemingway's sly syntax.

23. Leslie A. Fiedler, *Love and Death in the American Novel* (New York: Dell, 1966), pp. 316–317. He continues that "Had Catherine lived, she could only have turned into a bitch; for this is the fate in Hemingway's imagination of all Anglo-Saxon women. . . . When Hemingway's bitches are American, they are hopeless and unmitigated bitches; symbols of Home and Mother as remembered by the boy who could never forgive Mama for having wantonly destroyed Papa's

Indian collection!" Fiedler remains a wonderful read; his assessments are not without value.

24. Fitzgerald's comments quoted in Scott Donaldson's *Hemingway vs. Fitzgerald*, pp. 126–130.

25. Hemingway's introduction to *Men At War* (New York: Crown, 1942), p. 10.

26. Ibid., p. 7.

27. Ibid., p. 6.

28. Quoted in Reynolds, *Hemingway's First War*, p. 39 (Manuscript #236).

29. Bernard Oldsey, "Hemingway's Beginnings and Endings," *Ernest Hemingway: Six Decades of Criticism* (E. Lansing: Michigan State University Press, 1987), pp. 113–138, this excerpt p. 113.

30. Michael S. Reynolds, *Hemingway's First War*, p. 238; hereafter cited in text.

7 Reception

We can gain some sense of the way *A Farewell to Arms* was received by the important critics of Hemingway's time through reading Ford Madox Ford's introduction to the novel, an introduction that he was asked to write for a 1932 edition of the book. Dated in that year, Ford's essay begins with the emphasis that had made the young American writer so important to the modernist literary world—his style. Ford's essay begins in the subjective: "I experienced a singular sensation on reading the first sentence of *A Farewell to Arms*."[1] Excited because Hemingway's writing was so exact, Ford claimed that he realized the young American writer had "the discipline that makes you avoid temptation in the selection of words and the discipline that lets you be remorselessly economical in the number you employ."[2] As a result, according to Ford,

> Hemingway's words strike you, each one, as if they were pebbles fetched fresh from a brook. They live and shine, each in its place. . . . So one of his pages has the effect of a brook-bottom into which you look down through the flowing water. The words form a tessellation, each in order beside the other.
>
> It is a very great quality. It is indeed the supreme quality of the written art of the moment. It is a great part of what makes literature come into its own at such rare times as it achieves that feat. Books lose their hold on you as soon as the words in which they are written are demoded or too usual the one following the other. The aim—the

achievement—of the great prose writer is to use words so that they shall seem new and alive because of their juxtaposition with other words. This gift Hemingway has supremely.[3]

As Ford concludes, "You could not begin that first sentence and not finish the passage."[4]

The inevitability of the words pleases the older modernist writer, as does Hemingway's ability to sustain his effects. The novel encourages Ford in his high assessment of the American writer's talent, partly because it reassures him. "*A Farewell to Arms* is a book important in the annals of the art of writing because it proves that Hemingway, the writer of short, perfect episodes, can keep up the pace through a volume" (253). Ford also comments about the stylistic perfection of the ending sentences of Hemingway's novel, saying, "that muted passage after great emotion still holds the mind after the book is finished" (252).

As these comments show, the thoroughly modernist Ford Madox Ford read *A Farewell to Arms* in a modernist way, emphasizing craft and its corollary, the way the writer's entire being contributed to his art. The opinions of other successful writers were what really mattered about the book's reception: that it was a popular success—and later a film—almost worked against its being considered good literary work. Hemingway seldom mentioned Henry James (except ironically),[5] but one of the long-term motives for his writing was to place himself in the company of the greatest American novelists.

The fact that Ford was writing the 1932 introduction to *A Farewell to Arms* also must have pleased Hemingway, since Ford's *The Good Soldier* until that time had been considered the best-written of the World War I fictions. It is indicative of Hemingway's reluctance to pay tribute to works that had influenced his own writing that he never mentioned Ford's novel (even in his long introduction to *Men at War*, when he was surveying writing about World War I and other conflicts). Ford's novel, like Hugh Walpole's *The Young Enchanted: A Romantic Story*, and Blasco Ibáñez's *The Four Horsemen of the Apocalypse*, foregrounded the interrelation of love and war, the romance in each work intensified—and terribly complicated—by the fact of characters living through a war.

Ford's novel is also ironically titled, with the modifier "good" working as does that same adjective in Gertrude Stein's "The Good Anna" to suggest reservations about the character's life choices. The modernist's need for a double text—a work seemingly about one theme yet possibly undercutting the accepted view of that situation—becomes a commonplace during postwar modernism.

That Ford had subtitled *The Good Soldier* "a tale of passion" came in for criticism in the manuscript of Hemingway's earlier *The Sun Also Rises*. Ford, there represented as Braddocks, is enthusiastic about taking his friends to the dancing club, a possible cover for a house of prostitution.[6] But *The Good Soldier*, with Ford's various configurations of fidelity and infidelity, may have had more influence on Hemingway's posthumously published *The Garden of Eden*—with its liaisons both lesbian and hetero-sexual—than on *A Farewell to Arms*. Hemingway's 1929 book, in fact, is a novel remarkable for its single-minded insistence on monogamy. The author's voice in most of the manuscript sections, which Fitzgerald and others had suggested that he cut, clearly speaks from a postwar perspec-tive. Ford had begun *The Good Soldier* in 1913, on his fortieth birthday, so the mores that he described would have been *prewar*: his definition of *pas-sion* was therefore that of an earlier generation. (The quality of passion may not change, but its representation in art must; that is the control of social conventions breaking into the writer's aesthetic.)

The deepest irony in any comparison between Ford's *The Good Soldier* and Hemingway's *A Farewell to Arms* is, of course, the fact that Ford's sol-dierly characters would never have deserted—either country or lover. One might see Frederic Henry's act of desertion as another of those cross-generational statements made by the younger American writer to the aging British one: *I can write about a deserter and make him heroic,* taunts Hemingway. The premise of *A Farewell to Arms*, a great irony in itself, might well have offended Ford.

Yet Ford chooses to praise the Hemingway novel. He avoids saying anything at all about its characters or its themes, however, and in his focus on Hemingway's style, may be keeping himself from voicing com-plaints about those matters. In fact, in his tactful praise, Ford never men-tions that *A Farewell to Arms* is a World War I novel.

By drawing from his admiration for Hemingway's *In Our Time*, Ford repeats a number of the critics' approaches to this 1929 novel: what made Hemingway such a bright spot on the literary scene was his consistent production. Once he began publishing, with the chapbook *in our time*, his work was steadily in the public eye; and once he became a property of Charles Scribner's house, his fiction could be found in both book form and in the pages of *Scribner's Magazine*. No matter that he lived in Paris during his early publishing years, the modernist literary scene wanted to be understood as international. Hemingway's living in Paris certainly brought more cachet to his literary standing than had he lived in Oak Park, Illinois.

Dorothy Parker, too, writing in the *New Yorker*, treated Hemingway's work as a totality. She used a metaphor to describe the enthusiastic reception Hemingway—and his works—had received: "Ernest Hemingway wrote a novel called *The Sun Also Rises*. Promptly upon its publication, Ernest Hemingway was discoverd, the Stars and Stripes were reverentially raised over him, eight hundred and forty-seven book reviewers formed themselves into the word 'welcome' and the band played 'Hail to the Chief' in three concurrent keys. All of which, I should think, might have made Ernest Hemingway pretty reasonably sick."[7] Parker's wit did not obscure the fact that Hemingway was a hot property: people were talking about him, reading his fiction, and telling stories to each other about the time they met him, or knew someone who had. His visibility as a part of the Stein circle was serving him well. If he could not be found at the Paris cafés, he would be sure to occasion either Stein's salon or Sylvia Beach's bookstore. And Hemingway had worked to make himself accessible.

One of Parker's points is that Hemingway's two magnificent story collections—*In Our Time* and *Men Without Women*—would never have won such acclaim without the novel appearing between them: "Literature, it appears, is here measured by a yard-stick." Once *The Sun Also Rises* was published, however, according to Parker, its author "was the white-haired boy. He was praised, adored, analyzed, best-sold, argued about, and banned in Boston; all the trimmings were accorded him. People got into feuds about whether or not his story was worth the telling. . . . They affirmed, and passionately, that the dissolute expatriates in this novel of 'a lost generation' were not worth bothering about; and then they devoted most of their time to discussing them. There was a time, and it went on for weeks, when you could go nowhere without hearing of *The Sun Also Rises*" (164).

To move this good-humored exaggeration into the future, witnessing the clear best-sellerdom of *A Farewell to Arms*, is to understand the foundation for Hemingway's popular fame. The intellectuals and the modernist critics who valued the new writing served as the base for Hemingway's celebrity but the readers who bought copies of *A Farewell to Arms* became the population who made him a key Scribner's property.

Of substance too is Parker's closing remark, that Hemingway shares much of his position as a twentieth-century American writer with Sinclair Lewis; both have what she calls "a reportorial talent." But she distinguishes between them by saying that "Lewis remains a reporter, and Hemingway stands a genius because Hemingway has an unerring sense of selection. He discards details with a magnificent lavishness; he keeps his words to their short path" (165).

Claude McKay too writes about that initial early impression within the literary world: "Ernest Hemingway was the most talked about of young American writers when I arrived in Paris. He was the white hope of the ultra-sophisticates. In the motley atmosphere of Montparnasse, there was no place for the cult of little hero worship. James Joyce was worshipped, but he had won out with a work that took men's eyes like a planet. But in Montparnasse generally writers and artists plunged daggers into one another. That atmosphere in its special way was like a good tonic. . . . It was therefore exciting that Ernest Hemingway had won the regard and respect of the younger creative artists and even of the older."[8]

McKay also talks about the way knowing Hemingway's books changed what kind of literature was being written by the serious poets and novelists of the time: "I was excited by the meteor apparition of Ernest Hemingway. . . . In Paris and in the Midi, I met a few fellows of the extreme left school, and also a few of the moderate liberal school and even some of the ancient fossil school—and all mentioned Hemingway with admiration. Many of them felt that they could never go on writing as before Hemingway" (168).

Given this atmosphere of Hemingway's early success, his personal plans to meet new (and usually famous) people were never difficult to implement. As J. Gerald Kennedy and Jackson R. Bryer comment in their opening essay of French Connections: Hemingway and Fitzgerald Abroad, "From their first conversation at the Dingo [in 1925, two weeks after The Great Gatsby was published], Hemingway impressed Fitzgerald as 'the real thing,' a genuinely talented writer with invaluable personal experience."[9]

For reviewer Paul Rosenfeld in The New Republic, Hemingway's early writing captured the innovation of modernist Paris. Rosenfeld places his writing "with cubist painting, Le Sacre du printemps, and other recent work bringing a feeling of positive forces through primitive modern idiom. The use of the direct, crude, rudimentary forms of the simple and primitive classes and their situations, of the stuffs, textures and rhythms of the mechanical and industrial worlds, has enabled this new American storyteller, as it enabled the group to which he comes a fresh recruit, to achieve peculiarly sharp, decided, grimly affirmative expressions; and with these acute depictions and half-impersonal beats to satisfy a spirit running through the age. Hemingway's spoken prose is characteristically ironic with a lyricism, aliveness and energy tremendously held in check. With the trip-hammer thud of *Le Sacre* his rhythms go."[10]

Established in only a few years, then, as an innovative modernist writer, Hemingway was comfortably wedged into a bracket that might sometimes include Sherwood Anderson and Gertrude Stein, sometimes European writers, sometimes F. Scott Fitzgerald but more and more often only himself. Experimentalism, as we have already seen, sold few books—even though critics admired the writer who was innovative. A *Farewell to Arms* could make money for Hemingway. If it could also be regarded as fine writing, he won on two counts. What Hemingway gained by leaving his spare modernist vignettes and turning to write his war story, the narrative he had been working on intermittently for years, was a way into more commercially profitable publishing opportunities.

For the period we now know as modernism began with World War I. Even if social observers had stopped repeating the rubric of "postwar," the war to end all wars was so firmly inscribed in everyone's mind and heart that recovering from the war was a universal problem. Why else were all these young Americans in Paris? To escape the ravages of their fundamentalist belief system—that if one worked hard and saved, he or she would become successful—once embroiled in war, they turned their backs on the homeland that had proven meretricious. Patriotism had sold them short. They had not been among those eight or ten million casualties, but neither had they answered their parents' insistence that they return home and become loyal, patriotic community members again. In his 1925 story "Soldier's Home," Hemingway had laid out the territory about as well as any writer before or since. As critic Marc Dolan explained, the myth of the American twenties, caught so truthfully by F. Scott Fitzgerald, depended on the icon of "lost generation": "from youthful exuberance (the 'younger generation' of the early 1920s) to self-absorbed decline ('a lost generation' in the late 1920s) to conspicuous decadence ('the lost generation' of the early 1930s). . . . This narrativized perception of the decades gave it a clear protagonist (the generation of the 1890s), a clear beginning (the enthusiastic days just after 'The War'), and a very clear end (the more resigned time just after 'The Crash').[11]

Most of the reviews of Hemingway's A *Farewell to Arms* repeated this idea. Before the Great War, and even during it, human values were simpler, more humane, more conventional. Man wants to serve his country, just as man wants to marry and have children: the dominance of "home" and keeping that "home" as country safe motivated most civilized human actions. Once Hemingway had written his war story, reviewers began seeing that his other published books were also "postwar" works, or at least narratives about the aftermath of war. As Ray B. West, Jr., opened his essay on Hemingway's writing, "Ernest Hemingway's first three important works were In Our Time, a collection of curiously related short storries; The Sun Also Rises, his first serious and successful novel; and A Farewell to Arms. All three deal with the same subject: the condition of man in a society upset by the violence of war."[12]

When West reads A Farewell to Arms, rather than finding that the war disappears toward the end of the novel, he instead claims, "The war is not over." War symbolizes modern man's realization that life does not end happily—neither is there a great deal of happiness along the way. "Even after the successful effort to leave Italy and enter Switzerland, the war (which is really a symbol for the chasm of nature—the biological trap) catches up with Frederic and Catherine. It is significant that Frederic's reason tells him he can escape—that he has escaped; his sensibility suggests that he is only playing truant. Frederic felt like a masquerader in his civilian clothes. That is to say in the modern sense, all happiness is a form of truancy."

Linking all parts of A Farewell to Arms to World War I enables the reader to comprehend the novel's dire tone of coming disaster. In that way, war is both background and foreground. Perhaps throughout his writing career, the war—for Hemingway—was the iceberg he was so continuously conscious of.

That Hemingway was irritated by the assumption that he wrote about World War I because he had served in it becomes clear from several of his personal letters. To Max Perkins in 1933, Hemingway reminds him that "I invented every word and every incident of A Farewell to Arms [sic] except possibly 3 or 4 incidents. All the best part is invented. 95 per cent of The Sun Also Rises [sic] was pure imagination. I took real people in that one and I controlled what they did. I made it all up."[13] Twenty years later, but in what seems to be an attempt to be helpful, Hemingway explains to his friend Charles Poore,

> Remember Charlie in the first war all I did mostly was hear guys talk; especially in hospital and convalescing. Their experiences get to be more vivid than your own. You invent from your own and from all of theirs. The country you know, also the weather. Then you have a map 1/50,000 for the whole front or section; 1/5000 if you can get one for close. Then you invent from other people's experience and knowledge and what you know yourself.

Then some son of a bitch will come along and prove you were not at that particular fight. Fine. Dr. Tolstoi was at Sevastopol. But not at Borodino. He wasn't in business in those days. But he could invent from knowledge [sic] we all were at some damned Sevastopol.[14]

In a 1951 letter to Thomas Bledsoe, Hemingway discusses another way of being "real" in the novel: "Every writer is in much of his work. But it is not as simple as all that. I could have told Mr. Young the whole genesis of The Sun Also Rises [sic] for example. It came from a personal experience in that when I had been wounded at one time there had been an infection from pieces of wool cloth being driven into the scrotum. Because of this I got to know other kids who had genito urinary wounds and I wondered what a man's life would have been like after that if his penis had been lost and his testicles and spermatic cord remained intact. I had known a boy that happened to. So I took him and made him into a foreign correspondent in Paris and, inventing, tried to find out what his problems would be when he was in love with someone who was in love with him and there was nothing that they could do about it."[15]

Hemingway's clear frustration as he tried to inform critics and readers about important aesthetic truths marks his last ten years of life. Ironically, the very critics that made him a prominent twentieth-century writer became a torment to him. His reference in this last-quoted letter to "Mr. Young" suggests the relationship he had been having with Philip Young, whose 1952 critical study of Hemingway's fiction is among the earliest published. As bibliographer Kelli A. Larson notes about the prominence of Young's work, "Young's early psychoanalytical approach to Hemingway's fiction has earned him the distinction of being one of the most often-cited scholars in the field. Interestingly, Young's wound theory— that Hemingway's fiction represents the author's lifelong struggle to psychically purge himself of the wound he received while in Italy during World War I—is nearly as widely known as the fiction itself. Ironically, Young's highly influential wound and 'code-hero' theories have made *him* the subject of critical analysis, beyond the conventional book review."[16]

Hemingway did not hesitate to make his objections clear to Young himself. In a 1952 letter, he explained "I have written the late Mr. Charles Scribner and Mr. Bledsoe why I am opposed to biography of living [sic] writers. . . . [Y]ou know it can be damageing [sic] to a man while he is writing in the middle of his work to tell him that he is suffering from a neurosis as to tell him that he has cancer? The man himself can say 'oh s[h]it.' But he has been damanged [*sic*] with everyone who reads him. And I have known writers who could be damaged by such statements to such an extent they could no longer write" [i.e., F. Scott Fitzgerald]. The letter continues with the fact that Hemingway's objection is largely a matter of principle, but it closes, "From my own stand point, as writer, I have so far had worry, annoyance, and severe interruption of my work from this book."[17] Throughout many of his letters during the 1950s, he complains about this kind of critical invasion, which is unnecessary, it seems to him. It was not a new position. After all, Hemingway had written in 1926 to Maxwell Perkins, "Critics . . . have a habit of hanging attributes on you themselves—and then when they find you're not that way accusing you of sailing under false colors."[18]

A Farewell to Arms plays into this long-lasting war with the critics in a significant way. It was, after all, the fiction in which the Hemingway character (Frederic Henry) received his wound. In one of the more dramatic pieces of writing in the novel, Henry's near-death experience was made memorable to readers of all kinds, not only to critics. The scene was one of Hemingway's first attempts to use a modified stream-of-consciousness technique. And even though he wrote a number of such interior monologues in the draft version of the novel, he eventually cut most of them. Henry's wounding scene, then, calls attention to itself through its style as well as through its content.

Even as American literary study in the decade of the 1950s was trying to focus on the text, avoiding the biographical that had for so many years been a part of literary criticism, Hemingway's texts seemed to draw much of their realism, much of their authenticity, from the biographical and the autobiographical. To apply the tenets of the so-called "New Criticism" to Hemingway's work meant omitting facets of his experience that appeared to be directly involved with his writing. Here, the burgeoning growth of Hemingway's celebrity (the fact that United States readers, as well as the international literati, knew who he was and what kind of writing he did) tended to interfere with critics being able to focus on the writing. Scott Donaldson makes the point that two of Hemingway's books during the 1930s—Death in the Afternoon and Green Hills of Africa—are defenses of his writing and his aesthetic: almost immediately after the publication of A Farewell to Arms, then, and in the aftermath of those reviews and critical essays about Hemingway and war, he began to mount what he saw as a necessary defense. The characterization Hemingway wanted to present was "Hemingway as modernist writer"—nothing more, and certainly nothing more invasive into his personal life. In Donaldson's words,

During the 1930s, as at no other time in his life, Hemingway indulged in presentation of himself (and his ideas about life and love and literature) in his writing, particularly in *Death in the Afternoon* and *Green Hills of Africa*. In a 1933 cartoon, William Steig caught the spirit of his public persona by depicting him holding a rose in his hairy tattooed fist. In the same year, Ernest expressed his legitimate impatience with the garbage spilled onto the page about him by various publicity agents. He got Max Perkins to issue a statement in protest against Paramount's stories about him in connection with the Gary Cooper-Jennifer Jones film version of *A Farewell to Arms*. "Mr. Ernest Hemingway has asked his publishers to disclaim the romantic and false military and personal career imputed to him in a recent film publicity release. . . . While Mr. H. appreciates the publicity attempt to build him into a glamorous personality like Floyd Gibbons or Tom Mix's horse Tony, he deprecates it and asks the motion picture people to leave his private life alone."[19]

The fight Hemingway was waging would not be won. He had succeeded too well in becoming the persona of his Paris life, his war experiences, his big-game hunting, and his bullfighting: the books he published, too, although they were not autobiographical for the most part, demanded that readers identify their author with their content. Rather than a biographical fallacy, Hemingway's reputation as great modernist writer was plagued by an autobiographical one.

FEMINIST AND SEXUALIZED CRITICISM AND HEMINGWAY'S WORK

Culturally, too, it was a simpler world. In the 1930s and 1940s and 1950s, between the two all-encompassing world wars, to write about "war" or to refer to that noun in any way meant immediate reader recognition. Everyone in the twentieth century, regrettably, knew what war signified. It remained for critics in the 1980s and the 1990s to begin to unpack the concept that "war" was inherently a masculine idea, a masculinist proving ground, a paradigm that had to omit any concept of the feminine in order to continue the patriotic emphasis on serving, as well as on saving.

In the early stages of feminist criticism, focus fell on writers who created major women characters; Ernest Hemingway's work was seldom mentioned. When in 1988 the first volume of Sandra M. Gilbert and Susan Gubar's three-book project, *No Man's Land: The Place of the*

Woman Writer in the Twentieth Century appeared, the world of literary response was troubled. Not only was the thesis of this work, the title of the first book of which was "The War of the Words," that the real conflict in the twentieth century was the battle between patriarchal (male) control and women's rebellion against it, but the authors chose very male terms to characterize that battle: not only "war" but "no man's land," the sad rubric for the trenches that had decimated so many Allied troops during World War I. Rather than see "man" as the object of contention during the linguistic controversy to replace "man" as signifier for all people—and use instead "human," readers saw it as a reference to the bloodshed of the First World War. Their choice of title seemed, somehow, disrespectful. "War" as a word was itself heavily freighted. How could women critics who wanted to write about some lost or less-appreciated works by women writers appropriate such a valuable term? It didn't matter that Gilbert and Gubar quoted from the very masculine D. H. Lawrence in their epigraph page, when Lawrence had written, "Perhaps the greatest revolution of modern times is the emancipation of women; and perhaps the deepest fight for two thousand years and more, has been the fight for woman's independence, or freedom, call it what you will. The fight was deeply bitter and, it seems to me, it is won."[20] The pages of *No Man's Land* are filled with what then seemed to be revolutionary concepts: the book, in fact, opens with these rhetorical questions: "Is a pen a metaphorical pistol? Are words weapons with which the sexes have fought over territory and authority?" (3)

It was bad enough that women critics assumed enough authority to modify the standard paradigms of literary criticism, but Gilbert and Gubar had also undermined the agreed-upon meanings of words to create their biting irony. In somewhat the same vein, as she writes about World War I, critic Jane Marcus suggests,

> It has always seemed to me very curious that historians do not mention the suffrage campaign as the training ground for ambulance drivers and VAD nurses in World War I. Bravery, physical courage, chivalry, group solidarity, strategic planning, honor—these things women had learned in the streets and jails of London, the *first* "forbidden zone" they had entered.[21]

While in early fiction about war the gender structure was almost entirely male—with women appearing either as nurses or camp followers—this different critical perspective unearthed the women characters who had been present all along. This perspective also enabled the long-suppressed writings about war by women authors to regain both print and validity. (Hemingway's "Catherized" insult about Willa Cather's war novel *One of Ours* was finally being challenged.)

Later, during the 1990s, when feminist criticism had become firmly entrenched within literary criticism, a different emphasis on the perceived sexuality of characters both female and male made itself visible. Gay and lesbian theory offered a purview into relationships and structures that a comparatively simple male/female dichotomy had seldom assessed. As Valerie Rohy said in her *Impossible Women: Lesbian Figures and American Literature*, the reason Hemingway's work is relevant to critics who use these Foucauldian tools is both the alignment of characters in his works, and the years of criticism that have created an even more gendered way of reading: "Hemingway is most useful to lesbian reading, that is, not as an instance of individual obsession or neurosis, but as an astute recorder of the compulsions and anxieties of masculine literary modernism and modernist culture."[22]

Charles Hatten's major essay on what he calls "reified desire" in *A Farewell to Arms* is a superior example of the complexity of this approach. Hatten admits that one reason this novel prompts so much critical debate is its sexism, focused through the Frederic Henry-Catherine Barkley relationship. But another reason is "societal anxiety over processes of sexual reification."[23]

He contends that *A Farewell to Arms* is not simply a romance, and that Catherine's "relation to sexuality is not obvious." The work instead "thematizes the difficulties of [male] sexual desire" in that Henry feels threatened by Fergie, Von Campen, and other women. The reader, then, feels that Frederic Henry is "embattled" in regard to the "feminizing social world" (77). Because Henry's desire *is* reified, cut off from the communal networks that once gave it meaning, Hemingway's emphasis in the book is "how the historically new experience of reified sexuality that it depicts and vindicates will provide [any kind of foundation] for an early twentieth-century version of masculine identity" (78). Accordingly, "the reified sexuality embodied in Barkley ultimately will undercut Henry's masculinity" (88). It is Barkley who initiates the sex, who creates variants on both their intercourse and their identity as a couple—behavior that must be threatening to Frederic. Hatten concludes, "Barkley wishes that their sameness in desire will erase their differences in gender identity. Her desire for transgressions of gender boundaries is a crucial part of the couple's situation later in the novel." Not surprisingly, the new gender role "oppresses Henry" (95).

Hatten deals as well with two points that few critics have studied. He attributes Hemingway's making Frederic a deserter to his wanting to show how little the traditional codes of being masculine apply: "It is one of Hemingway's more daring moves to ask his readers to sympathize with a deserter from the Allied side . . . but only in this way can he make clear the emptiness of earlier public versions of masculinity" (92). And he sees that Henry's behavior while Catherine is in childbirth is nonmasculine because it is entirely passive. He can only wait. This is Hatten's argument:

> [D]ying stoically, she defeats Henry in the competition for status that began with her acceptance of their relationship's basis in desire. In dying bravely—she confronts the ultimate fear-inducing situation of death and masters it—in a feminine version of the battlefield, she achieves exactly the sort of heroic stature that persistently eludes Henry. (96)

The novel, then, grants heroism to a woman. "Barkley both defeats him at his own male game of bravery and deprives him of the traditional masculine role of protector of a woman." Yet, because Catherine plays by the male rules, "masculinity as an ideal is retained" (96).

Hatten also studies the language of A Farewell to Arms, and concludes that because Barkley is a woman, she can express her experiences. As she dies, she voices the disillusionment that brings together the war plot and the romance. Hatten sees that Hemingway's "selfconsciously virile prose" yet bears "an undercurrent of sentiment that contradicts conventional masculinity" (98).

Because Hemingway uses Catherine to express "this mostly masculine mood," he succeeds—according to Hatten—in conveying "his sense that masculinity in actuality . . . remains fragile and vulnerable" (97). Michael North, in his Reading 1922: A Return to the Scene of the Modern, supports Hatten's position as he notes that "There was the widespread male fear that 'nice wives' were no longer 'like that,' or worse, that they were 'like that' in something like the sense that Stein intended."[24] The questioning of apparent sexual alleigances showed the underlying fear that "women were changing and out of the more complex fear that something long taken for granted, something soft and comforting in a harshly instrumental world, something 'nice,' in a word, was being lost." North concludes, "The apparent division between the male world of tough talk and linguistic experiment and the conventionally female world of everyday sentimental language was . . . complex" (203).

Debra A. Moddelmog's *Reading Desire: In Pursuit of Ernest Hemingway* builds an even more extensive argument to keep readers from running immediately for the autobiographical interpretation. She explains that her book grew out of her surprise that critics and readers alike seemed hesitant to explore Hemingway's "sexual identity or his desires"—almost as if the great author's caveats about never invading his privacy had truly fenced this area off from investigation.[25] This critic invokes the interrogation of an earlier study, that by Nancy R. Comley and Robert Scholes, who suggest in their *Hemingway's Genders* that they were not trying to prove that Hemingway was gay, but rather that such a question "is too simple. . . . What we have been trying to show is that Hemingway was much more interested in these matters than has usually been supposed—and much more sensitive and complex in his consideration of them."[26] Broken open by the posthumous publication of Hemingway's *The Garden of Eden* in 1986, all critical reticence about sexual matters began to evaporate.

The significance of Moddelmog's book is that it questions so many tenets about Hemingway and his writing that readers had assumed were classically in place. What does being heroic mean? Why is a man's relationship with a woman so difficult? While she does not specifically read *A Farewell to Arms*, Moddelmog notes that the male characters in Hemingway's writing are seldom described (at least not so much as are the women characters) except in the matter of their shared wounds: "In most Hemingway novels, the male hero's injury is described in more detail than are the features of the man who endures it" (124). In all these figures, the wound connotes "the physical and moral superiority of white normative masculinity and heterosexuality. At the same time, the need to repeat this pattern reveals an underlying hysteria about this superiority." Drawing from Michael S. Kimmel's work,[27] she identifies Hemingway as seeming to desire "the male gaze, a homoerotic enactment" rather than just male friendship (172); she also reads Catherine Barkley as (at least) an "erotic go-between" in the case of Rinaldi and Frederic. While this is Peter F. Cohen's argument,[28] Moddelmog sees the suffusion of desire to run in several overlapping tracks—not only in *A Farewell to Arms* but in all Hemingway's writing. Her overall contention is that Hemingway's fiction consistently "problematizes" the areas of "masculinity/femininity, homosexuality/heterosexuality" by bringing "traditional significations of gender and sexuality into conflict." In both *The Garden of Eden* and *The Sun Also Rises*, and a number of works between them, Hemingway "exposes the intellectual limitations that result when 'gender' and 'sexuality' are read as innocent acts of nature and as fixed binaries"(92–93).

Part of the historical intrigue with Hemingway's concepts of masculinity and femininity, male and female, is that in many respects, Hemingway seemed very traditional—if not "smelling of the museums," in Gertrude Stein's words, at least late Victorian. Mark Spilka added to our understanding of how traditional Hemingway was, and of how rooted in the nineteenth century, in both British and United States culture, he remained: part of that intractable rootedness stemmed from the fact that Hemingway saw himself as an intellectually imposing writer. A deeper part, as Spilka points out in his *Hemingway's Quarrel with Androgyny*, resulted from his admiration for the great literatures. Hemingway could never truly become an innovative modernist because at heart he wanted to become a latter-day Rudyard Kipling, or even an Emily Brontë.[29]

LIONEL TRILLING AND THE HUMANISTS VERSUS THE MODERNS

Even before the concept of war, and war as an exclusively male activity, was being challenged by complex new critical ideas, the critical establishment had to find a way to intervene in the highly moralistic attempts to rid American literature of the pernicious influences of the moderns. Piqued at first by Hemingway's *The Sun Also Rises*, and then threatened further by William Faulkner's *Sanctuary*, the relentless narrative of Temple Drake's rape by a gang of bootleggers, readers who abjured the influence of the new generation (which they saw as a thoroughly lost one) took refuge in Comstockery. Books—like Henry Miller's, for example—could be banned; writers could be forced out of the establishment through angry reviews or poor sales—or both.

Lionel Trilling was one of the influential critics at mid-century who tried to give conservative readers ways to understand the modernists' experimental work. Robert Penn Warren was another. Men who revered good writing, and who were writers themselves, were faced with the dilemma of making the remarkable twentieth-century writing being done in the United States (work that was quickly appreciated abroad, as countless translations into foreign languages showed) somehow palatable, even of interest to traditionally trained readers and book buyers. One of Trilling's strategies was to make Hemingway (and Faulkner) religious enough to partake of the spirit of the age, the new, the twentieth century. There was currency in difference if it could be explained correctly.

Trilling's point was that Hemingway, like the greatest of novelists and short-story writers, is able to convey emotional truths that cannot be challenged. He discounts Faulkner's efforts to a certain extent (as if Faulkner's South were a country so remote from the East Coast that its values were incomprehensible) but makes great claims for Hemingway as the inheritor of the Russian novelists Tolstoy and Dostoyevski. He speaks of Hemingway's "negative capability, this willingness to remain in uncertainties, mysteries, and doubts,"[30] a stance that is not unintellectual, Trilling says, but rather the most intellectual (or perhaps the most philosophical) of all current postures. As Trilling delivers his basic premise—that American writers have seldom been philosophical, or certainly not religious in any formal way—he leaves Hemingway behind and continues his march into more expected meditative ground. The hint of existentialism marks Trilling's postwar prolegomenon, but it is interesting that his best examples of the fusion of emotion with intellect—and one aspect of what he sees as the newly modern—place Faulkner and, particularly, Hemingway squarely at the center of what is coming. As he says modestly, "The subject is extremely delicate and complex and I do no more than state it barely and crudely. But no matter how I state it, I am sure you will see that what I am talking about leads us to the crucial issue of our literary culture."[31]

Trilling's attempt to hold steady within a literary world that was being buffeted once more by winds of change—this time, by the postwar existentialism of Europe—staved off the kind of boredom that appeared to envelop Hemingway studies in the 1950s. Even as Philip Young, Carlos Baker, Charles Fenton, and Earl Rovit were publishing studies of Hemingway that would enhance the use of his writings in America's classrooms, within the complacent suburbs of United States cities, his narratives seemed less and less relevant: why did any reader care to be linked with the bullfighter in "The Undefeated"? what was the excitement about all the drinking in The Sun Also Rises, now that Prohibition was only a memory? where were those trout streams—that "Big Two-Hearted River"—in the environs of heavily industrialized America? Rather than being seen as a writer of violence, Hemingway began to feel a bit nostalgic. And most nostalgic of all was the painful war experience of what had become Hemingway's centerpiece work, A Farewell to Arms.

Hemingway's career flourished once again with the 1952 publication of his novella, The Old Man and the Sea, which captured the United States public when it appeared in a single issue of Life magazine, with Hemingway's face on its cover, and also was a Book-of-the-Month Club selection. That work brought him both the Pulitzer Prize for fiction (in 1953) and the Nobel Prize for literature in 1954, just five years after that award had gone to William Faulkner. Yet while the public had found Hemingway again in the 1950s, literary critics at mid-century were less interested in Hemingway's work than they had been during the 1920s and the 1930s. Abby H. P. Werlock points out that although Hemingway remained of interest to general readers, "among university professors Hemingway lost ground to William Faulkner at mid-century (from the 1940s into the 1960s)."[32]

Hemingway's brilliance in his choice of Santiago, the natural Cuban man of the life of endurance, allowed him to avoid portraying the United States or any of its social strata. If Hemingway had found American intellectuals to be effete, even unbearable, he could—until the last few pages of his parable—omit them entirely. (The fact that the observers of Santiago's skeletal catch could not identify it, or could only misidentify it, spoke to Hemingway's several letters from this period about the knowledge and integrity—especially the lack of the latter—of the critics who were, in his words, hounding him. About one critic he wrote "The man . . . is one of those who think that literary history, or the secret of creative writing, lies in old laundry lists."[33] By locating his story in the Cuban waters, Hemingway saved himself from attacking a number of American critics and scholars; in effect, Hemingway became nostalgic, or at least distant, himself. The ground swell of enthusiasm that led to his acquiring the prizes he had never before won showed that his choice of topic, and its treatment, was apt.

Had critical reaction to Hemingway's works ended with exploring the author's relationship to past American and British writing, to style, to violence, to literature as it coexisted with philosophy, or to the writer's own carefully constructed persona, there would be little need for this chapter. But after Hemingway's suicide in July 1961, critical opinion began to change. The fact of the author's taking his own life—no matter how ill or depressed he had come to be—colored readers' reactions to his writing. So long as the code formula remained in place, the actuality of Hemingway's life—and then his unexpected death—undermined what his various fictions supposedly taught. How bravely could Santiago bring in that stripped skeleton, when his own eyes showed him that bones meant nothing? How "undefeated" could the Hemingway legend remain, now that the author had killed himself?

ALCOHOLISM AND THE HEMINGWAY OEUVRE

Hemingway criticism began taking several other new directions. From John W. Crowley's 1994 study, *The White Logic: Alcoholism and Gender in American Modernist Fiction* came the concept that there is such a pattern in fiction as "the drunk narrative." Crowley describes the fictional portrayal of drinking as a way of both bonding among characters and a means of warding off the attentions of homosexuals. Crowley contends that "Hemingway uses drinking . . . to establish a hierarchy of moral merit for his characters."[34] (It is the "good drunks" we admire, for whatever reasons.) Drunkenness, however, carries with it "the threat of gender uncertainty. . . . [T]he male rummy is as unmanly as Brett [in *The Sun Also Rises*] is unwomanly" (57). What makes this chapter of Crowley's book important for Hemingway critics is that while he locates drinking as one of the essential male bonding devices, he concludes that, in Hemingway's fiction, "the strongest bonds among men are formed less by means of alcohol than in spite of it. Drinking as a proof of manhood is ultimately motivated for Hemingway by the power and presence of women beyond the charmed male circle" (62).

Crowley's study deals more thoroughly with his authors' writing than did those seminal studies of writers and their drinking (Tom Dardis' *The Thirsty Muse: Alcohol and the American Writer* [New York: Ticknor & Fields, 1989] and Donald W. Goodwin's *Alcohol and the Writer* [New York: Penguin, 1990]). Still more intricate in the way the authors interface Hemingway as alcoholic with his writing is a recent essay by Ellen Lansky, in which she links Hemingway with Djuna Barnes and uses the more easily understood *The Sun Also Rises* to pair with Barnes' *Nightwood* in order to show the debility of the alcoholic characters (and perhaps their creators, Hemingway and Barnes).[35] But it is Matts Djos in *The Hemingway Review* who makes the best case for the visible influence on Hemingway's style, themes, and characters of the concept that drinking indicates masculinity, and that one who survives a life of alcoholism is somehow heroic.[36] And Scott Donaldson adds in the definitive comparison of the illness of alcoholism in the lives of both Hemingway and Fitzgerald in his *Hemingway vs. Fitzgerald: The Rise and Fall of a Literary Friendship* (Woodstock, N.Y.: Overlook, 1999).

Just as Moddelmog was surprised that so few critics had interrogated Hemingway's sexual preferences, in relation to the fictions he wrote about sexuality, so today's reader might wonder at the fact that few readers had been concerned until the 1990s with the enormous amount of drinking in Hemingway's fiction—and in his life. Even while Shari Benstock's 1986 *Women of the Left Bank, Paris, 1910–1940* (Austin: University of Texas Press) was changing the landscape of what readers knew about all of modernism but particularly about expatriate writers—men as well as women—many critical patterns seemed to be set in stone. That a writer such as Hemingway frequented Natalie Barney's lesbian salon, or was content being the pet of not only Stein but Sylvia Beach and other strong American women in Paris, seemed of less concern to critics than his choices among endings for A *Farewell to Arms*. The dilemma was that even if the material to change readers' thinking was published, few readers made the necessary connections. Many of the books published during the later 1980s and the 1990s were somewhat retrospective, and they made it possible for critics to repeat the same kinds of commentary, to show the same kinds of attitudes, as they had learned in their first readings of Hemingway's fiction thirty, forty, or fifty years earlier.

HEMINGWAY AND RACE

Another theme that has recently come into Hemingway criticism, though slowly, is attention to the way Hemingway treats race difference. When Toni Morrison chose to write about Willa Cather and Ernest Hemingway in her Harvard lectures, published in 1992 as *Playing in the Dark: Whiteness and the Literary Imagination*, her commentary provoked much attention. (Since Morrison had written her M.A. thesis on Virginia Woolf and William Faulkner, had she spoken about those writers, her choices would have seemed less radical.) She allowed her audience to test her theory with Hemingway, a writer not usually discussed in terms of race. One of Morrison's points was that Hemingway frequently used people of color to emphasize the whiteness of his main characters; in her discussion of his *To Have and Have Not*, she refers to his choices of naming the black (or at times referring to him as "nigger") but more explicitly to the way Hemingway identified the black as representative of "outlaw sexuality." As Morrison explains,

> Here [*To Have and Have Not*] we see Africanism used as a fundamental fictional technique by which to establish character. Within a milieu that threatens the dissolution of all distinctions of value—the milieu of the working poor, the unemployed, sinister Chinese, terrorist Cubans, violent but cowardly blacks, upper-class castrati, female predators—Harry and Marie (an ex-prostitute) gain potency, a generative sexuality. They solicit our admiration by the comparison that is struck between their claims to fully embodied humanity and a discredited Africanism. The voice of the text is complicit in these formulations: Africanism becomes not only a means of displaying authority but, in fact, constitutes its source.[37]

In Morrison's schema, Hemingway's *The Garden of Eden*—in its pub-lished version—becomes a labyrinth of Africanist tropes (especially the eroticism of hair and skin) that gives confused gender and racial signals to any reader. His *True at First Light* would only compound the problem.

Morrison's focus aided younger critics in their perceptions. Carl P. Eby's essay "'Come Back to the Raft Ag'in, David Honey!': Hemingway's Fetishization of Race in *The Garden of Eden* Manuscripts" appeared recently in his important book, *Hemingway's Fetishism: Psychoanalysis and the Mirror of Manhood*, to clarify the way sexuality and sexual concerns influenced much about Hemingway's fiction. Similarly, Amy Lovell Strong's investigation of Hemingway's Indian imaginary provided new ground. Her "Screaming through Silence: The Violence of Race in 'Indian Camp' and 'The Doctor and the Doctor's Wife'" appeared first in *The Hemingway Review*, 1996.[38]

THE NEWEST TRENDS IN CRITICISM
OF *A FAREWELL TO ARMS*

To describe the critical reception of *A Farewell to Arms* as if those 1929 and 1930 reviews were even the start of the story is to simplify the way Hemingway lived his life as writer. There is a great deal more. Very recent essays on the novel specifically also show the influence of new critical approaches. Jennifer A. Haytock's "Hemingway's Soldiers and Their Preg-nant Women: Domestic Ritual in World War I," crosses from textual analysis into genre definition (*Hemingway Review* 19 [Spring 2000], pp. 57–72). Steven Trout's "'Where Do We Go From Here?' Ernest Heming-way's 'Soldier's Home' and American Veterans of World War I" contextu-alizes the fictional dilemma of Harold Krebs within the actual lives of returning men (*Hemingway Review* 20 [Fall 2000], pp. 5–21). Matthew C. Stewart's "Ernest Hemingway and World War I: Combatting Recent Psy-chobiographical Reassessments, Restoring the War," (*Papers on Language and Literature* 36 [2000], pp. 198–217) gives a new historicist reading. Mil-ton A. Cohen's "Soldiers' Voices in *In Our Time*: Hemingway's Ventrilo-quism?" provides a linguistic approach to the various speakers of the stories and vignettes (*Hemingway Review* 20 [Fall 2000], pp. 22–29). Gary Har-rington's "Partial Articulation: Word Play in *A Farewell to Arms*" is a lin-guistically based psychoanalytic reading of dialogue (*Hemingway Review* 20 [Spring 2001], pp. 59–75). For an emphasis on race and ethnicity, Ronald Berman's *Fitzgerald, Hemingway, and the Twenties* (Tuscaloosa: University of Alabama Press, 2000), has a quantity of new information.

NOTES

1. Ford Madox Ford, "Introduction to Ernest Hemingway, A *Farewell to Arms*" (1932), p. 246.

2. Ibid., p. 251. Notorious in his later criticism of Ford, in the posthumously published *A Moveable Feast*, Hemingway at this stage of his career knew enough to avoid running headlong into Ford's personal and literary power.

3. Ibid., p. 250.

4. Ibid., p. 251.

5. Peter L. Hays' recent essay, "Hemingway's *The Sun Also Rises* and James's *The Ambassadors*" is the definitive reading of the similarities between these novels [*Hemingway Review* 20, no. 2 (Spring 2001), pp. 90–98]. And see Kirk Curnutt, *Ernest Hemingway and the Expatriate Modernist Movement* (New York: Gale, 2000).

6. Claude Caswell makes this point, that many of Hemingway's references to entertainment in Paris have to do with prostitution ("City of Brothelly Love: The Influence of Paris and Prostitution on Hemingway's Fiction," in *French Connections: Hemingway and Fitzgerald Abroad*, ed. J. Gerald Kennedy and Jackson R. Bryer (New York: St. Martin's, 1998), pp. 75–100.

7. Dorothy Parker, "Review of *Men Without Women*," *New Yorker* (October 27, 1927), pp. 92–94, in *Ernest Hemingway: Six Decades of Criticism* (E. Lansing: Michigan State University Press, 1987), pp. 163–165.

8. Claude McKay, *A Long Way from Home* (New York: Lee Furman, 1937), pp. 249–252, in Ibid., pp. 167–169.

9. J. Gerald Kennedy and Jackson R. Bryer, "Recovering the French Connections of Hemingway and Fitzgerald," *French Connections* (New York: St. Martin's, 1998), pp. vi–xv, this p. viii.

10. Paul Rosenfeld, "Tough Earth," *New Republic* (November 1925), pp. 22–23, in *Ernest Hemingway: Six Decades of Criticism* (E. Lansing: Michigan State University Press, 1987), pp. 61–63.

11. Marc Dolan, *Modern Lives: A Cultural Re-reading of "The Lost Generation"* (West Lafayette, IN: Purdue University Press, 1996), p. 160.

12. Ray B. West, Jr., "The Unadulterated Sensibility," *The Art of Modern Fiction* (New York: Holt, Rinehart & Winston, 1949), pp. 139–151.

13. Hemingway to Maxwell Perkins, 1933, *Letters*, p. 400.

14. Hemingway to Charles Poore, 1953, *Letters*, p. 800.

15. Hemingway to Thomas Bledsoe, 1951, *Letters*, p. 745.

16. Kelli A. Larson, "Bibliographical Essay: Lies, Damned Lies, and Hemingway Criticism," *A Historical Guide to Ernest Hemingway* (New York: Oxford University Press, 2000), pp. 213–234, this p. 216.

17. Hemingway to Philip Young, 1952, *Letters*, pp. 760–761.

18. Hemingway to Maxwell Perkins, 1926, *Letters*, p. 240.

19. Scott Donaldson, *Hemingway vs. Fitzgerald* (Woodstock, NY: Overlook, 1998), pp. 290–291.

20. Sandra M. Gilbert and Susan Gubar, *No Man's Land*, Vol. I, *The War of the Words* (New Haven: Yale University Press, 1988), epigraph page.

21. Jane Marcus, "Corpus/Corps/Corpse: Writing the Body in/at War," *Arms and the Woman: War, Gender, and Literary Representation* (Chapel Hill, University of North Carolina Press, 1989), pp. 124–167, this excerpt p. 135.

22. Valerie Rohy, *Impossible Women, Lesbian Figures and American Literature* (Ithaca, N.Y.: Cornell University Press, 2000), p. 67.

23. Charles Hatten, "The Crisis of Masculinity, Reified Desire, and Catherine Barkley in *A Farewell to Arms*," *Journal of the History of Sexuality* 4, no. 11 (1993), pp. 76–98; hereafter cited in text.

24. Michael North, *Reading 1922: A Return to This Scene of the Modern* (New York: Oxford University Press, 2000), p. 203.

25. Debra A. Moddelmog, *Reading Desire: In Pursuit of Ernest Hemingway* (Ithaca, NY: Cornell University Press, 1999), p. 3; hereafter cited in text.

26. Nancy R. Comley and Robert Scholes, *Hemingway's Genders: Rereading the Hemingway Text* (New Haven, CT: Yale University Press, 1994), pp. 143–144.

27. Michael S. Kimmel, "Masculinity as Homophobia: Fear, Shame, and Silence in the Construction of Gender Identity," *Theorizing Masculinities*, ed. Harry Brod and Michael Kaufman (Thousand Oaks: Sage, 1994).

28. Peter F. Cohen, "'I Won't Kiss You. . . . I'll Send Your English Girl': Homoerotic Desire in *A Farewell to Arms*," *Hemingway Review* 15, no. 1 (Autumn 1995).

29. Mark Spilka, *Hemingway's Quarrel with Androgyny* (Lincoln: University of Nebraska Press, 1990), and see Richard Lehan, "Hemingway Among the Moderns," *Hemingway in Our Time*, ed. Richard Astro and Jackson J. Benson (Corvallis: Oregon State University Press, 1974), pp. 191–212.

30. Lionel Trilling, "Contemporary American Literature in Its Relation to Ideas," *The American Writer and the European Tradition*, ed. Margaret Denny and William H. Gilman (New York: McGraw-Hill, 1950), p. 149.

31. Ibid., Trilling specifically notes that in Hemingway's writing "a strongly charged piety toward the ideals and attachments of boyhood and the lusts of maturity is in conflict not only with the imagination of death but also with that imagination as it is peculiarly modified by the dark negation of the modern world" (p. 148).

32. Abby H. P. Werlock, "Review of *A Historical Guide to Ernest Hemingway*," *Hemingway Review* 20, no. 2 (Fall 2000), p. 108.

33. Hemingway to Dorothy Connable, 1953, *Letters*, p. 131.

34. John W. Crowley, *The White Logic: Alcoholism and Gender in American Modernist Fiction* (Amherst: University of Massachusetts Press, 1994).

35. Ellen Lansky, "The Barnes Complex: Ernest Hemingway, Djuna Barnes, *The Sun Also Rises*, and *Nightwood*," *The Languages of Addiction*, ed. Jane Lilienfeld and Jeffrey Oxford (New York: St. Martin's, 1999), pp. 205–224.

36. Matts Djos, "Alcoholism in Ernest Hemingway's *The Sun Also Rises*: A Wine and Roses Perspective on the Lost Generation," *A Casebook on Ernest Hemingway's* The Sun Also Rises, ed. Linda Wagner-Martin (New York: Oxford University Press, 2001), pp. 139–53.

37. Toni Morrison, *Playing in the Dark: Whiteness and the Literary Imagination* (New York: Vintage, 1992), p. 80.

38. Both the Eby and Strong essays are reprinted in my *Hemingway: Seven Decades of Criticism* (E. Lansing: Michigan State University Press, 1998), pp. 329–348 and 29–44.

8 Bibliographic Essay

This essay deals with the world of secondary criticism, the work profes-
sional critics and scholars have done for seventy-five years as they expli-
cate, critique, and interpret the writing of Ernest Hemingway. There is an
immense quantity of criticism, and new electronic delivery modes add
materials to the print archive exponentially. As bibliographer Albert J.
Defazio wrote recently, Hemingway scholars need to set up a cyber system
that would become "a communication super-highway." Because the field
of Hemingway criticism is "expanding at such a rate that we all, no matter how dedicated, simply can't keep up with the information," Hemingway scholars "should organize our information, make it available, and
provide a human mechanism for sifting knowledge from the information"
("Biblio-Files: Notions from a Decade of Annotation," *Hemingway
Review* 20 [Fall 2000], 97–103).

Defazio's own Hemingway bibliographies, published twice a year in the
journal *Hemingway Review* help readers stay current; so too do his survey
chapters on Hemingway and Fitzgerald, written each year for *American
Literary Scholarship: An Annual* (Durham, N.C.: Duke University Press,
year by year). This series of scholarly books involves an intricate process:
all the criticism in print is recorded in the MLA bibliography. The editor
of each chapter in *American Literary Scholarship: An Annual* is provided
with the listing of all material published in, for example, 1998. During
1999, the editor finds and reads each book and essay, and then writes a
chapter that assesses that material published in 1998. This compendium

of useful chapters then appears in book form during the year 2000. Because of the lag time between the MLA record being complete and the editor doing all the work required, there is a two-year hiatus for readers. For example, the *American Literary Scholarship* volume published in the summer of 2002 will include assessments of criticism that was published during the year 2000.

Susan Beegel, the Hemingway scholar who edits *The Hemingway Review*, is also a good bibliographer. Her most recent work of this nature is "Conclusion: The Critical Reputation of Ernest Hemingway" included in Scott Donaldson's *The Cambridge Companion to Hemingway* (Cambridge, UK: Cambridge University Press, 1996).

Another important Hemingway bibliographer is Kelli A. Larson, whose recent publications include her bibliographical essay in *A Historical Guide to Ernest Hemingway* (New York: Oxford University Press, 2000) and "Stepping into the Labyrinth: Fifteen Years of Hemingway Scholarship," in *Hemingway: Up in Michigan Perspectives*, ed. Frederic J. Svoboda and Joseph J. Waldmeir (E. Lansing: Michigan State University Press, 1995), 275–82. These essays are a continuation of her work as the author of *Ernest Hemingway: A Reference Guide, 1974–1989* (G. K. Hall, 1991). Standard bibiographical print sources are the first of these Hall reference guides, Linda W. Wagner's *Ernest Hemingway: A Reference Guide* published in 1977, annotations through 1974 and the original bibliographic work, Audre Hanneman's *Ernest Hemingway: A Comprehensive Bibliography* (Princeton, NJ: Princeton University Press, 1967) and its supplements. The very first "bibliographic" work was of primary sources, Louis H. Cohn's *A Bibliography of the Works of Ernest Hemingway* (New York: Random House, 1931).

All responsible critics should also be bibliographers, and most are. But the practice in book publication during the 1980s and the 1990s has been to delete what had been the customary ending section, a bibliographic listing of useful sources, whether or not those sources were quoted from within the text. To save both space and money, most books in the past twenty years have included only material that appears in actual notes, either footnotes or endnotes. It thus became possible for younger students of Hemingway's writing to be well-grounded in criticism and yet entirely unfamiliar about books that had long been considered key, even seminal, studies of the writer's work. Perhaps worse, these important studies—no longer read—themselves became the targets of criticism: we have already seen how Philip Young's 1952 *Ernest Hemingway* (New York: Rinehart) became the whipping boy for all psychoanalytic criticism, even though most of what Young contends in his book is eminently credible.

EARLY BOOKS OF SECONDARY CRITICISM

To discuss Philip Young's *Ernest Hemingway* is to point to the state of criticism on this writer at the midpoint of the century. Aside from informed essays by half a dozen critics, among them Malcolm Cowley, Robert Penn Warren, and Edmund Wilson, much of the secondary criticism in print during the 1940s and the 1950s was in the form of book reviews. (Book reviewers are, by definition, popular writers, journalists rather than scholars, and their aim is to publish in newspapers and magazines—in order to sell, or to discourage the reader from buying, a book.) Young's study was written in a less formal—almost a novelistic—style, and was commercially published; it was intended for the general reader. The book touched on the issues readers were most curious about: the sparse Hemingway style, the character of "Nick Adams" as a young Hemingway surrogate, the vitiating wound and its consequences, the "code" of seemingly stoic behavior men must adopt, and Hemingway's place in American letters, particularly the correspondence between his work and Mark Twain's fiction.

Young has been maligned for his tendency to exaggerate events in Hemingway's life: his account of the 1918 wounding, for example, leaves *three* of "the Italian soldiers who were with him" dead—"All three of them had their legs blown off," (135). The one who was still alive, "Living but legless," was carried by the badly wounded Hemingway "back toward the trenches." It was at that moment that Hemingway was machine-gunned. Unfortunately, in 1952 when Young's book appeared, Carlos Baker's biography was not even started. What information existed about Hemingway's life came from the stories people—including Hemingway—told, and from the writer's fiction. The collapsing of *A Farewell to Arms* onto the life of the author created a number of errors. (Admittedly, Young's prose style here created another layer of fictionality.)

The fact that Young was explaining Sigmund Freud, especially his *Beyond the Pleasure Principle* and its concepts of "repetition-compulsion," within his commentary on Hemingway's writing was his attempt to educate readers. But it could also be seen as a reductionary strategy: once the reader knew Freud, all of Ernest Hemingway became clear. (This appeared to be Hemingway's objection to Young's work.)

It bears reminding today's readers that Freud's work was less familiar to mid-century readers than it has become today. And another element of the content for Young's 1952 study was the fact that the United States was in its own recovery period following World War II. Young's emphasis on war injuries—and characters' involvement in military struggles—was more germane to the times than it might appear to be today in this twenty-first century. Two of Hemingway's most significant novels—*A Farewell to Arms* and the 1940 *For Whom the Bell Tolls*—were war novels. When Young takes the military model to describe what he calls "the myth of America"—"the breakdown of peace" that dominated much of the twentieth century, in his concluding chapter, his method seems reasonable.

Charles A. Fenton's *The Apprenticeship of Ernest Hemingway: The Early Years* was another commercially published study (brought out by Viking in 1954). Fenton had attempted to research the writer's development through his various kinds of journalism and the still-garbled information about his childhood, adolescence, and young manhood. He too was interested in the role World War I had played in Hemingway's development; Fenton's only other published work was an anthology of short fiction from World War II. His approach in writing about the wounding in 1918, however, was to quote Hemingway on the situation, rather than to provide his own descriptions of events; for example, from *Green Hills of Africa*, Fenton quotes Hemingway, "I thought . . . about what a great advantage an experience of war was to a writer. It was one of the major subjects and certainly one of the hardest to write truly of and those writers who had not seen it were always very jealous and tried to make it seem unimportant, or abnormal, or a disease as a subject, while, really, it was just something quite irreplaceable that they had missed." Moderate in style, Fenton's chief contribution in this book is a detailed assessment of Hemingway's journalism, particularly the extensive writing he did in the 1920s about European wars.

Criticism increased terrifically once Hemingway published *The Old Man and the Sea* and won both the Pulitzer Prize for fiction and the Nobel Prize for literature in 1954. That such accolades were, sadly, followed by Hemingway's visible decline, by rumors of his serious illness, and by his 1961 suicide, provided even more reason for studies to be written. By the 1960s, a number of important critical books were seeing print: in 1963, both Carlos Baker's *Hemingway: The Writer as Artist* (Princeton, NJ: Princeton University Press) and Earl Rovit's *Ernest Hemingway* (New

York: Twayne) appeared. Each one provided valuable, and consistently well-supported, information. Baker, as his title indicated, tried to unearth the driving principles for Hemingway's achievement in writing. Like Fenton, Baker read the short fiction and the journalism as well as the so-considered "major" novels. Rovit covered all of Hemingway's writing, and a chapter on the author's biography, because that was the mandate of the important Twayne series of criticism on writers. Although necessarily formulaic, the Twayne books have been invaluable additions to secondary criticism, particularly on contemporary or lesser-known writers. Both of these studies remain significant.

Joseph M. DeFalco adopted much of Young's critical point of view in his 1963 book, *The Hero in Hemingway's Short Stories* (Pittsburgh: University of Pittsburgh Press). Issues of heroism were central both during the 1960s and in criticism of *A Farewell to Arms* specifically. It was in Leo Gurko's 1967 study, *Ernest Hemingway and the Pursuit of Heroism* (New York: Crowell) that the definition of *hero* became more complicated. Reading structurally, Gurko rightly saw that Hemingway's narrative method was not encyclopedic: "Instead, he evaluated his men and women by their reaction to some deliberately contrived strain. . . . The crisis situation, the breaking point, is his chief, almost his sole concern" (228). Despite that insight, Gurko finds Frederic Henry, along with Catherine Barkley, to be heroic in *A Farewell to Arms*.

Delbert E. Wylder, however, writing in his 1967 *Hemingway's Heroes* (Albuquerque: University of New Mexico Press), left Frederic out of the equation and emphasized that in the course of the novel Catherine becomes the prototypical Hemingway "hero" (66–95). With the obvious masculinist bias in reading Hemingway, few people would have made that move to describe Catherine as a superior hero. Wylder's book might be said to be the first feminist reading of *A Farewell to Arms*, as well as other of Hemingway's novels. Wylder sees his book as providing a direction different from the Young-inspired Freudian approaches: "The progressive hero concept, though continually being modified, is also restrictive at times, especially when the hero is too closely tied to the life of the man Ernest Hemingway and the legend he helped to create. . . . [T]he Hemingway novels are quite different in conception and technique and . . . the protagonists are distinctly different characters" (223–224).

Robert W. Lewis had found the qualities of Frederic Henry less than heroic, too, in his 1965 *Hemingway on Love* (Austin: University of Texas Press). Other mid-1960s books that dealt less often with this novel included Constance C. Montgomery's useful *Hemingway in Michigan* (New York: Fleet, 1966) and Philip Young's *Hemingway: A Reconsideration* (University Park, PA: Pennsylvania State University Press, 1966). For Sheridan Baker, writing in *Ernest Hemingway* (New York: Holt, Rinehart, 1967), the issues of interpretation went far beyond which character was or wasn't heroic. And for Richard B. Hovey, writing in his controversial (again, fairly psychoanalytic) book *Hemingway: The Inward Terrain* (Seattle: University of Washington Press, 1968), most of Hemingway's fiction was of interest chiefly because of the way it interfaced with what was known of the author himself.

Perhaps the most useful book of 1968 was Robert O. Stephens's *Hemingway's Nonfiction* (Chapel Hill: University of North Carolina Press). Encyclopedic in his knowledge, Stephens brought to bear in discussions of the ostensible nonfiction—including the problematic *Death in the Afternoon* and *Green Hills of Africa*—all kinds of information about Hemingway's fiction, as well as his life. And perhaps the most useful book of 1969 was Jackson J. Benson's *Hemingway: The Writer's Art of Self-Defense* (Minneapolis: University of Minnesota Press). Avoiding the too-biographical and too-psychoanalytic approaches, Benson yet forced readers to see how much the artistry of Hemingway's work became his persona, that Hemingway saw himself as only a writer. What that self-definition meant to twentieth-century American literature has seldom been so well expressed, and so thoroughly explored.

Like Wylder's, Benson's reading also makes use of gendered and sex-linked interpretations. Part of its strength comes from his acknowledgment that Hemingway does use and emphasize the masculine point of view. Benson sees that choice as just one segment of Hemingway's overall criticism of "emotionalism in general," along with the "entire 'romance' attitude toward life" (28). This critic thinks that Hemingway's primary interest throughout his fiction was on depicting male-female relationships as ideal, sexual, and joyful: "Hemingway embraces pleasure as the substance of love" (29).

In 1972 Arthur Waldhorn's *A Reader's Guide to Ernest Hemingway* (New York: Farrar, Straus, Giroux) also provides a well-informed textual reading. His view of *A Farewell to Arms* is as "Hemingway's first full-scale treatment of mortality" (114). For all its comparisons with the short stories and *The Sun Also Rises*, however, *A Farewell to Arms* "does not end in total negation. Like Jake and Nick, Frederic is an apprentice who must master the paradox that life can be full even though empty. And he must learn too that courage and compassion animate humanity even when uncontrollable forces threaten to quench the last glimmer of hope" (115).

BOOKS ABOUT A FAREWELL TO ARMS

In addition to collections of critical essays devoted entirely to *A Farewell to Arms*, there are three books that study the novel exclusively. The first, and most helpful, is Michael S. Reynolds' *Hemingway's First War: The Making of a Farewell to Arms* (Princeton, NJ: Princeton University Press, 1976). Divided into three sections, the study tries to replace the almost legendary tales of the author and this novel as historical treatments of World War I. Part I disabuses the reader of most of the biographical fallacies; it also treats the manuscript versions of the novel. Part II assembles a number of documentary and historical accounts of the battles of the First World War and creates a multidimensional set of source materials that Hemingway might well have known. Part III reads the novel itself, first as "travel literature" and then as the complex novel other critics had found it to be. By giving readers a great deal more information than had ever been available, even if some of the links had to remain speculative, Reynolds clarified, and corrected, most readers' views of *A Farewell to Arms*.

The publication of this book pointed critics to the fact that the Hemingway Collection was being catalogued and indexed in the Boston area, ready to be placed into the John F. Kennedy Library once that building was completed. For the first time, a number of letters by the author as well as countless manuscripts and draft pages of the Hemingway texts were accessible to scholars. Bernard Oldsey's *Hemingway's Hidden Craft: The Writing of A Farewell to Arms* (University Park: Pennsylvania State University Press, 1979) makes exhaustive use of those manuscripts. In its graceful and compact presentation of draft materials, Oldsey's book created a new kind of Hemingway criticism: one more factual, more based in sometimes tedious reading and comparing of versions of a page, a paragraph, a story, and one less subject to the whims of the reader-critic. Hemingway's own drafts, complete with their changes, became the authority for this kind of criticism of the work.

Oldsey's book presents in appendixes versions of both the opening and the many endings. Its four textual chapters concern Hemingway's listing and choices of titles for the novel, an assessment of how large a role the author's biography plays in the formulation of *A Farewell to Arms*, and a thorough discussion of both the openings of the novel and its closings. His very interesting Part III describes what seems to be the fact that Hemingway had once started *A Farewell to Arms* with Frederic Henry's arrival in Milan, where getting him to a hospital room is done with great difficulty. Oldsey concludes, "Hemingway composed the opening and the eleven other essential chapters that constitute Book One of *A Farewell to Arms* as an afterthought" (58). Once in the hospital room, interestingly, in this first version, there is no Miss Barkley at all.

Robert W. Lewis's much later *A Farewell to Arms: The War of the Words* (New York: Twayne, 1992) is a useful compendium of much extant criticism. It seldom goes beyond accepted readings, although Lewis devotes many pages to Hemingway's characterization of both Frederic and Catherine.

THE BIOGRAPHIES OF ERNEST HEMINGWAY

Running concurrent with these critical studies have been the numerous biographies of Ernest Hemingway. Soon after his death, in 1962, two books by family members were published: Leicester Hemingway's *My Brother: Ernest Hemingway* appeared from World Publishing (Cleveland) and Marcelline H. Sanford's *At the Hemingways: A Family Portrait* was published by Little Brown Boston. Leicester's account described his being the younger brother (younger by fifteen years) who was himself a frustrated writer; Marcelline's tried to put a placid, even boring, face on a group of people whose lives were bound to be incompatible (the reissue of *At the Hemingways* includes letters between Ernest and Marcelline, and is contextualized differently because of that correspondence).

The first biography of the writer was Carlos Baker's *Ernest Hemingway: A Life Story* (New York: Scribner's, 1969). In many respects valid still, Baker erred in deferring too much to Mary Hemingway and the family; but that is a charge to be taken by most first biographers. In factual information, compressed scene, and the ability to draw consummate conclusions from a quantity of fact, Baker wrote a superb book. He might have treated Hemingway's writing to a greater extent, but he had already written both his own study and served as editor of a collection of criticism on Hemingway's four major novels. Baker was the most authoritative critic, as well as *the* biographer.

Other family members published memoirs during the 1970s (Madelaine Hemingway Miller's *Ernie: Hemingway's Sister "Sunny" Remembers* [New York: Crown, 1975] and son Gregory Hemingway's *Papa: A Per-*

sonal Memoir [Boston: Houghton Mifflin, 1976]) as did Mary Welsh Hemingway, the widow, in 1976: her definitive but disappointing *How It Was* (New York: Knopf). The only other biography was Scott Donaldson's 1977 *By Force of Will: The Life and Art of Ernest Hemingway* (New York: Viking). In 1983, Bernice Kert provided much previously unknown information in her study of Hemingway's wives and his mother, *The Hemingway Women* (New York: Norton).

In 1985 Jeffrey Meyers published his somewhat derivative *Hemingway: A Biography* (New York: Harper & Row), followed in 1987 by the controversial one-volume Kenneth Lynn, *Hemingway* (New York: Simon & Schuster). It was Lynn's emphasis on the "twinning" of Ernest and Marcelline, complete with the alternation of overalls and dresses for school, that began to counter the long-standing notion of the wound as seminal. Lynn formulated these childhood experiences as an even more pervasive "wound." Two excellent biographers were beginning multivolume projects: in 1985, Peter Griffin's *Along with Youth* (New York: Oxford University Press) appeared, followed in 1986 by Michael Reynolds' *The Young Hemingway* (Cambridge, MA: Basil Blackwell). (Second volumes by each appeared several years later: Peter Griffin's *Less Than a Treason* [New York, Oxford, University Press 1990] and Michael Reynolds' *Hemingway: The Paris Years* [Cambridge, MA: Basil Blackwell, 1989]. Reynolds' third volume, *Hemingway: The American Homecoming*, appeared from Blackwell in 1992.)

Among recent biographies are James R. Mellow's one-volume *Hemingway: A Life Without Consequences* (Boston: Houghton Mifflin, 1992), which was uniformly well-received; Gioia Diliberto's *Hadley* (New York: Ticknor & Fields, 1992), a second biography of Hemingway's first wife; the last two volumes of the Michael Reynolds' monumental (and definitive) project—*Hemingway: The 1930s* (Norton, 1997) and *Hemingway: The Final Years* (New York: Norton, 1999); and Scott Donaldson's biography of two writers as their lives intersected, *Hemingway vs. Fitzgerald, The Rise and Fall of a Literary Friendship* (Woodstock, NY: Overlook, 1999). Michael Reynolds died before completing his one-volume edition of the biography; it is unknown whether that work will be completed by someone else.

THE JOURNALS, LETTERS, AND LIBRARY LISTINGS

According to Susan Beegel, editor of *The Hemingway Review*, "The 1970s also marked the real beginning of a phenomenon known as the

'Hemingway industry.'" So many critics were now at work on Hemingway that the available spectrum of generalist journals could not accommodate their productivity. In 1970, Matthew J. Bruccoli founded *The Fitzgerald-Hemingway Annual* to provide an additional forum for publication. When this journal folded in 1979, Kenneth Rosen picked up the torch and created *Hemingway Notes*, a publication devoted exclusively to Hemingway studies and still going strong today as *The Hemingway Review* ("Conclusion: The Critical Reputation of Ernest Hemingway," *The Cambridge Companion to Hemingway*, ed. Scott Donaldson [Cambridge, UK: Cambridge University Press, 1996], 283).

The greatest impetus to continuing study of Hemingway, particularly to biography of the writer, was the 1981 publication of *Ernest Hemingway: Selected Letters, 1917–1961*. Edited by Carlos Baker, against the express wish of the author, the letters fueled readers' ire as well as their interest. The information in the letters has been invaluable, and plans are in place by the Ernest Hemingway Foundation to collect and publish what will be a multivolume edition of the many as-yet-unpublished Hemingway letters. Other valuable sources that appeared during the 1980s were Michael Reynolds' *Hemingway's Reading, 1910–1940* (Princeton, NJ: Princeton University Press, 1981) and James D. Brasch's and Joseph Sigman's *Hemingway's Library: A Composite Record* (Boston: Garland, 1981).

THE POSTHUMOUSLY PUBLISHED WORKS

Although Hemingway died in 1961, Scribner's publishing house kept his works before the public. In 1964 his Paris memoir, *A Moveable Feast*, had been published; in 1970, his unfinished novel, *Islands in the Stream*; and in 1972, edited by Philip Young, *The Nick Adams Stories*, including segments of texts that had not been previously in print.

Once Scribner's published Hemingway's unfinished novel *The Garden of Eden* in 1986, edited by Tom Jenks, many more psychoanalytic, feminist, and sexualized readings appeared. The simple descriptor "macho" seemed false: the author was clearly interested in same-sex liaisons and passions, despite his façade of disdain for arrangements other than the heterosexual. The recent publication of Hemingway's *True at First Light*, a work sometimes referred to as "the African book," edited by his son Patrick Hemingway, will not impact secondary criticism quite so much—but it does make the reader return to themes of race, the primitive, and the exotic. The single best book on these posthumously published works is Rose Marie Burwell's *Hemingway: The Postwar Years and the Posthumous Novels* (Cambridge, UK: Cambridge University Press, 1996).

With the appearance of *The Garden of Eden* in 1986, the composition of secondary criticism on Hemingway's works began to change: an appreciable increase in women critics who were publishing was evident. According to Susan Beegel, "Following publication of *The Garden of Eden*, the number of women in Hemingway studies doubled again, and today women account for 29 percent of published scholarship" (*Cambridge Companion*, 290–291). As Linda Wagner-Martin mentioned in her introduction to her third "decades" of criticism collection, "Nearly all critics included in both the earlier books [*Ernest Hemingway: Five Decades of Criticism*, 1974, and *Ernest Hemingway: Six Decades of Criticism*, 1987] were male—a statement that reflects on the sexual composition of scholars and teachers in post-secondary institutions as much as it does on the composition of collective Hemingway scholars. The *Seven Decades* collection, in contrast, is comprised of more than 40 percent women scholars' work" (*Hemingway: Seven Decades of Criticism* [E. Lansing: Michigan State University Press, 1998], 11).

Any listing of recent books of secondary criticism would disappoint the reader who immediately begins to expect work by women scholars to flood the market. There are, however, hundreds of excellent essays by those scholars, and with time, they will publish books. Meanwhile, Lawrence Broer and Gloria Holland have compiled a book of essays on Hemingway by only women scholars. *Hemingway and Women: Female Critics and the Female Voice* was published in 2002 by Alabama University Press. Linda Wagner-Martin's *A Historical Guide to Ernest Hemingway*, published in 2000 by Oxford University Press, included new essays by Jamie Barlowe, Marilyn Elkins, Susan Beegel, Frederic Svoboda, Kelli A. Larson and the editor. Such critics—among others—such as Nina Baym, Linda Patterson Miller, Wendy Martin, Mimi Reisel Gladstein, Ann Edwards Boutelle, Carol Gelderman, Blanche Gelfant, Cathy N. Davidson, Susan Shillinglaw, Pamela Smiley, Sibbie O'Sullivan, Susan S. Lanser, Charlene Murphy, Kathy Willingham, Jacqueline Tavernier-Courbin, Rena Sanderson, Hilary K. Justice, Alice H. Farley, Fern Kory, Barbara Lounsberry, Judy Jo Small, Genevieve Hily-Mane, Elizabeth Dewberry, Nina M. Ray, Shari Benstock, and Mariam B. Mandel as well as those already mentioned in this reference guide, have contributed important essays. Jamie Barlowe-Kayes' essay "Re-Reading Women: The Example of Catherine Barkley" describes the ways criticism by women scholars is sometimes overlooked within the field (in my *Ernest Hemingway: Seven Decades of Criticism*, 1998, 171–184).

In the last decades of the twentieth century, key critical studies included Joseph Flora's *Hemingway's Nick Adams* (Baton Rouge: Louisiana State University Press, 1982), Gerry Brenner's *Concealments in Hemingway's Works* (Columbus: Ohio State University Press, 1983), Norberto Fuentes' *Hemingway in Cuba* (New York: Lyle Stuart, 1984), John Raeburn's *Fame Became of Him: Hemingway as Public Writer* (Bloomington, IN: Indiana University Press, 1984), Mark Spilka's *Hemingway's Quarrel with Androgyny* (Lincoln: University of Nebraska Press, 1990), Paul Smith's *A Reader's Guide to the Short Stories of Ernest Hemingway* (New York: Hall, 1989), Robert Scholes and Nancy R. Comley's *Hemingway's Genders: Rereading the Hemingway Text* (New Haven, CT: Yale University Press, 1994), Robert E. Fleming's *The Face in the Mirror: Hemingway's Writers* (Tuscaloosa: University of Alabama Press, 1994), Carl Eby's *Hemingway's Fetishism: Psychoanalysis and the Mirror of Manhood* (Albany: State University of New York Press, 1999), and Debra A. Moddelmog's *Reading Desire: In Pursuit of Ernest Hemingway* (Ithaca, NY: Cornell University Press, 1999).

To close this bibliographical essay, two very important collections of essays deserve mention. Edited by J. Gerald Kennedy and Jackson R. Bryer, some of the essays from the 1994 Hemingway-Fitzgerald conference in Paris appear in *French Connections, Hemingway and Fitzgerald Abroad* (New York: St. Martin's, 1998). Whether the essays treat one or the other of the pair, each does a commendable job of being current, well-grounded, and critically sophisticated. Among the most interesting are Claude Caswell's "City of Brothelly Love: The Influence of Paris and Prostitution on Hemingway's Fiction," Ruth Prigozy's "Fitzgerald, Paris, and the Romantic Imagination," Felipe Smith's "The Figure on the Bed: Difference and American Destiny in *Tender Is the Night*," James Plath's "*The Sun Also Rises* as 'A Greater Gatsby': 'Isn't it pretty to think so,'" Nancy R. Comley's "Madwomen on the Riviera: The Fitzgeralds, Hemingway, and the Matter of Modernism," and the introduction by the editors, as well as J. Gerald Kennedy's closing essay, "Figuring the Damage: Fitzgerald's 'Babylon Revisited' and Hemingway's 'The Snows of Kilimanjaro.'"

Just as consistently strong a collection is Scott Donaldson's *The Cambridge Companion to Hemingway* (Cambridge, UK: Cambridge University Press, 1996), including invited essays by such Hemingway critics as Paul Smith, Thomas Strychacz, James Nagel, Robert E. Fleming, Keneth Kinnamon, Rena Sanderson, Allen Josephs, Susan Beegel, J. Gerald Kennedy, Michael Reynolds, and Elizabeth Dewberry. In Kennedy's "Hemingway, Hadley, and Paris: The persistence of desire," he traces much of the biography that prepares the reader for the kind of bitter sorrow that readers of Hemingway's *A Farewell to Arms* experience. Kennedy's argument is that Hemingway metamorphosed Paris to have been—in the 1920s—his beguiling mistress. Not that it was Paris that cost him his marriage or the loss of Hadley—whose loss he mourns throughout *A Moveable Feast*, as well as *Islands in the Stream*. In Kennedy's assessment, Hemingway's life had connected "his love of Paris, his commitment to writing, and his troubled marital relations. Those three preoccupations seemed intertwined by geographical and historical destiny. . . . Hemingway returned to Paris obsessively as a locus of longing."

In Kennedy's analysis, "If his fictional treatment of the city reflects the complications of his private life, it also reveals the unmistakable persistence of his desire for Paris, a desire linked in his writing with a succession of influential female characters" (200).

While Kennedy does not extend his reading to include either *A Farewell to Arms* or the character Catherine Barkley, it is possible to transfer that great sense of loss to Hemingway's novel of love and war, particularly since he was composing it in the years immediately after his divorce from Hadley.

It is Michael S. Reynolds' essay, "*A Farewell to Arms*: Doctors in the House of Love" in the *Cambridge Companion* that allows the reader a more informed return to Hemingway's 1929 novel. With material Reynolds had not used in his earlier writing about this book, his essay provides a storehouse of medical information for today's reader. But it does more, and as Reynolds admits in Note 8 to his essay: "Although I stand by my early work, I am no longer reading the same text I did in my youth. If I contradict myself, I contradict myself" (125).

What knowledge about medical practices early in the twentieth century means to the reader of *A Farewell to Arms* is that Frederic Henry cannot be excused for putting Catherine in danger. Medical science was not arcane: Frederic, like Hemingway, had ways of learning how to protect his beloved. But more importantly, as Reynolds says, "For a novel supposedly about love and war, we see little of war, and who can see love, that supreme abstraction? More clearly in focus is the human condition: the drive to propagate in the close proximity of death played out against the backdrop of ritual violence. The story that Frederic is left to narrate does not reflect well on the displaced American. He has done nothing particularly brave, nothing heroic. . . . Never do we see him sacrifice himself for Catherine. Their escape into Switzerland is to save his life, not hers" (124). Reynolds concludes, "We are all permanently at risk, trusting in doctors, medical and metaphorical, to preserve us in a world where we have little control: we are born into the world's hospital, each of us a terminal case" (125).

As this necessarily brief tour of secondary criticism suggests, scholars of Hemingway's works continue to produce good, provocative, writing about the fiction that continues to hold its central place in American (and world) twentieth-century literature.

Index

About the Author

LINDA WAGNER-MARTIN is Hanes Professor of English at the University of North Carolina at Chapel Hill. She has published numerous books, including the *Historical Guide to Ernest Hemingway* (2000) and was president of the Ernest Hemingway Foundation and Society.

**Recent Titles in
Greenwood Guides to Literature**

James Joyce's *Ulysses:* A Reference Guide
Bernard McKenna

John Steinbeck's *The Grapes of Wrath:* A Reference Guide
Barbara A. Heavilin

Gustave Flaubert's *Madame Bovary:* A Reference Guide
Laurence M. Porter and Eugene F. Gray